Psychoanalytic Approaches to Supervision

CURRENT ISSUES IN PSYCHOANALYTIC PRACTICE
Monographs of the Society for Psychoanalytic Training

CURRENT ISSUES IN PSYCHOANALYTIC PRACTICE

*Monographs of the
Society for Psychoanalytic Training
Number 2*

Psychoanalytic Approaches to Supervision

Edited by

Robert C. Lane, Ph.D.

BRUNNER/MAZEL, PUBLISHERS • NEW YORK

Library of Congress Cataloging-in-Publication Data
Psychoanalytic approaches to supervision / edited by Robert C. Lane.
        p.   cm. — (Current issues in psychoanalytic practice : no. 2)
    Includes papers from three symposia held in 1987 and 1988 as well
as additional contributed papers.
    Includes bibliographical references.
    Includes index.
    ISBN 0-87630-603-2
    1. Psychoanalysis—Study and teaching—Supervision—Congresses.
I. Lane, Robert C.   II. Series: Current issues in psychoanalytic
practice (Brunner/Mazel Publishers) : no. 2.
    [DNLM: 1. Organization and Administration.   2. Psychoanalysis.
W1 CU788LD no. 2 / WM 460 P97503]
RC502.P73   1990
616.89'17—dc20
DNLM/DLC
for Library of Congress   90-1971
                                                                  CIP

Published by
BRUNNER/MAZEL, INC.
19 Union Square
New York, NY 10003

Manufactured in the United States of America

10   9   8   7   6   5   4   3   2

Contents

Contents

Foreword

Current Issues in Psychoanalytic Practice takes pride and pleasure in producing this issue on supervision. Our Guest Editor, Robert C. Lane, has done a superb job in gathering an array of distinguished psychoanalytic educators who have provided us with many stimulating insights on many dimensions of the supervisory process.

Many of us who practice psychoanalysis and psychotherapy have contended that doing supervision is much more difficult than performing psychotherapy. Not only must the supervisor deal with transference and countertransference issues, resistances to learning and counterresistances to teaching, but how to intervene in supervision is much less prescribed and much less clear. Should the supervisor be a therapist or quasi-therapist? How much should the supervisee's dynamics be discussed in supervision? Does the supervisor have the right to recommend further analysis? These are some of the questions that perplex educators in the mental health profession and have not yet been completely answered.

Dr. Lane and his colleagues have moved us further in our understanding of the complexities of the supervisor-supervisee relationship and have enlightened us regarding the many different patterns of learning and achieving, as well as blocking and failing.

One of the unique aspects of this issue is that the supervisee is individualized, and his or her experiences are given a high priority. Further, in virtually all of the papers, the teacher emerges as an equal partner trying to understand his or her own role in the supervision process.

We are very indebted to Dr. Lane for this unique and eloquent contribution. We are sure the understanding of all of our readers will be enhanced by it.

HERBERT S. STREAN, D.S.W.
Editor

Contributors

Elaine G. Caruth, Ph.D.   Training and Supervising Analyst and Faculty, Los Angeles Institute for Psychoanalytic Studies; Associate Clinical Professor, Department of Psychiatry (Child), UCLA Neuropsychiatric Institute.

Saralea E. Chazan, Ph.D.   Instructor, New York Hospital-Cornell Medical Center, Westchester Division; private practice, New Rochelle, New York.

Anna Duran, Ph.D.   Associate Staff Therapist, Postgraduate Center for Mental Health; Adjunct Associate Professor, Graduate School of Business, Columbia University; author of articles on cross-cultural competencies, educating emotions and clinical reasoning skills through cross-cultural dialogues, subjective experiences with difference, and developing expertise in understanding client problems.

Patricia R. Everett, Ph.D.   Psychologist, Hawthorne Cedar Knolls, Division of Jewish Board of Family and Children's Services, and author of art history articles.

Reuben Fine, Ph.D.   Organizer and First President, Division of Psychoanalysis, American Psychological Association; Director Emeritus, New York Center for Psychoanalytic Training; Member, National Academy of Practice in Psychology; author of numerous books and papers.

Suzanne M. Gassner, Ph.D.   Psychoanalyst in private practice; Member, Mount Zion Hospital Psychotherapy Research Group; co-author of a book about problems in higher education and author of many articles on psychology, psychoanalysis and social work; Past Chairman, Department of Human Growth and Development, University of Massachusetts, College of Public and Community Service.

Franklin H. Goldberg, Ph.D.   Director of Psychological Services, Jewish Child Care Association, New York City; Faculty and Supervisor, Manhattan Institute for Psychoanalysis; Past President of the Clinical Division, New York State Psychological Association.

George D. Goldman, Ph.D.   Clinical Professor of Psychology, Supervisor of Psychotherapy, and Director of Clinical Services, Postdoctoral Psychotherapy Center, Adelphi University; private practice, Jericho, NY, and New York City; editor of 15 books in the area of psychoanalysis and psychotherapy; Past President, Division of Psychoanalysis, and Division of Psychologists in Independent Practice, American Psychological Association.

James W. Hull, Ph.D.   Assistant Director of Training, New York Hospital-Westchester Division, Cornell Medical Center; Assistant Professor of Psychology, Cornell University, Department of Psychology; Member, Society for Psychoanalytic Training.

Bertram P. Karon, Ph.D.   Professor of Clinical Psychology, Michigan State University; President, Division of Psychoanalysis, American Psychological Association; Former Director, Center for Psychoanalytic Studies, Michigan Society for Psychoanalytic Psychology; Past President, Psychologists Interested in the Study of Psychoanalysis; Past President, Michigan Society for Psychoanalytic Psychology; most important publication, coauthored with G. R. VandenBos: *Psychotherapy of Schizophrenia: The Treatment of Choice.*

Robert C. Lane, Ph.D.   Resident Psychoanalytic Scholar, Nova University, School of Professional Psychology; Clinical Professor of Psychology, Postdoctoral Program in Psychotherapy, Adelphi University; Director of Training, Long Island Division, New York Center for Psychoanalytic Training.

Wilma Cohen Lewis, Ph.D.   Faculty and Supervisor, Postgraduate Center for Mental Health; and Faculty and Associate Supervisor, Training Institute for Mental Health.

Martin Mayman, Ph.D.   Professor, University of Michigan, Department of Psychology; Teaching Faculty, Michigan Psychoanalytic Institute; Past Faculty Member, Topeka Institute for Psychoanalysis; private practice, Ann Arbor, Michigan.

Dale Mendell, Ph.D.   Faculty and Supervisor, Psychoanalytic Institute, Postgraduate Center for Mental Health; Faculty, Senior Supervisor, and Training Analyst, Training Institute for Mental Health; Editor, *Early Female Development: Current Psychoanalytic Views.*

Joseph W. Newirth, Ph.D. Associate Professor, The Gordon F. Derner Institute of Advanced Psychological Studies, Adelphi University; affiliated with The National Institute for the Psychotherapies and The Manhattan Institute for Psychoanalysis.

Norman C. Oberman, Ph.D. Training Analyst, Supervising Analyst, and Dean of Studies, Los Angeles Institute and Society for Psychoanalytic Studies.

Ruth Ochroch, Ph.D. Clinical Professor of Psychology, Ph.D. Clinical Psychology Program, New York University; Diplomate in Clinical Psychology, American Board of Professional Psychology; Member and Board Member, Division of Psychoanalysis, American Psychological Association.

Arnold Wm. Rachman, Ph.D. Training and Supervising Analyst, Psychoanalytic Institute, Postgraduate Center for Mental Health; Clinical Associate Professor, Postdoctoral Program in Psychoanalysis and Psychotherapy, Adelphi University.

Jeanne M. Safer, Ph.D. Faculty and Supervisor, Postgraduate Center for Mental Health and National Institute for the Psychotherapies; ABPP Diplomate in clinical psychology; book reviewer for *The Psychoanalytic Quarterly* and *Psychoanalytic Books.*

Stephen M. Schiff, Ph.D. Supervising Psychologist, Pace University Counseling Center; Adjunct Assistant Professor of Clinical Psychology, Teachers College, Columbia University.

Edith Schwartz, Ph.D. Member, Board Member, and Faculty, New York Freudian Society; Fellow and Faculty, Institute for Psychoanalytic Training and Research; Member and Faculty, National Psychological Association for Psychoanalysis; Member, International Psychoanalytic Association.

Jerome Singer, Ph.D. Professor of Psychology and Director of Graduate Studies, Department of Psychology, Yale University; Life Member, William Alanson White Psychoanalytic Society; author of numerous books and articles, including recently published: *Repression and Dissociation: Implications for Personality, Psychopathology and Health.*

George Stricker, Ph.D. Professor of Psychology and Dean, Derner Institute of Advanced Psychological Studies, Adelphi University; Diplomate in Clinical Psychology; Editor, *Clinician's Research Digest;*

author or editor of 13 books, the two most recent: *From Research to Clinical Practice* and *Handbook of Quality Assurance in Mental Health.*

Gayle Wheeler.   Ph.D. candidate, Psychoanalytic Institute of Northern California; private practice, San Francisco, California.

Warren Wilner, Ph.D.   Clinical Professor of Psychology, Postdoctoral Program for Psychoanalysis, Adelphi University, the Postdoctoral Program for Psychoanalysis, and New York University. Faculty, Manhattan Institute of Psychoanalysis; Supervisor, William Alanson White Institute and National Institute for Psychotherapies.

Fred Wolkenfeld, Ph.D.   Clinical Professor of Psychology, Training and Supervising Psychoanalyst, New York University Postdoctoral Program in Psychotherapy and Psychoanalysis; Training and Supervising Psychoanalyst, Psychoanalytic Training Institute of the New York Freudian Society; Associate Clinical Professor of Psychiatry, Albert Einstein College of Medicine.

Psychoanalytic Approaches to Supervision

Introduction

Robert C. Lane, Ph.D.
Guest Editor

   This issue contains articles contributed by psychologists affili-
ated with a number of psychoanalytic institutes, principally in New
York, but also sprinkled throughout the country. The Psychoanalytic
Training Institute of the New York Freudian Society is represented by
Robert C. Lane, Edith Schwartz, and Fred Wolkenfeld; the Institute for
Psychoanalytic Training and Research by Edith Schwartz; and the
New York Center for Psychoanalytic Training by Reuben Fine, James
W. Hull, and Robert C. Lane. The William Alanson White Institute is
represented by George D. Goldman, Joseph W. Newirth, Jerome L.
Singer, and Warren Wilner; the Manhattan Institute for Psychoanaly-
sis by Franklin H. Goldberg; the Adelphi Postdoctoral Training
Program in Psychotherapy and Psychoanalysis by Saralea E. Chazan,
Reuben Fine, George D. Goldman, James W. Hull, Robert C. Lane,
Joseph W. Newirth, Arnold Rachman, George Stricker, and Warren
Wilner; the New York University Postdoctoral Training Program in
Psychotherapy and Psychoanalysis by Franklin H. Goldberg, Ruth
Ochroch, and Fred Wolkenfeld; and the Nova Postdoctoral Institute
for Psychoanalysis by Robert C. Lane. The Postgraduate Center for
Mental Health's Training Program in Psychotherapy and Psychoa-
nalysis is represented by Anna Duran, Wilma Cohen Lewis, Dale
Mendell, Arnold Rachman, Jeanne M. Safer, and Stephen M. Schiff.
The Los Angeles Institute for Psychoanalytic Studies is represented
by Elaine G. Caruth, and Norman C. Oberman; the Mount Zion
Psychotherapy Research Group by Suzanne M. Gassner; the Topeka
Psychoanalytic Institute and the Michigan Psychoanalytic Institute
by Martin Mayman; and the Michigan Society for Psychoanalytic

1

Training by Bertram P. Karon. Patricia R. Everett is a psychologist in private practice.

A variety of papers on supervision is presented within the text. These include: A paper on the selection of patients for supervision (Everett & Stricker); a paper on a therapist's perception of phases in supervision and what they meant to her (Chazan); papers on the supervisory process (Caruth, Goldberg, and Oberman); a panel on the difference between psychoanalytic psychotherapy and psychoanalysis (American Psychological Association; Schwartz); and supervision by Erich Fromm on a case (Goldman). There are a number of original theoretical papers on supervision, including Caruth on dyadic (preoedipal) and triadic (oedipal) issues in supervision, Fine on the "analytic superego," Lane and Hull on the "good hour" in supervision, Newirth on "countertransference anxiety," Oberman on the "analytic identity," and Wilner on the "primary experience." There is a paper on parallel process (Wolkenfeld), and a number of papers from a conference on cross-gender supervision. The discussions of panels by Mayman and Singer are "must" reading for everyone in the field.

This issue is introduced with a paper on how patients are selected for supervision. Everett and Stricker stress the importance of the process of selecting patients for supervision or control by the candidate/therapist. This area has been relatively unexplored in the literature. The authors discuss the "preferred" or "favorite" patient when there are a number of possible patients to present. When there are very few eligible patients to present, the choice may be made by circumstances for the candidate. The authors also discuss the emerging variables, such as personality attributes and therapeutic skills of the supervisee, that potentially exert an influence on the selection of patients to be presented. They review therapeutic styles and parallel process and make recommendations for future research.

Chazan defines three phases within the development of the supervisee-supervisor relationship. Phase One marks the beginning of finding a space where subsequent creativity will take place. Phase Two ensues as the dyad begins to formulate a structure together, which defines their understanding of the therapeutic process. Phase Three is the culmination of these efforts resulting in renewed personal and professional identifications. Chazan feels the end goal is reached when the supervisee is welcomed as a colleague and begins to apprentice others in continuation of the craft.

Fine proposes the term "analytic superego" for the resistance in the supervisory process. This term encompasses both the analytic prohibitions (the basic rules of neutrality, anonymity, etc.) and those projected into the supervisory process by either of the participants. Fine examines the various reactions to the supervisory process and the supervisor that lead to presenting inaccurate data. These include the wish to please the supervisor, defiance, blocking on aggressive or sexual material, concealing, and other reactions. He offers us interesting personal anecdotes and impressions of well-known analysts. Included are his simultaneous supervision with Geza Roheim and Theodore Reik, and thoughts about Sullivan and Freud. He cautions us about the intrusion of unresolved conflicts into the supervisory session. Finally, he points out that despite its many pitfalls, supervision "is still the most practical method of teaching psychoanalytic technique."

Goldberg holds the view that supervision as "a focus of study" has received relatively little attention and recommends a course in analytic school dealing with supervision (see Schwartz). He presents some of the critical issues in supervision, describes various approaches and concepts, and raises a number of salient and perplexing questions on the supervisor's role and style in the supervisory process. He discusses how one selects a supervisor, how analysts of different persuasions conduct supervision, and the focus of supervisory attention (the patient, the therapist, the process, and transference-countertransference). Goldberg advocates that the supervisee find his or her own system of belief and style, after being exposed to a variety of systems and styles.

Lane and Hull apply the framework of Ernst Kris's "good hour" in therapy to the supervisory situation. They stress Kris's emphasis on an infantile prototype, usually of an oral nature, in the gaining of insight and how this effects the state of the transference. They then apply Kris's three aspects of ego functioning, temporary and partial regression, objective self-observation, and control over the discharge of affects, which are often attached to childhood memories, to the good hour in supervision. They present three clinical cases and raise some very important theoretical issues.

Wilner, in a very original paper, digresses from the model of the regulatory principal of interpretation or secondary process thinking, to that of primary experience in doing supervision. What is said to Wilner "becomes a context of action and interaction rather than of meaning." He permits and/or recommends that the therapist and supervisor live out and express what they are experiencing in "a way that never may be interpreted or commented upon." The paper introduces a new and daring concept, which "cannot be employed indiscriminately" and needs the guidelines described in his paper. He offers us four clear supervisory vignettes to illustrate the various points made in his discussion.

Goldman shares with us a very personal experience, that of his supervision on a case of dependency with Erich Fromm. Fromm's insight into the personality of this very dependent patient is an excellent lesson in how to handle this type of patient. What Fromm said in 1958 is just as true today. This paper will be picked up and read again and again. Fromm's words, often poetic, will linger.

Schwartz, in her paper, deals with the differences between psychotherapy and psychoanalysis. After defining terms, she sees the supervision of psychoanalysis as being more systematic than that of psychotherapy, with the key difference being the degree of regression induced in the patient. To her, treating the more disturbed patient in psychotherapy is more difficult to teach, requires more speculative exploratory work, and countertransference problems are often of a more difficult nature. She raises and attempts to answer a number of very significant questions, such as: What happens in supervision? How do we differentiate the "dumb" spots from the "blind" spots? What are the therapeutic and pedagogic responsibilities of the supervisor? Finally, she suggests a supervisory course be offered in the beginning of institute training.

Wolkenfeld, one of the early writers on parallel process, points out his thesis early in his paper, "that any supervisory situation of dynamic psychotherapy, individual or group, on a one-to-one or in a continuous case seminar situation will provide the necessary conditions for the inevitable emergence of parallel reenactments." He proceeds to give examples of parallel reenactment and to discuss its ramifications and definitions. He points out that it is "not always clear which way the mirror is facing" (it may be supervisor to therapist rather than therapist to supervisor).

Wolkenfeld tells us that the essential mechanism of parallelism is "identification" and how all three principles in the triad—patient, analyst, and supervisor alike—are involved in multiple identificatory processes for the unfolding and success of the analytic and supervisory processes. Wolkenfeld also gives us a treat in his discussion of the concept of psychic reality and how it relates to the psychoanalytic treatment process and parallel process in supervision. He concludes by telling us that the main objective of supervision is not the teaching of technique and theory, important as it is, but the refinement of the supervisee's psychoanalytic mode of listening and the internalization of a psychoanalytic attitude. He emphasizes the latter's relationship to transference reactions, drive derivatives and defenses, the analytic process and supervision, and parallel process.

The Postgraduate Center's symposium on Gender Issues in Psychoanalytic Supervision offers an interesting area for exploration in which there will be much further research. Mendell suggests that where there is a female patient and male therapist, a female supervisor is uniquely suited as the supervisor of choice. She can assist the male therapist to recognize, understand, and perhaps help to modify his female patient's behavior. Safer points out, "It is also important not to jump to the conclusion that only a woman can understand another woman." She cautions against assuming there is a "uniquely feminine" or "masculine" style of supervision or of analysis and that a same or opposite sex supervision dyad has an identifiable quality independent of the personalities of the participants. Rachman gives a fascinating example of his own initial experience with cross-gender supervision and how he handled it. Lewis tells us that what appears on the surface to be a gender issue, after further work, often turns out to be a transference issue, possibly triggered off by the sex of the supervisor, as well as by age and other concrete factors. She also offers anecdotes from her own supervision.

The last two papers in the symposium are contributions from candidates in the Postgraduate Program. Duran tells us supervision is an interpersonal process reflected in attitude toward gender, people and places, social concepts, language habits, communication processes, supervisory goals, style, and expectations. She raises several important questions about gender, the double standard, and the impact of social concepts, and conscious and unconscious attitudes on the therapeutic and supervisory processes in general. Schiff discusses the task of the analyst in understanding the contribution of cross-sexual supervision. He postulates that differences between analyst and patient, such as gender, "have the potential to enhance the treatment or, conversely, may serve as an obstacle to the analyst's ability to accurately perceive the patient's case."

The American Psychological Association's symposium on Supervision in Psychotherapy versus Supervision in Psychoanalysis offers us many interesting papers. Ochroch outlines the problem in her introductory paper. She discusses definitions, principles of supervision, and differences in the training necessary for and the type of patient seen in psychoanalytic psychotherapy and psychoanalysis. Gassner describes how the Mount Zion Psychotherapy Research Group conducts supervision. She introduces us to a new psychoanalytic theory: "control mastery," headed by Harold Sampson and

Joseph Weiss. Her goals in supervision are to help candidates learn how to use the first few sessions to develop a case formulation, to evaluate its accuracy and to revise it if necessary, and to apply the case formulation to arrive at case guidelines.

Karon, in his very rich paper replete with personal anecdotes, talks about "real" therapy, whether it be psychoanalytic psychotherapy or psychoanalysis. He gives many examples of definitions and explanations of what may constitute differences according to different theoreticians. His discussion of "parameter phobia" is indeed helpful, as are the examples he offers us. Karon is a pioneer in his acceptance of cases rejected by others, in his openness, in his emphasis on truth and authenticity, in his method of presentation, and in his work with the disturbed patient.

Newirth points out the importance of the therapist's understanding of his or her own dynamics and receiving intensive supervision. He indicates that the development of the supervisee's ability to use the "self" as a major emotional force is the most important aspect of supervision. Newirth uses an object relations developmental model in discussing styles of supervision. He emphasizes the creation of a holding environment, continual growth, the development of the self, and interpersonal relations rather than drive and conflict resolution. He elaborates on concerns in supervision that lead to countertransference anxiety: being abandoned in the analytic situation, the recognition that the supervisory situation is one of mixed purposes and loyalties, concern with loss of boundaries, and depressive anxiety and guilt as a result of the therapist's recognition of hateful feelings toward the patient. Finally, he reviews some important concepts of Searles and Winnicott on identity and the development of the self.

Singer, in his very clear discussion, directs our attention to the need for more time to be given to the social and interpersonal realities within the supervisory relationship. He feels supervision has the functions of attending to the the pulse of the therapy as well as teaching and evaluating. Singer raises many important questions about graduate school supervision and what it should and should not entail. He points out that graduate students are not psychoanalytic candidates. He recommends less use of jargon and time spent on theory, and offers a clear statement of the current state of knowledge about graduate training. He describes three supervisory styles, commenting on them in terms of the three presenters, and he recommends more research on the effectiveness of different supervisory styles. Singer closes by raising some important questions concerning the need for supervision and the psychoanalytic features that should be emphasized in working with students in supervision.

Wheeler, in her introduction to the Division of Psychoanalysis of the American Psychological Association symposium on the Psychoanalytic Supervisory Process, stresses the state of mind of the analyst at work, or the analyst's "work ego." The analyst works with his or her unconscious, referred to by Isakower as the "instrument" of analysis. She proposes pedagogic skill, tact, and patience as necessary qualifying credentials for supervision. The supervisor's "knowledge of theory and practice" are supplemented by multiple identifications and capacity for empathy.

Caruth, in her exciting paper, deals with different approaches to supervision, the supervisory process, techniques of supervision (technique and content-oriented supervision versus an emphasis on countertransference and inner processes), and parallel process. She discusses the dyadic preoedipal area of narcissistic vulnerability and oedipal issues in relation to triadic aspects. She contrasts and compares certain aspects of the supervisor-supervisee relationship to the analyst-analysand relationship. Caruth is particularly illuminating when discussing "dumb" spots, and "deaf" and "blind" spots, overlapping triangles, gossip, matching and mismatching, and accountability to the training institute.

Oberman points out that despite the brilliance of supervisors and giftedness of candidates, there may be a lack of adequate understanding and guidance in the supervisory process. Whereas many supervisors place the personal and professional growth of candidates first and foremost, this often proves not to be the case. Supervisors, not having the benefit of the candidate's associations, are often unaware of the nature of the transference or the candidate's conflicts. Oberman sees the capacity to form a learning alliance as a prerequisite for supervision. He perceives the training program in general, and the training analysis in particular, as recapitulating the parent-child relationship, and by so doing limiting the resolution of the Oedipus complex.

In addition to the acquisition of basic skills, he views the establishment of an analytic identity as an important goal of training. Candidates are interested in "curing" themselves, not just the patient, and this "cure" is the achievement of an analytic identity. Oberman feels that the tools with which analysts work do not necessarily help them understand the process. After pointing out the internal processes that analysts struggle with in establishing their analytic identity, and indicating how rarely this is described in the literature, Oberman presents a beautiful example of how this process takes place. He concludes by pointing out that the supervisor must demonstrate to candidates that they "already have the means within themselves to be an analyst, but now must learn to apply it."

Mayman in his discussion of the previous two papers advises that the supervisor should not allow him- or herself to be drawn into the patient-therapist dialogue, and to avoid any identification with the patient in this transference. He feels no candidate can listen "intuitively, empathically, openmindedly and effectively to the patient if one ear is cocked for the supervisor's criticism." Mayman recommends that the supervisee put what he or she learns in supervision completely out of mind, as he or she often feels impelled to tell it immediately to the patient, with disastrous effects. The proper timing of interpretations takes "training, experience, and in-touchness" with the patient. The therapist should have his or her finger on the pulse of the treatment process, be cautious about interpretations, learn to wait, and to show forbearance, overcoming enthusiasm to share what he or she has learned.

Mayman asks supervisees to present material freshly, spontaneously, without process notes, allowing the material to structure itself as therapy goes along. He completes his article by giving a number of rules of thumb: respond empathically to the patient; look through the transference at what the patient is saying; go with the affect; interpret defense before content.

We were indeed fortunate that Mayman as well as Singer discussed their ideas about supervision rather than sticking strictly to the task of discussing the papers given by members of their panels. It is interesting to see how their papers dovetail and complement each other.

Deep gratitude is expressed to Lucy Freeman, who read all the papers and made many helpful suggestions; to Herbert Strean, who offered the opportunity to put together and edit this issue on supervision and who wrote the foreword; to all the contributors for their contributions; to Joseph Krasnansky, the Managing Editor of Current Issues in Psychoanalytic Practice, for his patience and cooperation; and especially to my wife, Jean Betty Lane, for her indulgence and support.

Selection of Patients
for Psychotherapy Supervision

Patricia R. Everett, Ph.D.,
and George Stricker, Ph.D.

The various theoretical approaches to psychodynamic psycho-therapy share an emphasis on supervision as the primary method of teaching and developing therapy skills (Ekstein & Wallerstein, 1958; Fleming & Benedek, 1966; Lambert, 1980). Therefore, the therapist's choice of which patients to discuss in supervision should be considered an important variable with potentially significant impact on both the patients' treatment and the therapist's professional growth. This topic has been essentially unexplored in writings on psychotherapy supervision. In this paper, we will first discuss the importance of the selection of patients for supervision and address the omission of this topic in the literature. We will then look at what has been written about preferred patients and those chosen for supervision. Next, we will consider what we might infer from the scant literature and focus on what might determine the therapist's choice of patients for discussion in supervision. Finally, we will pose questions and make recommendations for future research.

Importance of Selection of Patients for Supervision

Individual supervision, no matter what the theoretical orienta-tion of the participants, essentially consists of two people, a supervisor and a supervisee, looking at the interactions between the supervisee and the patient in order to help the supervisee be more effective as a therapist (Arlow, 1963; Hess, 1980). If, as many (e.g.,

Lambert, 1980) believe, supervision is "aimed at helping the student therapist to modify *specific* behaviors with *particular* clients" (p. 425, italics added), the selection of certain patients for supervision is intended to have a significant bearing on the treatment of those discussed. Concurrently, the therapy of those patients not covered in supervision might be affected by the absence of discussion, perhaps in an adverse way. The choice of patients for supervision also has a potential bearing on the direction and extent of an individual supervisee's development as a therapist.

These decisions regarding the extent to which patients are covered in supervision assume greater importance when we consider the large number of psychotherapy patients treated by students and candidates in training, who are highly dependent upon supervision to provide focus, meaning, and clarity to their therapeutic work. They receive only a limited amount of individual supervision time per week with an experienced clinician. Questions then arise regarding the most effective use of that supervision time if, indeed, the selection of patients for discussion is considered a relevant variable in their treatment.

There are those supervisors who would argue that supervision should be targeted more toward the therapist's growth and therapeutic abilities than toward specific patient problems. They hold that the effects of supervision are generalizable, that is, that undiscussed patients can benefit from the therapist's receiving supervision on other patients (Gustin, 1958). This might be true of important general features of the therapist, such as self-confidence, ability to handle aggression, and empathic capacity. However, each patient brings a unique set of problems to therapy and engenders complex countertransference feelings in the therapist, particularly in the neophyte. Discussion of these specifics should aid the therapist's functioning with, and understanding of, that patient. Arlow (1963) cites the value of supervision in helping the therapist discover his or her "blind spots." If a supervisee withholds talking about a certain patient, blind spots that might be specific to the interaction with that patient are not made available for discovery in supervision. In a similar vein, Issacharoff (1984) focuses on the supervisee's countertransference in supervision. It follows that if a therapist refrains from discussing a patient, the specific countertransference feelings, which may, in themselves, lead the therapist not to bring up that patient, will be excluded from supervision.

Literature on Selection of Patients

While the literature on supervision includes innumerable general references to the patient in supervision and many citations of specific patients discussed, without exception the authors do not address the question of how that particular patient came to be the focus of the supervision under consideration (Ekstein & Wallerstein, 1958; Fleming, 1967; Friedlander et al., 1984). Therapists in training usually have to select certain patients from among many to discuss with a single supervisor. The question of how and why patients are selected for focus in supervision becomes pressing as we consider its potential impact on the treatment of the patient and training of the therapist.

The essential omission from the literature of the topic of selection of patients for supervision is significant. Articles and books on supervision address such areas as models for teaching (Ekstein & Wallerstein, 1958; Friedlander et al., 1984), countertransference in supervision (Goin & Kline, 1976; Issacharoff, 1984), stages in supervision (Grater, 1985; Hess, 1987), and parallel processes (Doehrman, 1976; Grey & Fiscalini, 1987; Sachs & Shapiro, 1976). Albott (1984) even acknowledges the importance of the setting of supervision in influencing the learning process and the selection of supervisors as a relevant variable. However, he does not mention choice of patients for supervision among these factors.

Articles that address the choice of supervisor and mention the selection of patients are all concerned with psychoanalytic training, where each supervisor and supervisee commonly cover only one patient. The focus of selection of patients for supervision is, thus, oriented toward which are appropriate cases for supervised psychoanalysis, not which patients from among many are chosen for discussion (Grinberg, 1970; Hirsch, 1984; Lebovici, 1970). For example, when DeBell (1963), in his review of writings on psychoanalytic supervision, refers to "selection of cases for supervision" (p. 564), he looks at the method of initially identifying and accepting a "suitable" patient in terms of "analyzability" for supervised psychoanalysis.

Why has the general area of choice of patients for supervision been overlooked in the literature and, perhaps as a corollary, often even in the supervisory relationship itself? This latter idea is difficult to consider in light of the lack of empirical research or theoretical speculation on the subject, but it seems likely that, within some supervisory dyads, the supervisee and supervisor actively avoid the issue of how much time is spent on each patient. Some supervisors prefer not to look at the process of supervision nor to touch on the supervisee's countertransference feelings. Such an avoidance could result in a lack of attention to the potential meaning of an unbalanced consideration of patients in supervision. Perhaps the therapist and supervisor collude in their failure to discuss why they focus on some patients rather than on others. They might both silently agree to exclude from supervision certain patients who, due to such factors as diagnosis, degree of liveliness, or sex, are not of real interest to either or both the supervisor and supervisee.

Instances when the topic of choice of patients for supervision is not addressed could be seen as revealing resistances in the supervisory relationship on the part of both parties. Both supervisor and supervisee might be resistant to exploring the factors determining their preferred patients. In addition, the supervisor often holds a bias toward certain categories of patients and may communicate a preference to the supervisee who, depending on his or her own needs and personality, might then aim to please the supervisor with his or her choice. For example, if a supervisor, even subtly, indicates a lack of interest in supervising adolescents, a supervisee might indulge the supervisor and discuss such patients minimally or not at all.

Another important dynamic established between supervisor and supervisee that might be upset by their attention to which patients are brought to supervision is the different ways of relating that develop around various patients. A supervisor and supervisee often share a unique relationship based on each patient. Addressing why other patients are not discussed might be seen by both members of the supervisory dyad as having the potential to rupture their established ways of interacting. The supervisor and supervisee might be comfortable with the existing character of their relationship and may resist inviting possible threats to it. Introduction of another case into the relationship might lead to altered ways of interacting that would be less comfortable for both supervisor and supervisee.

Problems in communication between supervisor and supervisee might parallel breaks in communication between therapist and patient and might also lead to an avoidance of the issue of choice of patients. Countertransference resistances could also be a reason why a therapist does not bring a particular patient to supervision, and this might extend to an overall resistance to talking about the process of selection both within the supervisory relationship and in the literature.

As many authors have noted, there is a tendency for the

experience of supervision to engender regression in the supervisee. It is even possible for oedipal conflicts to be enacted, as the supervisor and supervisee play out parent-child roles and, with the patient included, are involved in a triangular relationship (Lower, 1972; Martin et al., 1978; Meerloo, 1952). And, as Searles (1955) points out, the supervisee may simply "resent" being in supervision. More specifically, the supervisee can be "tenaciously resistive to, if not actively resentful and derisive of" (Searles, 1965, p. 591) the supervisor's attempts at helping the supervisee recognize the progress in his or her work with patients.

The supervisory situation provides a ripe environment for struggles over control, which are fueled by unconscious hostilities on the part of both members of the supervisory dyad (Meerloo, 1952). The supervisor must rely totally on the supervisee for his or her version of the patient's story, a dependence that the supervisor might not want to admit. The supervisee, on the other hand, is forced to submit his or her performance for evaluation by a superior authority who has never even seen the patient under discussion. When considered in the context of these various conflicts over control in the supervisory relationship, the choice of which patients to discuss in supervision can represent the last vestige of control that a student therapist possesses. By holding onto that special and often undiscussed control over which patients are brought to supervision and which aspects of the session are introduced, to a certain extent the supervisee can direct his or her own learning needs and determine the boundaries of the interaction with the supervisor.

The control dynamics in the supervisory relationship can be considered in light of Winnicott's (1965) discussion of the development of the "true self" and "false self," in which the child is seen as constructing a "false self" to adapt to the demands of his or her environment, thereby hiding his or her "true self." Similarly, the supervisee can be viewed as struggling to preserve a sense of self, and thus erecting a "false self" to ward off the impingements of the supervisor and, at the same time, to please the supervisor. The supervisee's presentation of a case will thus always be, to a greater or lesser degree, a false one, designed to protect his or her "true self," or core, from the intrusions of the supervisor. Selection of patients for supervision, then, becomes imbued with real meaning for the supervisee as a secret source of control that is often not explicitly acknowledged. For this reason, as well, with all its unconscious components, writers on supervision might avoid addressing the topic of choice of patients. As supervisees might want to preserve their secret source of control, and supervisors might not want to admit a situation that seems to undermine their control, writers might avoid attending to such charged process issues in the supervisory dyad.

Literature on Preferred Patients

Although both the empirical and theoretical literature on psychotherapy is filled with references to the preferred patient, such a preference on the therapist's part might not have a bearing on which patients are discussed in supervision. However, since some therapists certainly spend more time in supervision on their favorite patients, we will take a brief look at the characteristics of preferred patients. Studies have found that therapists prefer patients of the opposite sex who are young, attractive, verbal, intelligent and successful, the so-called YAVIS patient (Schofield, 1964). These patients reportedly tend to be considered for, and remain in, longer treatment (Imber et al., 1955; Lorr et al., 1958). There are implications of such a preference for the treatment of the patient, as some studies have found a positive correlation between the likability of the patient and the therapeutic outcome for that patient (Garfield, 1986).

There are real problems associated with a therapist's choosing to work with some patients over others, or to concentrate on some, at the expense of others, in supervision. In an article exploring the factors involved in determining the "analyzability" of a patient, Hirsch (1984) warns against blindness to the countertransference issues associated with this decision. He admits, "Analysts, like most other people, prefer to work with the greater likelihood of success. When the supply of patients is sufficient, analysts will generally tend to choose the least risky of the lot. Well-functioning patients will be chosen over poorly functioning ones because they are more likely to help the analyst feel effective" (p. 171). Hirsch sees such a determination partially as the result of transference and countertransference forces operating in the therapist: similar issues might be involved in a therapist's selection of patients for supervision.

Literature on Selection of Patients for Supervision

The literature on psychotherapy supervision, as already mentioned, contains only a few references to the selection of certain patients from among many for supervision. Wagner (1957) mentions that, in supervision, the psychiatric resident is allowed to "choose his patient from a limited number of selected cases" (p. 762), but he does not address what factors go into that decision. Greenberg (1980) notes that supervisees must make choices regarding how best to use supervision, including which patients to focus on. However, he fails to explore how the supervisee arrives at these choices and what might be the treatment implications for those patients covered or not covered in supervision. Selzer, Murphy, and Amini (1961) refer to an instance where a positive change occurred in a patient when a new supervisor assumed direction of the case. Unlike the previous supervisor, who divided the weekly supervisory hour among three patients, the new supervisor spent the entire hour on this one patient. Certainly, the change in the patient is overdetermined, but it is interesting to note the possibility that the amount of time spent in supervision had a bearing on the treatment.

Two recent empirical studies investigated the selection of patients for supervision, with a focus on the characteristics of those patients chosen for supervision and the potential effects of such a selection on their subsequent treatment (Burgoyne et al, 1976; Steinhelber et al., 1984). Although various methodological problems, such as lack of random assignment and lack of multiple ratings of variables, characterize both studies, the results suggest measurable differences between those patients who are discussed in supervision and those who are not. Therefore, we will briefly review each study individually.

Burgoyne et al. (1976) investigated the factors that distinguish patients who are more frequently discussed in supervision. The researchers derived their consideration of this question from the observed YAVIS syndrome. The therapists in the study were 17 residents at a hospital outpatient clinic. The results showed that these residents were supervised on 66% of a total of 89 patients who had been in therapy for more than 8 months. Very few older, less educated, and poorer patients were presented for supervision. Patients with a psychotic diagnosis were less likely to be discussed in supervision, while those with personality and/or character disorders were more likely to receive such attention. Only a "strong trend" ($p<.06$) existed to suggest that patients who were "liked" had more frequently supervised treatment. The therapist's reports of involve-ment with the patient, however, were significantly related to consis-tent and frequent supervision.

Steinhelber et al. (1984) claimed to present the first empirical investigation of the effects of supervision on patient outcome. The researchers looked at the amount of supervision time devoted to a particular patient as it related to patient outcome. The subjects in the study were 51 therapists in training at an adult psychiatric outpatient clinic, who treated a total of 237 patients. Although the results indicated no statistically significant differences to support the hypothesis that the amount of supervision would be positively associated with patient outcome, the authors reported some of their findings as consistent with those of Burgoyne et al. (1976). High supervision was more likely to be given to patients with a diagnosis of personality disorder, neurosis, or transient situational reaction, and low supervision to those with psychotic affective disorders, schizophrenia, and borderline personalities. Steinhelber and colleagues also found an association between younger patients and higher frequency of supervision. Cases in which psychotropic medications were combined with psychotherapy were supervised less often than those not involving such drug treatments.

These two studies mark an important beginning in the investigation of characteristics that distinguish patients who are discussed frequently in supervision from those who are not. Together, both studies also offer a different perspective on two widely investigated areas of research: length of psychotherapy and patient selection for psychotherapy. Whether or not patients continue in therapy has been considered primarily a client variable, with a focus on determining the patient characteristics that lead to premature termination. In support of this long-held view, a large number of studies have found a relationship between social class and length of stay in psychotherapy (Berrigan & Garfield, 1981; Imber et al., 1955). Lower class patients drop out significantly more often than those from middle and upper classes. Adding another possible element to this equation, Burgoyne et al. (1976) and Steinhelber et al. (1984) consider continuation in therapy to be a function of the amount of supervision a patient's therapist receives. Their findings also support the long-held belief that patients from higher social classes are more often accepted for therapy (Bailey et al., 1959; Schaffer & Myers, 1954). This inequity in patient selection is extended by Burgoyne et al. and Steinhelber et al. to the realm of supervision, where it appears that lower class patients may be similarly discriminated against. Such an imbalance in discussion of patients in supervision is potentially highly significant, as patients whose treatment is least successful appear to be those least likely to be presented for supervision.

Inferences from the Literature

Now that we have reviewed what little has been written on the selection of patients for supervision, what might we infer from this information? And what can we extrapolate from the supervision literature that will shed light on the possible factors affecting the therapist's choice of patients for discussion in supervision? Although it is not always the supervisee who designates the patient for focus, as at times the supervisor initiates the choice or institutes a structured approach to ensure more or less equal time spent on each patient, we will focus here on factors that influence the supervisee's choice.

Four primary factors influence the therapist's selection of certain patients from among many for discussion in supervision: patient variables, therapist variables, supervisor variables, and those processes unique to the supervisory relationship. There is certainly interaction among these categories, but we will consider each separately and suggest areas of overlap.

Patient variables that bear on the therapist's decision regarding who will be the focus of supervision include the patient's age, socioeconomic status, diagnosis, education, sex, race, personality, attitude toward therapy, psychological-mindedness, and transference issues. Patient variables may interact with therapist variables in affecting the choice for supervision in relevant areas of patient-therapist similarity, such as primary emotional conflicts, birth order, or values. For example, a therapist might be more motivated to talk about a patient who has neurotic issues similar to his own, as a way of helping himself with those areas of conflict.

Therapist variables that might determine the choice of patients for supervision seem to center on personality attributes and therapeutic skills of the supervisee. Certainly, the meaning of supervision for each individual supervisee will bear on the decisions regarding patients. This will affect both the choice of patients to present and the selection of material from the session to be presented. If the supervisee sees supervision as a place to be corrected and punished for mistakes, he or she might withhold discussion of certain aspects of the sessions with patients. Conversely, if supervision is conceptualized as existing to help with the development of skills, he or she will be more open to the experience and to exposing his or her own behavior as a therapist. Searles (1979) talks about psychiatric residents being "afraid" to relate to their supervisors their feelings of intense identification with their schizophrenic patients for fear of being judged "crazy" themselves. Thus therapists' beliefs about how they will be evaluated by colleagues and supervisors can prevent them from reporting such disturbing aspects of treatment with patients.

Turning to specific personality variables, therapists who are excessively fragile and sensitive to criticism might only bring up patients who make them look good, or focus on parts of the therapy sessions that cast their performance in a relatively good light. On the other end of the spectrum are therapists who exhibit a "neurotic need for self-punishment" (Lebovici, 1970, p. 386) and therefore present only those patients with whom they feel inept. Therapists' self-awareness and experiences in their own therapy might also be important elements entering into their patient choices for focus in supervision. As regards therapists' skills, such factors as confidence and ability to handle aggressive or sexual material will affect comfort in supervision and thus willingness to address difficult material, errors, and countertransference feelings. All of the above factors can be either brought to supervision by the therapist or activated by either the personality of the supervisor or the experience of supervision, to which we now turn.

Lebovici (1970) points out, "Supervision is not the teaching of technique. It is a relationship between two persons which requires knowledge of all the subtle transference displacements that are facilitated" (p. 392). The supervisory relationship, then, includes the personality characteristics of the supervisor and the supervisee, and the climate of interaction between them. Emch (1955) defines supervision as an "experience overtly taking place between two people" and poses the question of "who else is there, either overtly or covertly" (p. 299). By using mathematical formulas to calculate possible combinations, Emch illustrates the large number of complex interplays between seven identified participants in the supervisory situation, including the therapist, patient, supervisor, therapist's analyst, and past supervisor. She arrives at a conceivable 126 pairs of relationships, all of which are capable of evoking conflict. The emotional impact on either or both members of the supervisory dyad of any one of these relationships, some of which are mainly unconscious, is potentially powerful, and thus may have an effect on the therapist's choice of which patients to discuss in supervision.

The personality of the supervisor certainly colors the relationship and has a bearing on the functioning of the supervisee within that relationship. Emch (1955) mentions the possibility of the personal problems of supervisors being played out in the supervisory relationship, with the supervisee becoming an unknowing victim of such conflicts, such as being caught in the cross fire of a supervisor's competitive battles within an institute. Lower (1972) also calls attention to personality factors in the supervisor and how they bear on the supervisory relationship. For example, a supervisor may subtly, and even unconsciously, encourage the supervisee to identify with him or her, and thus may push the therapist toward choosing for discussion a patient who will interest or please the supervisor rather than one who has meaning to the therapist. Grinberg (1970) refers to "supervisor psychopathology" and its specific manifestations in the supervisory situation, such as the supervisor with paranoid features who consequently withholds communication of his or her ideas and experience. The supervisee, therefore, will experience a range of feelings in reaction to the supervisor, which might affect choice of patients for coverage.

Closely related to personality characteristics of the supervisor is the style with which he or she conducts supervision and the resulting relationship between supervisor and supervisee. Fleming and Benedek (1966) use the term "learning alliance" to refer to supervision and to suggest its effectiveness when operating in an ideal climate of trust and cooperation relatively free of neurotic conflicts on the part of both members. However, there are many threats to this learning alliance that create tensions in the supervisory relationship and therefore might have a bearing on the supervisee's choice of patients for discussion.

Many authors have looked at supervisory styles (Cherniss & Egnatios, 1977; Friedlander & Ward, 1984), but we will concentrate here on two articles that suggest and explore the supervisee's experience of various approaches (Levenson, 1984; Rosenblatt & Mayer, 1975). Since its inception, practitioners and recipients of supervision have debated whether its main goal should be to teach or to treat the supervisee. Supervision currently takes many forms and locations along this didactic-therapeutic continuum. The orientation of a particular supervisory relationship may have a bearing on the patient as a result of the frequency of being the topic of discussion. The personality of the supervisee also enters here to affect his or her responses to various styles of supervision.

Levenson (1984) identifies six "rough" categories of supervisory styles that provide useful ways of considering various individual approaches to supervision. These types range from "holding or confirming," where the supervisor rarely intervenes and does not direct or control what the supervisee wants to explore, to the "metatherapeutic approach," which finds the supervisor primarily focused on the supervisee's countertransference, to the "Zen method," in which the supervisor confronts and harasses the supervisee until his or her preconceptions and rigidity are released.

Rosenblatt and Mayer (1975) outline four "objectionable supervisory styles" arrived at through student therapists' evaluations of their experiences as supervisees. The "constrictive" approach does not grant the supervisee sufficient independence, while the "amorphous" type offers little direction. In "unsupportive" supervision, supervisors are cold, withholding, and, at times, hostile. "Therapeutic" supervision, with its focus on exploration of the supervisee's personal issues and interpretation of dynamics, leaves supervisees most distressed and vulnerable.

Certainly, these varied styles of supervision might lead the supervisor and supervisee to assume a variety of roles within different supervisory relationships, such as collaborators, analyst-patient, or active supervisor-passive supervisee. We can imagine that the supervisee would feel very different about him- or herself and the supervisor in each of these situations. The supervisee might feel either enabled or inhibited about discussing difficult patients or issues. For example, a supervisee who is unsure about the effectiveness and appropriateness of supervision as therapy is paired with a supervisor of the therapeutic type. This supervisee might be hesitant to discuss a patient about whom he has intense and painful countertransference feelings, for fear of having to expose these emotions. Certainly, any supervisory approach might draw very different responses and lead to the assumption of different roles, depending on the personality characteristics of the supervisee. Thus, the manner in which the supervisor conducts supervision will likely have an impact on the supervisee's decisions about which patients to discuss. Further, it should be noted that many training programs offer candidates a choice among supervisors, and that choice is likely to be influenced by these same factors.

As Lower (1972) spells out, the supervisory situation itself may reawaken conflicts in the supervisor as well as in the supervisee, revolving around such areas as oedipal or narcissistic issues. Neurotic conflicts that the supervisee acts out with the supervisor certainly might affect the presentation of case material by the therapist, who might withhold discussion of certain patients or particular aspects of a specific patient. For example, the supervisee may sense the supervisor's narcissistic involvement and might not want to expose his or her own weaknesses, for fear of disappointing the expectations of the supervisor. Or, the supervisee might assert his or her separateness from the supervisor by not complying with the implicit demands of supervision. Alternatively, as Searles (1955) points out, the supervisor might feel competitive with the supervisee and/or the supervisee's analyst, and may thus inject anxious or aggressive content into the supervisory relationship.

In their discussions of parallel process phenomena, Searles (1955), Doehrman (1976), and Gediman and Wolkenfeld (1980) acknowledge that, just as the relationship between patient and therapist can affect the relationship between supervisee and supervisor, the process can work in the other direction, whereby aspects of the supervisory relationship are reflected in that between patient and therapist. This attention to the potential emotional effect on the patient of the supervisee's experience in supervision is rare in the literature and is important to consider in light of our question regarding factors that have an impact on the supervisee's choice of patients for supervision.

Epstein (1986) acknowledges the potential negative effect of supervision on the supervisee and on his or her conduct of therapy with the specific patient being discussed. Epstein points out the "authoritarian tilt" of the supervisory relationship. Its two members often collude not to discuss the negative emotional impact on the supervisee of the process of supervision and the experience of a particular supervisor. These negative effects of supervision may extend to influencing the supervisee's choice of patient for discussion.

As others, such as Munson (1987) and Albott (1984), have pointed out, sex roles as well as power issues may exert a strong negative influence on the supervisory relationship. Thus, the supervisee's choice of patients to discuss in supervision may reflect a struggle, perhaps an unconscious one, over gender issues and the imbalance of power within the supervisory relationship.

Recommendations for Future Research

Studies have suggested a measurable difference between those patients who are discussed frequently in supervision and those who are not. If a patient is not brought up in supervision, what factors in his or her character or interaction with the therapist or outside of the treatment might contribute to such an omission? What is going on in nonpresented therapies that renders them less presentable? Is a patient who is not presented necessarily overlooked or negatively affected? These questions all point to: What is the effect, if any, of more frequently supervised therapy on the patient? Further investigation into this relationship between supervision and patient outcome is crucial, as ultimately this is the only reason the topic of selection of patients for supervision is important.

A current study (Everett, in progress) is looking at this question of the relationship between the amount a patient is discussed in weekly individual supervision and the overall therapeutic progress of that patient, as rated by both the therapist and the patient. The study is also investigating the characteristics that distinguish those patients who are more frequently brought up in supervision from those discussed less often.

The idea of equal supervision time for each patient should be empirically studied to determine its actual importance and impact on the treatment. If it is a goal of supervision to consider each patient for an approximately equal amount of time, is sufficient time allotted for each patient to be covered? How can more supervision time be allotted in graduate training programs, or existing supervision time be more efficiently used? If the selection of patients for supervision is found to have a significant influence on the treatment, does this selection diminish or increase in importance as the therapist gets more experienced? Perhaps therapists' needs change as they acquire more experience and are able to generalize more from one patient to others. With this in mind, as Lambert (1980) suggests, more research should focus on experienced therapists, since most studies have relative neophytes for subjects.

References

Albott, W. L. (1984). Supervisory characteristics and other sources of supervision variance. *Clinical Supervisor, 2*(4), 27–41.

Arlow, J. A. (1963). The supervisory situation. *Journal of the American Psychoanalytic Association, 11,* 576–594.

Bailey, M. A., Warshaw, L., & Eichler, R. M. (1959). A study of factors related to length of stay in psychotherapy. *Journal of Clinical Psychology, 15,* 442–444.

Berrigan, L. P., & Garfield, S. L. (1981). Relation of missed psychotherapy appointments to premature termination and social class. *British Journal of Clinical Psychology, 20,* 239–242.

Burgoyne, R. W., Santini, S., Kline, F., & Staples, F. R. (1976). Who gets supervised? An extension of patient selection inequity. *American Journal of Psychiatry, 133,* 1313–1315.

Cherniss, C., & Egnatios, E. (1977). Styles of clinical supervision in community mental health programs. *Journal of Consulting and Clinical Psychology, 45,* 1195–1196.

DeBell, D. C. (1963). A critical digest of the literature on psychoanalytic supervision. *Journal of the American Psychoanalytic Association, 11,* 546–575.

Doehrman, M. J. G. (1976). Parallel processes in supervision and psychotherapy. *Bulletin of the Menninger Clinic, 40,* 9–104.

Ekstein, R., & Wallerstein, R. (1958). *The teaching and learning of psychotherapy.* New York: Basic Books.

•Emch, M. (1955). The social context of supervision. *International Journal of Psychiatry, 36,* 298–306.

Epstein, L. (1986). Collusive selective inattention to the negative impact of the supervisory interaction. *Contemporary Psychoanalysis, 22,* 389–417.

Everett, P. R. (in progress). Selection of patients for psychotherapy supervision and its relation to outcome. Dissertation, Adelphi University, New York.

Fleming, J. (1967). Teaching the basic skills of psychotherapy. *Archives of General Psychiatry, 16,* 416–426.

Fleming, J., & Benedek, T. (1966). *Psychoanalytic supervision.* New York: Grune & Stratton.

Friedlander, M. L., & Ward, L. G. (1984). Development and validation of the supervisory styles inventory. *Journal of Counseling Psychology, 31,* 541–557.

Friedlander, S. R., Dye, N. W., Costello, R. M., & Kobos, J. C. (1984). A developmental model for teaching and learning in psychotherapy supervision. *Psychotherapy, 21,* 189–196.

Garfield, S. L. (1986). Research on client variables in psychotherapy. In S. L. Garfield & A. E. Bergin (Eds.), *Handbook of psychotherapy and behavior change* (3rd ed., pp. 213–256). New York: Wiley.

Gediman, H. K., & Wolkenfeld, F. (1980). The parallelism phenomenon in psychoanalysis and supervision: Its reconsideration as a triadic system. *Psychoanalytic Quarterly, 49,* 234–255.

Goin, M. K., & Kline, F. (1976). Countertransference: A neglected subject in clinical supervision. *American Journal of Psychiatry, 133,* 41–44.

Grater, H. A. (1985). Stages in psychotherapy supervision: From therapy skills to skilled therapist. *Professional Psychology: Research and Practice, 16,* 605–610.

Greenberg, L. (1980). Supervision from the perspective of the supervisee. In A. K. Hess (Ed.), *Psychotherapy supervision: Theory, research and practice* (pp. 85–91). New York: Wiley.

Grey, A., & Fiscalini, J. (1987). Parallel process as transference-countertransference interaction. *Psychoanalytic Psychology, 4,* 131–144.

Grinberg, L. (1970). The problems of supervision in psychoanalytic education. *International Journal of Psychoanalysis, 51,* 371–383.

Gustin, J. C. (1958). Supervision in psychotherapy. *Psychoanalysis and Psychoanalytic Review, 45,* 63–72.

Hess, A. K. (1980). Training models and the nature of psychotherapy supervision. In A. K. Hess (Ed.), *Psychotherapy supervision: Theory, research and practice* (pp. 15–25). New York: Wiley.

Hess, A. K. (1987). Psychotherapy supervision: Stages, Buber, and a theory of relationship. *Professional Psychology: Research and Practice, 18,* 251–259.

Hirsch, I. (1984). Toward a more subjective view of analyzability. *American Journal of Psychoanalysis, 44,* 169–182.

Imber, S. D., Nash, E. H., & Stone, A. R. (1955). Social class and duration of psychotherapy. *Journal of Clinical Psychology, 11,* 281–284.

Issacharoff, A. (1984). Countertransference in supervision: Therapeutic consequences for the supervisee. In L. Caligor, P. M. Bromberg, & J. D. Meltzer (Eds.), *Clinical perspectives on the supervision of psychoanalysis and psychotherapy* (pp. 89–105). New York: Plenum.

Lambert, M. J. (1980). Research and the supervisory process. In A. K. Hess (Ed.), *Psychotherapy supervision: Theory, research and practice* (pp. 423–450). New York: Wiley.

Lebovici, S. (1970). Technical remarks on the supervision of psychoanalytic treatment. *International Journal of Psychoanalysis, 51,* 385–392.

Levenson, E. A. (1984). Follow the fox. In L. Caligor, P. M. Bromberg, & J. D. Meltzer (Eds.), *Clinical perspectives on the supervision of psychoanalysis and psychotherapy* (pp. 153–167). New York: Plenum.

Lorr, M., Katz, M. M., & Rubenstein, E. A. (1958). The prediction of length of stay in psychotherapy. *Journal of Consulting Psychology, 22,* 321–327.

Lower, R. B. (1972). Countertransference resistances in the supervisory situation. *American Journal of Psychiatry, 129,* 156–160.

Martin, G. C., Mayerson, P., Olsen, H. E., & Wiberg, J. L. (1978). Candidates' evaluation of psychoanalytic supervision. *Journal of the American Psychoanalytic Association, 26,* 407–424.

Meerloo, J. A. M. (1952). Some psychological processes in supervision of therapists. *American Journal of Psychoanalysis, 6,* 467–470.

Munson, C. E. (1987). Sex roles and power relationships in supervision. *Professional Psychology: Research and Practice, 18,* 236–243.

Rosenblatt, A., & Mayer, J. E. (1975). Objectionable supervisory styles: Students' views. *Social Work, 20,* 184–189.

Sachs, D. M., & Shapiro, S. H. (1976). On parallel processes in therapy and teaching. *Psychoanalytic Quarterly, 45,* 394–415.

Schaffer, L., & Myers, J. K. (1954). Psychotherapy and social stratification: An empirical study of practice in a psychiatric outpatient clinic. *Psychiatry, 17,* 83–93.

Schofield, W. (1964). *Psychotherapy: The purchase of friendship.* Englewood Cliffs, NJ: Prentice-Hall.

Searles, H. F. (1955). The informational value of the supervisor's emotional experiences. *Psychiatry, 18,* 135–146.

Searles, H. F. (1965). Problems of psycho-analytic supervision. In *Collected papers on schizophrenia and related subjects* (pp. 584–604). New York: International Universities Press.

Searles, H. F. (1979). Transitional phenomena and therapeutic symbiosis. In *Countertransference and related subjects* (pp. 503–576). New York: International Universities Press.

Selzer, M. L., Murphy, T. C., & Amini, F. (1961). Change of supervisor and psychotherapeutic progress. *Archives of General Psychiatry, 5,* 186–192.

Steinhelber, J., Patterson, V., Cliffe, K., & LeGoullon, M. (1984). An investigation of some relationships between psychotherapy supervision and patient change. *Journal of Clinical Psychology, 40,* 1346–1353.

Wagner, F. F. (1957). Supervision of psychotherapy. *American Journal of Psychotherapy, 11,* 759–768.

Winnicott, D. W. (1965). Ego distortion in terms of true and false self. *The maturational process and the facilitating environment* (pp. 140–152). New York: International Universities Press.

On Being Supervised and Supervision

Saralea E. Chazan, Ph.D.

In the realm between here and there, becoming and arrived, there exists a land of discovery. Between realms, light shines through interspaces and enlightens relationships not before perceived, which later become consolidated into spontaneous understandings. These are the feelings of an apprentice, who stands on ground still unsteady and surveys myriad horizons, waiting to see what will settle in and take hold as part of new realities. The supervisory relationship stands at the nexus point of this emergent structure. It leads from past therapeutic contacts to anticipated future mastery. To the supervisee, the supervisor is both an immediate presence and a representative of shared wisdom of the profession. Through him/her new bonds are established to the literature, which embody diverse perspectives, while providing sustaining support and guidance to the novice. In thinking back on my experience in receiving and giving supervision, three phases can be defined. Each phase can be identified within a single supervisory relationship and across supervisory experiences referring to the stages within one individual's professional growth. The three phases will be described below and comprise the content of this paper.

Phase One: The Creation of a Space

In order to give a place to playing, Winnicott (1971) postulates a potential space between the baby and mother. This potential space varies in accordance with life experiences in relation to the mother

25

and is distinctly separate from the biological inner world of mother and child and the shared external reality. It is this potential space, created by both partners together, which contains the play. Play, according to Winnicott, is a universal form of communication which contributes toward growth and health. He defines psychoanalysis as a highly specialized form of playing in the service of communication with oneself and others. It is the creation of this space that forms a home base for the supervisee. It is a focal point to which he or she will repeatedly turn in exploration and experimentation, while learning his/her craft. It is a space where work and play are fused as one, as personal and professional identity become closely bonded.

As in any new beginning, the novice supervisory relationship is at once uncertain and full of promise. Some initial ponderings include: Will he/she like me? Can we work together? Can I trust him/her? Can I reveal my doubts? How will he/she react to my mistakes? Are we at all alike? Will I be understood? Will I be appreciated? These questions are asked by both supervisee and supervisor as they begin to form the linkages necessary to create a place, a space within which new forms can emerge. Paradigms from the past are important in contributing to this process. These past influences include all the experienced meaningful relationships of both partners. The transference is from families-of-origin, personal therapies, and professional contacts. Points of mutual referencing are important in charting the extent of size and depth of the space to be utilized. Dyads will differ in their tolerance for difference and contrast. Within some dyads it will be the differences that prove most illuminating, while with others it is the gradual revelation of similarities that seems crucial. When this space has been firmly established there is an understanding reached of what, where, when, and why. The relationship then enters the next phase, which we shall refer to as "structure building."

Phase Two: Structure Building

The building of structure can be best understood following the model outlined by Mahler et al. (1975). At first the supervisor-supervisee relationship is experienced as twinning. The supervisor functions as an alter ego strengthening the supervisee's feeling of competence through similarity and shared meaning. "I am like him/her; he/she is like me." The narcissistic supplies gained in this way are intended to help the supervisee to attempt to view relationships from a new perspective enhanced by the supervisor's understanding. Flexibility and empathy are essentials for the supervisor to adapt him/herself to the supervisee's individual style and blend with, rather than negate, ongoing patterns. As the supervisee begins to practice the new understandings and techniques based upon these understandings, he/she experiences a burst of competence and freedom to venture forth and experiment with new approaches. The supervisor is there to guide and at the same time encourage exploration. The spheres of exploration are manifold and consist of personal, as well as professional, trials. The supervisor, as supraordinate guide, is felt as a presence in all relationships past, present, and anticipated. This interlocking of spaces through the supervisory relationship forms the basis for later integration of work and play.

During the period of repeated forays of exploration, return to home base, and receipt of feedback, the supervisee is able to continue the construction of his/her therapeutic model. The meaning of mistakes, injury, and recovery are part of the process. Differences of opinion, disappointment, power struggles, and tests of strength are hallmarks of this period. Disillusionment and despair are trying to both members of the dyad. Resistance to change indicates strength, as well as blockage to progress. The supervisor now is required to exercise tact, empathy, and tolerance for difference. Caution is needed to avoid the pitfalls of narcissistic domination and imposition of authority.

Appreciation of the smallest progress evidenced is experienced as enhancing by the supervisee and permits assimilation of criticism, without an overwhelmingly negative backlash. It is at this juncture that opposition is expected as a normal part of growth. When the conflict becomes a struggle of wills, a negative pattern of supervisee reaction may ensue. If the supervisor can guide his/her apprentice to a better understanding of these feelings, the experience may be directly therapeutic, freeing energies for the renewal of creativity. As the falls become fewer and the hurts become less, there is new consistency to understanding and a new phase in reunion is reached.

Phase Three: Reciprocity and "Well-being"

Erik Erikson (1959), in describing identity formation, characterized the psychosocial gains of adult ego development with the terms "intimacy," "generativity," and "integrity." Intimate engagements in forms of generativity and integrative experiences, which reflect values accrued from a lifetime, invite opportunities for ego functions in spheres free from conflict: "The older generation thus needs the younger one as much as the younger one depends on the older; and it would seem that it is in this mutuality of the development of the older and younger generations that certain basic and universal values such as love, faith, truth, justice, order, work, etc., in all of their defensive strength, compensatory power and independent creativity become and remain important joint achievements of individual ego development and of the social process" (p. 155).

Thus, according to Erikson, on the level of mutuality, a reciprocity becomes firmly established. The supervisory experience leads, then, to a dependable inner experience of "well-being" and professional identification. The supervisee is recognized as colleague and becomes a member in full standing of his/her profession. Although not every supervisory relationship ends on this note of mutuality, it is the final goal of all supervision. The supervisee is now "good-enough" in the eyes of his/her mentors and can begin the supervision of others. Struggles and expressions of difference now take the form of organizational forums, intellectual debates, and political issues. The space has widened beyond the dyad to an ongoing reaching out beyond and within the self to the definition of boundaries of professional identity.

Summary

Three phases are defined within the development of the supervisor-supervisee relationship. Phase One marks the beginning of finding a space where subsequent creativity will take place. Phase Two ensues as the dyad begins to formulate a structure together that defines their understanding of the therapeutic process. Phase Three is the culmination of these efforts resulting in renewed personal and professional identifications. The end goal is reached when the supervisee is welcomed as colleague and begins to apprentice others in continuation of the craft.

References

Erikson, E. (1959). *Identity and the life cycle.* New York: International Universities Press.

Mahler, M., Pine, F., & Bergman, A. (1975). *The psychological birth of the human infant.* New York: Basic Books.

Winnicott, D. W. (1971). *Playing and reality.* London: Tavistock.

Supervision and the
Analytic Superego

Reuben Fine, Ph.D.

The problems inherent in supervision were already sensed by Hanns Sachs, the first training analyst, when the Berlin Institute, the first training institute, was set up in 1920. The issue he saw was one of education versus indoctrination. He wrote:

The future analyst must learn to see things which other people easily, willingly and permanently overlook, and must be in a position to maintain this capacity to observe, even when it is in sharpest contradiction to his own wishes and feelings . . . As one sees, analysis requires something which corresponds to the novitiate of the church. (Fenichel, 1920, p. 73)

It is easy to see from this remark that severe resistance can be expected in the supervisory process. This has been our experience, though it is rarely discussed, since emphasis is usually on education. For the resistance in supervision, I propose the term "analytic superego," which, by analogy with the individual superego, embodies those commands and prohibitions the future analyst believes emanate from his/her position as an analyst. Some of the aspects of this analytic superego, such as the avoidance of social relationships with the patients and the maintenance of analytic neutrality, are written into the role, but others are projected into it by the individual analyst, and sometimes by the supervisor.

When you deal with a superego figure you have to learn to please him. Long ago Kubie (1958) discovered the obvious: The therapist in training does not present sessions accurately to the supervisor. For

29

this there are two reasons: First, the mechanical task of remembering everything—what the patient says, what the analyst says, and everything else—is humanly impossible. So the supervisor is confronted with selections. Second, since the aim is to please, the material is subjected to a variety of distortions and biases by the presenting therapist for the simplest reason of all—the desire to get through the program. In the following observations, this process of distortion should be held clearly in mind.

The various ways in which the therapist deals with the supervisor run parallel to the various ways in which he/she deals with other superego figures in any realm of life. The therapist can try to please, can be defiant, can block off material which reveals too much, conceal mistakes, or can revel in mistakes, in opposition to the supervisor's wishes. All the other defenses against superego pressure can be found in one form or another. First of all there is slavish imitation. In one case the supervisor could add nothing to what the therapist had to say, since the invariable reply was, "I've already done that." One naturally asks: If he gave every interpretation that the supervisor suggested, what need was there for supervision? In another case this was exactly the attitude of the therapist. She stated that she did much better without supervision, that she handled her cases well, and that it would be best to forgo supervision with her. Instead, she was dismissed from the clinic.

During my own training, at one time I was in supervision simultaneously with Geza Roheim and Theodor Reik. Reik was a very supportive man. Everything I did he found excellent. He also pushed a rather peculiar interpretation of the sex act: that if the man feels more sensation at the base of his penis he is closer to his homosexual feelings. Roheim on the other hand seemed to approve of nothing that I did. He was the most profound analytic thinker I have ever met, perhaps the most profound since Freud. The first analyst to work in a primitive community, he had a profound knowledge of psychoanalysis in all its aspects. Perhaps because of this, he was always critical of the interpretations I offered my patients. Yet in reflecting on this experience, it was from Roheim that I learned the most. However, learning from a supervisor who never gives any approval requires a strong ego. In retrospect, I think he was too critical, because of the lack of resolution of some of his own conflicts. A bookish boy, he had become a learned lonely man, relating only to his wife. When she died, he died shortly thereafter (within a few months).

The opposite to the therapist who is slavishly obedient is the one who is determinedly defiant. A student of mine once had in treatment an adolescent boy of 15 who never arrived on time. The therapist bawled the boy out every time, insisting that was the right way to do things. He had been through four supervisors who could not reach him and four committees which had failed him. Yet he persisted in his stubborn defiance.

Another set of problems relates to the severity of the impulses. In these days of ego analysis, which was intended to augment, not replace, id analysis, some therapists virtually omit the id altogether. For example, Kohut says almost nothing about the id, so that self psychologists and cultural psychotherapists often leave out any reference to classical theory.

On the other hand there are many therapists who make adequate use of their supervisory work and apply it to themselves without telling the supervisor about it. In one case, a young woman who dealt adequately with a lot of id material realized that her husband was very repressed; in the course of the supervision she divorced him and found a more libidinal man. Later she told me that her change was directly attributable to the supervision.

Then again, there are those who insist on an id interpretation of every action. Greenson (1967) cites an example of a woman who cancelled a session because her 3-year-old son was ill. The analyst, who was in supervision with Greenson, interpreted this as a resistance, saying that she wanted to be the child. Greenson told his supervisee to return to analysis. Whether he did so is not recorded, but the patient left analysis abruptly the next week.

Feelings about the patient are often hard to handle because of the analytic superego. If the supervisor likes the therapist in training too much, he or she is "abandoning neutrality," which is confused with a lack of feeling. Neutrality means that the analyst takes a neutral position with regard to the patient's conflicts, not an absence of feeling, which is humanly impossible. This applies to both sexuality and hostility.

If a man is confronted by an attractive woman who reveals her deepest secrets to him, he is apt to respond positively. Yet many therapists are deeply afraid of having any sexual feelings toward the patient. For them, whenever an erotic association comes to the fore, they turn it back to childhood immediately, which makes the patient feel like a child. A prominent analyst once told me that he wished Freud had set up a rule for how soon after an analysis is completed the therapist should be permitted to approach his patient romantically.

Many therapists make the mistake of confusing the erotic

feelings of the patient with mental illness. In a hospital outpatient situation, an attractive psychiatrist was assigned a patient who fell in love with her. He bought her flowers, tried to follow her around the hospital, bought her tickets for the lottery, even moved closer to the hospital in order to be closer to her. She was a depressed young woman (hospitalized at one time for depression) and terribly upset by all this attention. She insisted that he was schizophrenic (which he certainly was not) and transferred him to another therapist (had it not been for the supervisor she would have even hospitalized him).

It takes much control for the therapist to avoid intruding personal unresolved confiicts into the therapeutic situation. One therapist, who had been a priest, was eager to convert all his patients to Christianity. One of his patients was a priest as well. Much to the therapist's surprise, the priest-patient in one session revealed that he had a small penis and asked for advice about it. So he was just like all other men. The therapist did not know how to handle this situation. According to his analytic superego, priests should not have sexual feelings or be aware of their genitals.

In another case, the therapist was overly concerned with ethics. Whatever interpretation was offered, he would say, "But is that ethical? After all, you can't be sure." This man was also in supervision with another man on the faculty of the institute. Another of his resistances was to compare the suggestions of two controls, since they were bound to be contradictory on a number of points. He seemed to learn nothing from his supervision.

Many analysts become jealous of their patients, who may dress better, or be more accomplished in life, or seem superior to their therapists in some other way. Habitually these analysts seek to disparage their patients' accomplishments in order to get the supervisor to look more favorably on them. Because of this competition, they tend to push the patients in directions unfavorable to their development.

The battle of the schools leads to many countertransference problems, which are already apparent in the lives of the founders. Sullivan, as Perry's biography (1982) convincingly shows, never had much of an education, either in medical school or before. He was essentially unfamiliar with Freud, many of whose works had not yet been translated. As a lonely child brought up on a farm, whose earliest language was Gaelic, he developed a peculiar language and a peculiar writing style. Nevertheless he made some epoch-making discoveries in the treatment of schizophrenia. His followers have generally adopted his position on schizophrenia, but fail to realize that his theories, for the most part, are simply reformulations of Freud.

On the other hand Freud was a very learned man, competent in a number of different fields (for example, he read Shakespeare in English). The ability to sit through the associations of a disturbed person six days a week also required an enormous ability to concentrate and remember what he had heard. For his followers he became an impossible ego-ideal, which accounts for many of the splits and controversies within the field. Also Freud, whose social life centered very heavily around his family, failed to appreciate the significance of interpersonal relationships to the same extent as Sullivan.

On the current scene, feminism has created new countertransference problems covered over by a reliance on "theory." Shere Hite (1987) in her latest work actually advises women to leave their men, as Aristophanes did some 2500 years ago, but Aristophanes wrote a comedy, while Hite offers her work as a serious tract. Many of the therapists who value her work take an automatic position that any problem in a marriage is due to the man, and that the only solution for most women is to get divorced.

In spite of all these errors (and many others), the careful process of individual supervision, as practiced in analysis, is still the most practical method for teaching psychoanalytic technique. If it is realized that the therapist is not only engaging in an intellectual exercise about the principles of psychoanalysis, but is also resolving his/her analytic superego, the greatest progress is achieved. In this way, the supervisory experience becomes just as therapeutic an endeavor as the actual analytic process.

References

Fenichel, O. (1930). *Zehn Jahre Berliner Psychoanalytisches Institut.* Vienna: Internationaler Psychoanalytischer Verlag, 1970.

Fine, R. (1982). *The healing of the mind* (2nd ed.). New York: Free Press.

Greenson, R. (1967). *The technique and practice of psychoanalysis.* New York: International Universities Press.

Hite, S. (1987). *Women and love.* New York: Knopf.

Kubie, L. S. (1958). Research into the process of supervision in psychoanalysis. *Psychoanalytic Quarterly, 27,* 226–236.

Levin, M. (1987). *Feminism and freedom.* Princeton, NJ: Transaction.

Perry, H. C. (1982). *Psychiatrist of America.* Cambridge, MA: Belknap.

Contemporary Issues in and Approaches to Psychoanalytic Supervision

Franklin H. Goldberg, Ph.D.

Psychotherapists and psychoanalysts rate their supervision as the most valuable aspect of their professional development (Hart, 1982). Yet, supervision as a focus of study, compared to a myriad of other concepts and processes in psychoanalysis, has received relatively little attention. In the past few years there have been several professional conferences concerned with supervision as well as a number of books and articles devoted to a more scholarly approach to the subject. Nevertheless, supervision remains a neglected area of study in analytic training. It is the purpose of this paper to present some of the critical issues in supervision viewed as a process and to describe various approaches and concepts differentiating analysts of disparate persuasions.

Despite the regenerated interest, supervisees still rarely question the process of supervision. They make their choice of supervisor supposedly on solid supervisory grounds such as reputation of the supervisor and theoretical orientation, although other considerations include geographical location, giving good evaluation reports, possible referral sources, and the notion that a supervisor may be "easy on you." These latter bases for supervisory choice may be just as cogent as those involving reputation (e.g., having "star" quality) and perhaps just as valid. It is uncertain how often supervisors reflect upon the process of supervision. Not many of us have actual training in supervision, as relatively few programs or courses are available in supervision for supervisors. Hess (1986) notes that

according to the ethical principles of the American Psychological
Association, psychologists may only provide services in areas for
which they are qualified by training and experience. Most of us are
"experienced" by dint of having been supervised, and because we
supervise.

There has been increasing thought given to the suggestion that
psychoanalytic candidates receive supervision training, as they are
but a step away from being supervisors themselves. In their seminal
study on psychoanalytic supervision, Fleming and Benedek (1966)
note that the skills that lead to successful teaching of psychoanalysis
are essentially the same as those the student needs to develop for
therapeutic work with patients. It remains debatable whether a
"good" analyst would automatically, or even with some training,
become a "good" supervisor. There is also a question whether we
analysts as supervisors actually practice what we preach. Should we?
Can we? Probably not! Levenson (1982) comments that he is often
"perplexed, bored, confused and at sea" in doing his therapeutic
work, but when he supervises, "all is clear." He attributes this
difference to supervision being concerned with a different level of
abstraction than analysis, namely at a higher level where clarity
increases. Conducting analysis involves immediate experience and
interaction, which cannot be duplicated in the supervisory session.
Of course, there is a similar process occurring within supervision,
which can also be the focus of attention. Indeed, it is often the case
that afterwards, in retrospect, going back over a particular session,
both the analyst and the supervisor can detect previously unrecog-
nized themes, interactions, transferences, even countertransference
happenings.

The supervisory situation has its own anxieties for the supervisee, namely, the threat of exposure, the issue of competence as a
therapist, and the evaluative component of the supervision. Supervisors, as noted by Lesser (1983), have their reputation as teachers to
uphold, to impress upon the supervisee their own capabilities and
particular point of view as well as maintaining their standing within
the training institute hierarchy. It is fairly well-known, but not often
elucidated, that we may be influenced more in our therapeutic work
by our analysts than by our supervisors. Perhaps not so much in
terms of concepts, but more subtly in our style. Your analyst usually
does not tell you what he or she is doing, but you pick up how he or
she does it, and that may affect how you do it. How many times in an
analytic session with a patient, particularly in our beginning work,
might we consciously think, "Now, how would my analyst handle this

or respond?" Or how many times might we do our version unconsciously based on what he or she did? These recollections might
prove to be much more powerful influences on our work than what a
supervisor tells you to do or says he or she does.

From a historical perspective, we can trace the shift in supervisory practice from an authoritative to a more collaborative approach. Freud in 1910 advocated that self-analysis was an important
part of learning in psychoanalysis, although previously there were
group meetings at his home to discuss cases. As several prominent
psychoanalysts have stated, the main problem with self-analysis is
countertransference. In 1912, Freud advocated a training analysis,
but it was not until 1921 that a training analysis became part of the
training program. Eitington, in 1926, stated that the difference
between a therapeutic and a training analysis is not just a difference
in technique, but rather, the latter has an additional aim, a supervisory one.

The early concept of supervision in all mental health disci-
plines—psychiatry, social work, psychology, as well as in psychoanalysis—was that the student would learn by imitation, as in an
apprenticeship model. The supervisor would take over the case and
more or less tell the supervisee how to handle it. Balint (1948) called
this kind of supervision "superego training." The issue that became
more and more prominent and remains today as the major controver-
sial topic in discussions of how to supervise is, do we "treat" or
"educate"? Is supervision "therapeutic" or "didactic"? Some analysts,
like Ekstein (1960), believe that "the clinical teaching of psychoanalysis is largely a matter of demonstrating techniques." Thus, the
supervisor shows the supervisee by elucidating and pursuing the
candidate's countertransference reactions as revealed in interaction
with the patient. Lesser (1983) questions the reality and value of
maintaining traditional distinctions between the psychoanalytic and
supervisory situations. Eitington (1937) stresses, "There is more to
supervision than analyzing the countertransference," and most other
analysts agree. DeBell (1963), as an outcome of discussions with
other analysts, states, "Everybody appears to oppose 'treatment' of
the supervisee yet everybody does it to varying degrees, some with
misgivings, some without." I think it is not a matter of whether or not,
but how and how far therapeutic approaches are applied within the
supervisory process; it being more a question of emphasis. A recent
study by Hess (1986) revealed that when supervision was viewed by
supervisees as psychotherapy, the supervisory experience was
regarded less favorably.

One might hypothesize that the main difference between Freudian and interpersonal approaches to supervision is that Freudians concentrate on didactic issues while interpersonalists focus upon countertransference. However, this position is not supported by the literature, in which most analysts advocate a balance between these two emphases. Indeed, it is possible that, as Bromberg (1982) suggests, "when it comes to supervision, most analysts have been more receptive to thinking in terms of interpersonal process—i.e., at least with regard to what is happening between the therapist and the patient, than in trying to see things solely as separate intrapsychic fields. In fact, I think the subject of supervision is one of the less conflict-ridden interfaces between different psychoanalytic theories."

In the writer's opinion, differences in supervisory approaches between various theoretical positions arise not out of differences in the goals of supervision and the need for both educative and therapeutic components, but in the selection of material, the types of interventions, the concepts used—in essence on the conceptual and philosophical distinctions between the theories themselves and each supervisor's interpretation of these theories. I would postulate, however, that there may be supervisory differences between Freudian and interpersonalist analysts in the latter's relative deemphasis on technique, in their focus on the transference-countertransference interplay in the analytic session, and in the use of the supervisory process itself as a tool in supervision. However, there may be more overlap than there is divergence. With respect to the latter emphasis on the supervisory process per se, Searles (1962) sees the supervisor more as colleague than as one who prescribes treatment, "achieving fuller awareness of the process taking place between ourselves."

Fiscalini (1985) advocates exploring the supervisory relationship for transference-countertransference manifestations as "one of the major ways in which the supervisee learns about psychoanalysis and forms his identity as a psychoanalyst." Coupled with Levenson's (1982) thesis that "the metapsychology one chooses—whether it is interpersonal or Freudian or object relations—is really more a matter of personal aesthetics and I would prefer the supervisee to find his own system of belief as long as he recognizes that successful therapy does not depend upon his indoctrinating the patient with his beliefs or translating his theoretical beliefs into systematic action, nor obversely does it prove his metapsychology to be correct," these statements seem to reflect the contemporary interpersonal psychoanalytic approach to supervision. From a Freudian perspective, DeBell (1963) indicates that supervisors can use confrontation and clarification in uncovering countertransference reactions in the analyst, but not genetic reconstructions or even pursuing the analyst's "associative connections." For these explorations, the supervisor often suggests that the analyst consider these further in self-analysis or in the personal or training analysis.

Issacharoff (1982), an interpersonal analyst, in a similar voice, believes that while interpretations in analytic situations necessarily encompass elements from the past, in the supervisory situation interpretations should be limited to emotional reactions to the patient and to the supervisor. Issacharoff also notes that the remark, which many of us have made often enough—"Take it up in your own analysis"—is futile most of the time. The supervisee may not choose to turn to his or her analyst to discuss the "problem" immediately, either because of resistance or the feeling that it is an arbitrary intrusion into his or her own analytic process. Interestingly, some analysts from both persuasions do, while others do not, advise supervisors to contact their supervisee's analyst if a problem arises. This overture seems more likely to be condoned when the supervisor is an active member of the training institute and evaluation is a major concern.

The supervisory experience will vary according to certain presumptions, styles, and foci of the supervisor. Primary, in my opinion, is the personality or character style of the supervisor, which underlies theoretical orientation and determines the content and course of supervision. Rarely does the supervisee have a determining role in what aspect of, or how, his work is reviewed, except when the supervisor is really not interested or involved. The functional relationship between supervisor and supervisee—determined by both—colors the interaction. Is it like a teacher to a student? Is the supervisor a Zen master? Or, is he or she merely "the expert"?

Early in the history of psychoanalysis, the supervisor often assumed full or at least partial responsibility for the conduct of the case. This does not appear to be prevalent today. Is the supervisory relationship more like therapist and patient, or is it collaborative or collegial? Many supervisors choose to move from one role to another, depending on the needs of the supervisee or the phase of supervision. Indeed, when supervisors are asked if there is a difference between their work with beginners as compared with more experienced supervisees, they often refer to a change from being more didactic to more therapeutic, to more collaborative, perhaps paralleling to some extent progress through an analysis.

Another way of viewing the supervisory process is by locating the focus of attention. Is the supervisor 1) patient focused, concerned mostly with dynamics, history, making the correct interpretations; 2) therapist focused, concerned with countertransference phenomena and character reactions; 3) process focused, concerned with the ongoing interactions between therapist and patient, transference and otherwise; or 4) is the focus in supervision on the supervisory process where supervisee transference and supervisor countertransference reactions would be addressed? How do we as supervisors work and how does it affect what is communicated to our supervisees? What is learned? Why do some supervisees claim to have benefited greatly from a so-called holding or confirming setting when they were in joint supervision and little was said? Levenson (1982), in describing his work with Clara Thompson, said, "She established a play-ground in which we found ourselves—you either swim or sink." What about the drownees? Maybe as Jacob (1981) suggests, it depends on one's "cognitive style," the particular way in which we learn, which he elaborates on as a "working style."

Beginning candidates in psychoanalytic training tend to prefer a more active rather than passive style, another dimension which differentiates supervisory approaches and effectiveness. Their anxiety, related to their inexperience, seeks more definitive guidelines. Maybe later on, with more experience, supervisees can move from a focus on technique to a focus on process. Friedman and Kaslow (1986) connect the developing sense of professional identity schemata to Mahler's separation-individuation model. According to their paradigm, the supervisee's professional identity emerges through the following stages: 1) excitement and anticipatory anxiety when the supervisor should provide a "holding environment"; 2) dependency on the identification with the supervisor; 3) activity and continued dependency; 4) exuberance and taking charge; 5) identity and independence—the adolescence phase where questioning the supervisor (i.e., rebellion) occurs; and finally 6) calm and collegiality.

A phenomenon that occurs often in supervision, and proved useful in furthering the analyst's self-understanding, has become the object of controversy among various theoretical positions. This is the notion of parallel process, which Issacharoff (1982) defines as "occurring when the supervisee is unconsciously enmeshed in an unresolved treatment difficulty, resistance, or impasse with his patient and communicates this behaviorally in the supervisory situation." The presumed mechanism for this often dramatic observation is identification. Gediman and Wolkenfeld (1980) consider this phenomenon to be triadic, a complex network or system between the patient, therapist, and supervisor in communication with each other. They further suggest the concept of a learning alliance as essential to supervisory progress much as the therapeutic alliance is essential to analytic progress.

There are interesting possibilities here in shifts in the therapeutic interactions resulting from shifts in the supervisory interaction. Are there more subtle and direct effects on the analysis via supervisory interventions? Hopefully! What is sometimes surprising is when our more sophisticated patients ask us in innocent candor, "You seem more active lately. Have you changed supervisors?" Yes, often we have! What is also disconcerting is when you go into the next therapy hour with your patient armed with a crystal-clear understanding of some treatment issue derived from a painstaking scrutiny in supervision of your therapeutic interactions with your patient, and after sharing this magnificent, mind-boggling, cure-inducing insight with your patient, he looks at you as if to say, "So what?" This certainly says something about the analytic as well as the supervisory process. Questions arise as to what supervisors think they do and what they really do, and what supervisees think they learn and what they really learn. These would be meaningful topics for more intensive scrutiny, perhaps at the heart of supervisory transactions.

Hart (1982), Levenson (1982), Fleming and Benedek (1966), and others describe the supervisory process in terms of phases. Do they really exist? Are we as supervisors attuned to them? For example, Levenson writes, "With beginning therapists I would work on structuring the therapy, delineating it, helping the therapist to pace and control the flow of material and helping him learn how to do an inquiry . . . the next level of supervision would have to do with elaborating the nature and intentionality of interpretation . . . the third level of inquiry, where analysts are senior and/or working with termination, I would examine their realistic participation with the patient."

Fleming and Benedek (1966) earlier had described three phases in supervision interestingly paralleling what is sometimes referred to as the three phases of analysis (namely the beginning, middle and end phases) and strikingly similar to Levenson's comments, although reflecting very different persuasions. They discuss the aim of supervision as developing the analyst as an instrument, an analyzing instrument, echoing Freud's (1912) analogy comparing the analyst's unconscious to the receiver of a telephone, in the sense of freeing oneself from resistances and avoiding blind spots in one's analytic work. They indicate that the first phase in supervision is devoted to: 1) learning to listen with free-floating attention; 2) making inferential interpretations of meaning that is beyond the awareness of the patient, but is explanatory of the patient's behaviors; 3) learning to estimate the patient's level of anxiety and resistance; and 4) learning to judge timing and dosing of reactions in tune with the equilibrium in the analyst-patient relationship. In the middle phase, the phenomenon of regression and transference would be focused on in supervision, and in the end phase, emphasis would be placed on termination, recognizing progress, and the technical problems of bringing an analytic relationship to a close.

Summary

In this paper, I have tried to touch upon what seem to be the most salient and perplexing questions about the supervisor's role or style in the supervisory process. I would urge that psychoanalytic and psychotherapeutic training programs include a course on supervision so that prospective supervisors can grasp some of the intricacies met with in conducting supervision and can familiarize themselves with the conceptual issues rather than just proceeding ad hoc, as is the usual practice.

References

Balint, M. (1948). On the psychoanalytic training system. *International Journal of Psychoanalysis, 29,* 163–173.

Bromberg, P. M. (1982). The supervisory process and parallel process in psychoanalysis. *Contemporary Psychoanalysis, 18,* 92–111.

DeBell, D. (1963). A critical digest of literature on psychoanalytic supervision. *Journal of the American Psychoanalytic Association, 11,* 546–575.

Eitington, M. (1926). An address to the International Training Commission. *International Journal of Psychoanalysis, 18,* 346–348.

Eitington, M. (1937). Report of general meeting of the International Training Commission. *International Journal of Psychoanalysis, 18,* 346–348.

Ekstein, R. (1960). Report of the panel on the teaching of psychoanalytic technique. *Journal of the American Psychoanalytic Association, 8,* 167–174.

Fiscalini, J. (1985). On supervisory parataxis and dialogue. *Contemporary Psychoanalysis, 21,* 591–608.

Fleming, J., & Benedek, T. F. (1966). *Psychoanalytic supervision.* New York: Grune & Stratton.

Friedman, D. & Kaslow, J. J. (1986). The development of professional identification in psychotherapists. *Clinical Supervision, 4,* 29–49.

Freud, S. (1912). Recommendations to physicians practicing psychoanalysis. *Standard Edition,* 12, 111–120. London: Hogarth, 1957.

Gediman, H. K., & Wolkenfeld, F. (1980). The parallelism phenomenon in psychoanalysis and supervision: Its reconsideration as a triadic system. *Psychoanalytic Quarterly, 49,* 234–255.

*Hart, G. M. (1982). *The process of clinical supervision.* Baltimore: University Park Press.

*Hess, A. K. (1986). Growth in supervision: stages of supervisee and supervisor development. *Clinical Supervision, 4,* 51–67.

Issacharoff, A. (1982). Countertransference in supervision. *Contemporary Psychoanalysis, 18,* 442–455.

Jacob, P., Jr. (1981). Application: The San Francisco Project—The analyst at work. In R. S. Wallerstein (Ed.), *Becoming a psychoanalyst.* New York: International Universities Press.

Lesser, R. M. (1983). Supervision: Illusions, anxieties and questions. *Contemporary Psychoanalysis, 19,* 120–129.

* Levenson, E. A. (1982). Follow the fox. *Contemporary Psychoanalysis, 18,* 1–15.

Searles, H. (1962). Problems of psychoanalytic supervision. In J. A. Masserman (Ed.), *Science and psychoanalysis* (Vol. 5). New York: Grune & Stratton.

The Good Hour
in Supervision

Robert C. Lane, Ph.D.,
and James W. Hull, Ph.D.

Kris (1956) describes some of the characteristics of the "good hour" in analysis. He states that the insight achieved during the good hour depends heavily on the integrative functions of the patient's ego. Gaining insight always has an infantile prototype, usually of an oral nature, which determines the state of the transference during the good hour. Thus, the patient relives certain aspects of infantile experience during the good hour, usually involving fantasies of nursing. The infantile prototype, and hence the state of the transference, may be negative, and the good hour may begin with a negativism that reflects this early experience. Kris feels that a good hour is always the result of previous analytic work, during which countercathectic energies and energies attached to repression have been set free. An intrapsychic reorganization takes place and these freed energies are placed at the disposal of the ego in a neutralized form. Kris emphasizes that transformed aggressive energy plays a specific and crucial role in the ego integration that occurs during insight. Finally, he describes three aspects of ego functioning, which usually are evident during the good hour: 1) the patient's ego engages in a temporary and partial regression, but maintains the ability to reassert control at the point that an interpretation is reached; 2) when an interpretation is offered, the patient's ego expands its function to include objective self-observation; 3) there is control over the discharge of affects, with specific affective experiences often being attached to a childhood memory that emerges during the good hour.

43

We feel that the good supervisory hour can be understood by applying the framework Kris has developed. In this paper we will present several clinical vignettes that include descriptions of good hours in supervision, and then relate aspects of these particular sessions to the concepts Kris has outlined.

Since the 1920s analysts have debated the nature of psychoanalytic supervision and how it differs from the candidate's personal analysis (Fine, 1979). Two positions have emerged regarding the control, or supervisory analysis. The first suggests that supervision and personal analysis are two separate aspects of psychoanalytic training, and that whenever personal material arises in supervision it should be referred to the candidate's personal analyst. Supervision in this instance focuses almost exclusively on the technical difficulties presented by the patient, and the therapist's countertransference reactions are not dealt with in any depth. The second approach places less distance between the teaching (supervisory or control) and personal (training) analysis. In this view, the supervisor may emphasize the candidate's countertransference reaction, thereby involving the candidate more personally in the supervisory process. At times the distinction between the teaching and personal analysis may become blurred. Fine (1979) says, with regard to the training-supervising analyst, "No procedure is as unique to the analytic situation, and no procedure has been fraught with so much dissention, as the existence of the training-supervising analyst. Theoretically these two functions are separate, but in practice they overlap to such an extent that they can be considered together." In a personal communication (1986), Fine expressed the view that, in essence, it is up to the supervisee: If he or she wishes to pursue these countertransference feelings in supervision, it would be awkward to say, "Take this up with your training analyst." Such feelings can have a great effect on the therapy, and the therapist must understand them in order to do his or her most effective work with the patient.

By applying Kris's model to the supervisory process, we are clearly opting for the second of these two approaches to psychoanalytic supervision. However, some qualifications must be emphasized. Two of the three cases we discuss involved control analyses, in which supervisor and candidate followed one case over an extended period of time, rather than a broader type of supervision in which several cases might be discussed. Also, each candidate in these examples was already well into, or finished with, his or her personal analysis. Finally, these candidates were also far enough along in their psychoanalytic training that mastery of basic principles of technique had been achieved. We are suggesting that in control analysis, with candidates in the more advanced stages of both their personal analysis and their formal psychoanalytic education, there can be great benefit from creating a semipermeable membrane between supervision and the candidate's personal analysis, as described in the second model. Specific suggestions for fostering this type of supervisory relationship have been described elsewhere by Lane (1985).

Case 1

A male therapist was treating a borderline woman who exhibited severe problems with impulsivity. She had been seen for 8 months in psychoanalytic psychotherapy on a three times per week basis. Recently she had been dealing with issues related to a strong emerging attachment to the therapist, as well as intense aggressive impulses directed toward him. In the weeks leading up to this particular supervisory session, the therapist had discussed a feeling that occasionally came over him while listening to this patient. At times he became extremely tired, had difficulty concentrating on what she was saying, and felt a slight sense of depersonalization. Several times the therapist and the supervisor had noted this countertransference reaction, but no clear pattern or explanation had been evident.

During the session he presented on this particular day, the therapist had experienced these feelings in an intense manner. After a few moments of reflection, the supervisor pointed out that this was indeed a countertransference reaction, but in part it was being induced by the patient. He discussed the patient's emerging positive and dependent transference feelings toward the therapist, and her ambivalence about being special to him. Because she felt both an intense longing to be loved in a symbiotic manner, allowing the expression of her most infantile feelings and needs, and at the same time was repulsed by these wishes, she had to distance the therapist by making herself detached, remote, and unavailable. The supervisor suggested that the therapist's detachment was partly a reaction to this patient's lack of contact, as well as a countertransferential response based on whom she represented to him and on his past method of dealing with anger over not being able to "find" the absent object.

This interpretation seemed accurate, and the therapist and supervisor briefly discussed associations produced by the patient during previous sessions, which seemed to confirm this view. Suddenly, however, the therapist had a different set of associations. He remembered some recent material, which had been the focus of his own analytic sessions, involving occasions when his mother had abruptly shifted the topic of conversation to her own accomplishments and had seemed to ignore his presence. At these moments, the therapist felt very tired and had a great deal of difficulty focusing on what she was saying. He also experienced mounting feelings of anger related to her not "being there" for him.

The therapist shared these associations with his supervisor. It gradually became clear to him that his own reactions of boredom, difficulty in concentrating, and depersonalization were a defense against becoming aware of anger in his patient and himself, anger rooted in the frustration of needs for attention and nurturance. Because this insight came spontaneously, it was felt as an inner reality, which made sense and agreed with his other thoughts, both about the case and his own analysis. In subsequent sessions with the patient, the therapist began to interpret her preconscious and unconscious rage, and to monitor more closely his own angry feelings. Over the following weeks she moved into an exploration of core issues around frustrated dependency wishes. The therapist's countertransference reaction of boredom and depersonalization occurred much less often, and when it did reappear, it alerted him to feelings of unconscious anger over unmet dependency needs, in both his patient and himself.

A later session from the treatment of this patient provides another example of a good supervisory hour. The patient began this session by describing feelings of longing for a man with whom she worked on a daily basis. She felt this longing in an especially intense manner at the end of the day, when he left to go home. She was not sure that she could stand this any longer; it reminded her of her mother, and left her with the feeling that she had been torn prematurely from her mother's womb. However, she also was exceedingly uncomfortable when this man wanted to talk to her. She was bewildered by this and stated, "It's what I've longed for so much, but when it's finally offered to me, I find it unbearable . . . when he is looking at me with those deep blue eyes, I get enraged and could shoot him." The therapist suggested that these were feelings she also had toward him. She agreed, saying, "If I could have you, I would want you all the time, I would never get enough, but I couldn't tolerate the thought that you would care for me." She commented that it was much better to be unconnected to people, and remembered herself as a baby, "sitting there naked, dirty, with nobody around. When somebody finally does come, I refuse to get out of the crib."

The supervisor pointed out that an oppositional stance was necessary for this patient, because it made her feel strong and aware of herself as a separate person. For her, negativism was a way of defending against intense fears of merging. Although this interpretation made sense to the therapist, and he and his supervisor went on to discuss the implications of this view, he was aware of feeling distinctly uneasy during this particular supervisory session. Toward the end of the session he subtly objected to the interpretation the supervisor had offered, and as he walked out he had the feeling that he had been oppositional that day. While puzzling over this during the drive home, he had a number of associations which seemed to clarify the situation. He remembered feeling during the previous weeks that his supervisor had been particularly giving. He had loaned the therapist some reading material, and at the beginning of the sessions was particularly warm in his greeting. The therapist had felt gratified by these expressions of feeling, but as he thought about this, it dawned on him that a dynamic had evolved in the supervision which directly paralleled that in the therapy. As had been the case with his patient, the therapist felt that when the needed nurturance and caring were provided, they provoked in him a negativism, as a defense against intense wishes to merge. On the basis of these associations and his further discussions with the supervisor, the therapist came to feel that he had achieved an "inner" understanding of the adaptive value of his patient's negativism, which left him more prepared to deal with this resistance in subsequent therapy sessions.

These two supervisory sessions clearly illustrate that in many respects, the good hour in supervision may resemble the good analytic hour as described by Kris. In the good supervisory hour, the supervisor's interpretations allow the therapist to achieve his or her own insight, which is felt as a tangible internal reality which connects a number of salient issues and themes. There is a clear infantile prototype in the therapist's own past, involving difficulties in the early oral relationship to the mother. In the first supervisory session described above, the supervisor provided a type of experience that differed significantly from the infantile prototype in the therapist's past, involving a narcissistic mother who was not aware of her child's needs. By focusing his intervention on the induced aspect of the countertransference, the supervisor conveyed empathy for the therapist's inner experience. Because the therapist felt understood, and the narcissistic and aggressive dynamic was not reenacted, this supervision came close to the "good feeding" the therapist had missed during childhood. The result was a higher order integration of ideas and experiences in the form of a significant insight during supervision. This example also illustrates Kris's idea that aggressive energies must be sufficiently neutralized for insight to occur.

Finally, one may note the operation of the three ego functions identified by Kris as characteristic of the good analytic hour. A controlled and partial regression on the part of the therapist allowed the emergence of relevant material from his own analysis. The ego function of self-observation allowed him to connect this material with his countertransference reactions to the patient and transference reactions to the supervisor. Finally, affect connected with the original experience appeared in a modulated way, in the context of a childhood memory. In the second supervisory session presented above, the therapist recapitulated in supervision his own and his patient's oppositional defense against wishes to merge. By understanding and respecting the adaptive value of such negativism, the supervisor helped the therapist to become aware of his own oppositionalism, and in this way understand and appreciate his patient's resistance. The oral prototype here is refusing to eat as a defense against the wish to devour and be devoured, in the service of emerging autonomy.

Case 2

A female therapist in control analysis asked if she could discuss a new case, as she had a strange reaction to the first hour with this patient. She found herself feeling "disorganized, itchy, bored, like laughing out loud inappropriately." The patient was describing how she had been mistreated, and the therapist found herself clenching her fists, also wanting to beat her. She had the fantasy that this would be like beating a child, and if she gave in to the impulse, the patient would break into little pieces. Also, she had written several pages of notes on this new patient, which was very unusual for her. During this supervisory session she continued to take notes. In the past her supervisor had felt that this therapist placed great importance on her sense of separateness, and although she valued his comments and deeply respected him, she was conflicted about whether to take in what he had to offer, which made it difficult for her to write down anything he said. He guessed she was afraid that if she took him in, there would be nothing left of her.

The patient was a blonde, pale-faced woman, not particularly attractive, who had a childlike appearance and seemed to be no more than 20 years old. Actually she was 40, separated, and the mother of two children. She complained of eating difficulties, both anorexia and bulimia, and a number of other symptoms. In recounting her history she told of having been abused and deserted by a neglectful and sadistic mother. On one occasion her mother left all the children alone in the house, a fire broke out, and several of her siblings were burned. The patient had played the role of mother surrogate for her younger siblings, particularly after her mother abandoned the family when she was 10. She described her father and other males as "good and gentle men who meant no harm." When the patient was 18 she met a handsome, intelligent, very wealthy professional man who begged her to marry him. After first putting him off, she eventually yielded and they were married. He seemed at first to be a "good and gentle man" who also had been raised by a stern, perfectionistic and rejecting mother. After the marriage, however, her husband turned to alcohol, drugs, and other women. They separated, and whenever she briefly returned to him, she contracted genitourinary infections from him. She eventually met another man who cared deeply for her and wanted to marry her, but at this time her husband professed his love once more and begged her to return. When she told him about the other man, he accused her of betraying him and proceeded with the divorce.

As the therapist related this material, she commented that this patient seemed like a caricature of a woman. She was like a "whipping boy" who was beaten by everyone, the personification of the masochistic woman. She seemed weak, indecisive, and wishy-washy, but in her machinations she somehow got men to need her. They pleaded until she was touched by their offerings and yielded. She seemed to know nothing about men, feeling they were all good and meant well. The therapist noted that she had felt these things during the first few minutes with her patient, as if she herself were particularly attuned to just these issues.

The supervisor pointed out that the therapist was clearly experiencing a countertransference reaction centering around who and what this woman and her surrounding circumstances meant to the therapist. Asked to speculate about what might account for such a strong response, the therapist immediately thought of her own mother, and this association both scared and stirred her. She related that her mother had had a strong need to be her father's ally no matter what, and consequently had put up with a great deal from him. She felt her mother had been "the biggest martyr ever," and she did not want to be anything like her. "She's everything I ever wanted *not* to be." She specifically did not want to use her femininity to get what she wanted, and would not fight back in this manner. This issue had come up in her recent analytic sessions, where she had been discussing difficulties with her boss, who, like her father, left no margin for error and always had to be right. She felt a need to come across not as weak and dependent, but as tough and able to stand up to him. She was uncomfortable with dependency wishes, which she associated with weakness and femininity, but also did not want to see herself as masculine like her father.

At this point, in response to questioning by the supervisor, the therapist realized that her mother had by no means been so helpless, but indeed had been very related to others. The supervisor pointed out that she was right, and that her patient also was neither weak nor helpless. After all, she was getting a divorce, had managed to obtain a graduate degree after many years, had found another man who was "crazy about her," and did manage to come to therapy. The therapist felt that in some ways this patient represented the opposite of herself. She said, "She and my mother both appear helpless on the outside, but are very powerful inside. I am the other side; I appear very powerful on the outside and feel inadequate on the inside. My patient is me inside out." The therapist went on to say that this session had helped her immeasurably, and that she didn't anticipate any further trouble with this patient. She was advised to discuss these issues in depth with her analyst.

As Kris pointed out with regard to the good analytic hour, this supervisory hour began with a negativism that the therapist felt toward her patient. Also noteworthy about the beginning of this hour was the therapist's sudden willingness to take notes, suggesting that some resolution of unconscious negativism toward the supervisor had taken place. In allowing herself to associate to her patient's overtly masochistic presentation, this therapist engaged in a partial regression of ego functioning combined with intense self-observation. She connected her patient's behavior with her mother's self-sacrificing attitude, and in this way became more aware of her difficulties identifying with her mother, whom she perceived as weak. She discussed her internal struggle between conflicting masculine and feminine identifications, based on the association of masculinity with strength and femininity with weakness. However, underneath this issue there was an earlier conflict, which was the infantile prototype for her experience. She was ambivalent about whether to take in anything at all, and attempted to deny hunger as well as that nurturance that was available, in order to avoid the danger of merging. By respecting this therapist's need to remain separate, the supervisor made it safe for her to take more in, as well as helping her realize there can be strength in a dependent feminine position, as well as weakness concealed behind an aggressive masculine stance. The therapist was eventually able to integrate her experience with her patient and supervisor into an important insight regarding one characterological issue she shared with her patient.

Case 3

A male analyst was very embarrassed when his female patient abruptly sat up on the couch, turned around, looked him "in the eye," and discovered he was taking notes. He had not told her he took notes, and now he felt she had "caught him in the act." He said it felt like being "caught by my mother, with my pants down, masturbating." When she looked around he had the pad on his lap and the pen in his hand. She had had two prior experiences in psychotherapy, both negative, and his immediate thought was that now she would think he was her third negative experience. After having seen her for 2 years on a weekly basis, and repeatedly dealing with her intense mistrust of him, he recently had "invited" her to come twice a week. Now he feared he "might have blown it."

During this particular therapy hour, the patient's resistance had been especially pronounced. She arrived late, said she didn't feel like being in his office, denied she was resistant, and gave him a difficult time in general. She complained that he was picking at her brain, pushing her, and ruining her relationship with her boyfriend. She was sarcastic, chided him, made derogatory references to her last therapist, and declared, "I don't have to come if I don't want to." There was a part of her that didn't "want to come," although "the bigger part" did. The word "come" was used many times, and it clearly reflected her erotic teasing feelings toward him. These attempts at teasing were familiar to the therapist, and in the past she had manipulated appointments, told him of sexual encounters with her boyfriend in an exhibitionistic way, and made directly provocative comments such as, "It's too hot in here for me."

This patient had entered therapy as a result of long-standing depression and difficulties with men. She had a history of alcohol and drug abuse and eating difficulties, which were related to her depression. She described her mother as dangerous, extremely controlling, and at times psychotic. Her mother had issued many warnings, made threats, and put curses on the patient, as well as engaging in other forms of magical thinking. She had been hospitalized several times for depression, and had repeatedly overdosed. On one of these occasions it was the patient who discovered her. The patient's response to all this was to feel very close to her mother and protective of her, telling her everything. She feared hurting her mother and dreaded separating from her. Like her mother, she interpreted events as due to magic and the occult. She wondered whether, like her mother, she might have to take medication because of a "chemical imbalance." At times, she directly verbalized the fear of getting parts of her crazy mother inside of her.

The patient's father was a delivery man who was described as crude and inappropriate. Often he would tease her about men in a sarcastic, sexualized manner. Her brother also engaged in a sexualized form of teasing with her. Her boyfriends tended to be needy, and she often found herself trying to rescue them. She was concerned because frequently they turned out to be impotent, and she would hate to feel that their impotence was due to her "killing them or their penis." Her present boyfriend was as protective of her as she was of her mother, but teased and played games with her like her father.

The supervisor pointed out the therapist's countertransference feelings toward this patient, including his very strong involvement, ambivalence, and guilt. He suggested that the therapist was reacting to his patient's obvious seductiveness, but also the excitement and guilt he felt might mean that she had come to represent someone close to him from his own past. In discussing these countertransference reactions, the therapist acknowledged that just as she had a strong curiosity about him, he in turn was extremely voyeuristic toward her. Her dress and movements, her teasing and provocative manner, her gestures, tone, and the forbidden quality of her descriptions, all succeeded in making him intensely curious about her, her body, and her activities. He said it was as if he ate her up with his eyes every time he looked at her, and this mutual looking and teasing game went on continually between them.

In response to further questions arising during supervision, the therapist realized that he was attempting to sell himself to his patient, and what he really wanted was to be the most important man in her life. He had true love feelings for her, thought of her outside the therapy room, and had rescue fantasies about her. He also became aware of his strong ambivalence toward her. He wanted to see her five times a week, but didn't want to see her at all, because he felt that she interfered with his personal life. He discussed his own fear of impotence, as a psychotherapist and as a man, and noted in this regard that he was neither interpreting her transference reactions, nor the displacement of these onto her boyfriend. He had not been addressing her teasing, provocative behavior, her mocking of his personal attributes, or her wish to make him a witness to her sexual activities with her boyfriend.

As he discussed his involvement with his patient and his guilty feelings, the therapist had the thought that there was a maternal quality about her, and in some ways she was like his mother. He remembered a number of incidents during his childhood when his mother had exhibited the same flirtatious, seductive, and provocative qualities. She would invite delivery men and workmen into her home for hot and cold drinks. He would become extremely jealous and resentful of this, and he linked this memory to his patient recounting her sexual exploits to him. Eventually the therapist became aware that his strong countertransference and counter-resistance was based partly on reactivated oedipal feelings set off by this seductive and teasing patient. He then was able to analyze one of his own slips and see that these feelings also involved his sister, of whom the patient reminded him. By the end of the supervisory hour he felt more in touch with these issues, and would anticipate less difficulty with this patient in subsequent sessions.

Once this analytic work had been completed, the underlying oral issues in the patient-therapist interaction came into clearer focus. During subsequent supervisory sessions the therapist said that he was aware that underneath her overt preoccupation with sexuality, his patient was a frightened little girl, with a very poor sense of worth. Her sexuality and baiting flirtatiousness covered up a strong wish to be fed and nurtured. She used oral metaphors, and her drug and alcohol usage had recently become more intense. Her sexuality also had a strong oral emphasis (wish to be held, cuddled, fondled) and a stress on oral-genital contact.

The therapist then reported one of his own dreams. In this dream he returned to his university with the patient and asked a person who was a senior analyst to help him connect a basketball net to a 12-foot pole. This person couldn't help him, and he left to get help elsewhere. On the way, the patient was hungry and wanted to stop for something to eat. The passed a restaurant and saw a couple eating an overstuffed tuna fish sandwich on pita bread. He was aware that two additional bagels came with the sandwich. He didn't stop to eat but continued on his way.

The dream portrays the therapist's oedipal problem and his

frustration over not being able to solve this. He wants to be phallic, but needs help to get the net and the pole coupled, and looks to his supervisor-analyst-father. The latter is unable to help, which leaves him impotent. Unable to solve this phallic problem, there is a resurgence of oral wishes, which are the core issue around which he and his patient are struggling. The dream reveals the therapist's wish to have an exclusive relationship with his patient, to take her with him wherever he goes, as well as his wish to take a bite of her and be eaten by her, and similar feelings that she had for him. Oral impulses and attempts to control these are revealed in other aspects of the manifest contents—she wants to eat, to be fed, but he can't allow himself to take in, and withholds from her. They witness an oral primal scene, in which the stuffed pita bread and bagels may be taken as a representation of the mother's body, for which both of them hunger. The pita bread is a representation of food, the vagina, and an allusion to the phallus.

In further discussion with the supervisor, the therapist came to the realization that both he and his patient feared being over-whelmed by their strong dependency needs, and the fantasy of engulfment which such needs imply. His fear led him to attribute a phallic castrating quality to his patient, and to worry about his own potency. In a complimentary manner she unconsciously felt she had taken in a poisonous mother, and instead of bringing pleasure to her lover (and her internalized mother) during intercourse, she would destroy him and his penis. The supervisor identified her deepest unconscious fear as the wish to eat and be eaten (oral incorporation and sadism) as well as to be touched by the dangerous mother. She needed to ward off the magic of the therapy as she had had to ward off her mother's bad magic. After an extensive discussion of these issues in subsequent supervisory sessions, the supervisor noted that the patient's provocativeness and other transference resistances were being more effectively addressed by the therapist.

Over the course of these sessions, the therapist was able to explore the sexualized transference-countertransference dynamic he was enacting with his patient. His intense interest and desire for a special and exclusive relationship with her, and her desires for a similar relationship with him, led to a teasing and provocative interchange in the therapy sessions, which recapitulated aspects of both of their early histories. There was a complimentary and parallel relationship between patient and therapist: He represented her father and brother, while she represented his mother and sister. As the source of his sexualized countertransference became clear to the therapist, largely through the emergence of childhood memories related to his mother's teasing, he was able to move into an exploration of his own unfulfilled oral needs, which corresponded to the underlying oral conflicts in his patient. At this level the patient was seen as a source of desperately needed nurturance. Aggression directed toward the orally frustrating object found expression in his technical errors (not addressing the transference), his overt wish to be rid of her, and his dream that the supervisor could not help him. (This provides one example of Langs's, 1982, point that therapist dreams shared in supervision are often an expression of anger.)

These supervisory sessions are another illustration of the relevance of the points made by Kris. The supervision began with a negative countertransference expressed toward the patient, rooted in early oral deprivation the therapist had experienced. As this conflict was analyzed in supervision, the therapist's aggression found representation in childhood memories about his frustrating mother, and a dream about the supervisor's inability to provide. Because these feelings became more conscious and available to the therapist, an internal reorganization was possible, which allowed him to address more successfully these same issues in his patient. The therapist's ability to engage in a partial regression of ego functioning, as well as his careful self-observation, were prerequisites for the gains he made in supervision.

Conclusion

In our review of the literature on supervision, including recent works such as those by Caligor, Bromberg, and Meltzer (1984) and Fleming and Benedek (1983), we have found no systematic application of Kris's criteria for the good analytic hour, even by those who emphasize the similarities between supervision and personal analysis. This is surprising, since Kris's paper is widely regarded as a classic, and in recent years increasing attention has been paid to the supervisory process.

It comes as no surprise that good supervision involves many of the same processes as good analysis, and that Kris's description of the good analytic hour has direct relevance to the supervisory process. As the above vignettes illustrate, the good supervisory hour often occurs when a particular type of resonance has been set up in the therapist-patient and therapist-supervisor interactions. At the moment of resonance, both patient and therapist struggle with the same dynamic issues and the therapist feels at an impasse because his or her own difficulties mirror those of the patient. At the same time, this struggle is brought into the relationship with the supervisor. The issues themselves frequently revolve around unresolved oral conflicts, and the struggle with a depriving and orally frustrating object constitutes the most common infantile prototype for the good supervisory hour. The therapist's difficulty in handling oral aggression is central to this dilemma and usually results in a negativism directed toward both the patient and the supervisor.

To the extent that the supervisor is unable to help the therapist begin to resolve these conflicts, an impasse in therapy and supervision is likely to occur, with aggression and defenses against it acted out by the patient, the therapist, and/or the supervisor. Lane (1985) has discussed the nature of such impasses in supervision. If the supervisor has worked through these issues in him- or herself, and has been able to establish a good, working analytic relationship with the therapist, these conflicts can be brought into supervision. Typically this involves a partial regression of ego functioning on the part of the therapist, as well as intense self-observation. Often the therapist's unmet oral needs and resulting aggression come to be expressed in a modulated fashion through the emergence of a memory from his or her childhood, or a dream shared with the supervisor. If this process is allowed to unfold, the therapist may eventually experience a greater sense of integration, as well as the feeling of achieving an important insight about him- or herself. Almost as a matter of course, the therapist is more adept at dealing with these same conflicts in the patient.

Summary

The ideas Kris developed to explain the good analytic hour can have direct relevance to the supervision of advanced candidates grappling with countertransference issues. The achievement of insight during supervision can involve the same processes as the achievement of insight during analysis. The resonance which gets set up during such supervisions, where the therapist relives the same conflicts with both patient and supervisor, gives supervision its particularly strong impact and can provide an opportunity for important analytic work.

References

Caligor, L., Bromberg, P., & Meltzer, J. (1984). *Clinical perspectives on supervision of psychoanalysis and psychotherapy.* New York: Plenum.

Fine, R. (1979). *A history of psychoanalysis.* New York: Columbia University Press.

Fleming, J., & Benedek, T. (1983). *Psychoanalytic supervision: A method of clinical teaching.* New York: International Universities Press.

Kris, E. (1956). Some vicissitudes of insight in psychoanalysis. *International Journal of Psychoanalysis, 37,* 445–455.

Lane, R. (1985). The recalcitrant supervisee: The negative supervisory reaction. *Current Issues in Psychoanalytic Practice, 2,* 65–81.

Langs, R. (1982). Supervisor crises and dreams from supervisees. *Contemporary Psychoanalysis, 18,* 575–612.

The Use of Primary Experience in the Supervisory Process

Warren Wilner, Ph.D.

My premise in this paper is that supervision occurs in two separate modes, which, in turn, conform to two distinct laws or regulatory principles. In order of what we find most familiar and acceptable, the first mode is that of interpretation and secondary process. We listen to what our supervisees tell us, look to see what the material means, and interpret it to them, with or without recommendations as to how they should follow through clinically. The second mode underscores the fact that supervisor and supervisee, therapist and patient, and the patient and the people in the patient's life are continually acting upon one another through words, gestures, and deeds. The model here is that of primary experience: a continual movement of psychic process and/or energy that acts as cause "seeking" an effect. In this mode, what is said becomes a context of action and interaction rather than of meaning.

Meaning is being viewed here in a particular way. It may be understood as the mean or supposed essence of an aggregate of psychic events: what these events refer to. Meaning, therefore, requires another level or referent in order to illuminate these events. In contrast, within the primary mode, actions and events simply succeed one another over time. There can only be one such event at a given instant; hence, there can be no mean or meaning to these events. As in Kierkegaardian thought, there is no synthesis possible for thesis and antithesis; one must choose one or the other (MacMurray, 1957). Meaning is never absent from the supervisory process; it is simply not present in the primary mode. In interpersonal terms, the supervisor functioning within this mode is, as

Wolstein (1974) has termed it, an observing participant in addition to being a participant observer.

The distinction I am attempting to draw between these two modes and formulations of writers such as Modell (1975), who proposes a dual instinct model in order to bridge the gap between the intrapsychic and object relational, and Levenson (1972), who writes of how therapists must permit themselves to get caught up in patients' psychological systems (to participate) and later emerge from them in order to be able to comment upon the interaction between patient and therapist, is that I don't necessarily view the therapist's final or essential position, nor even that of the supervisor in the present context, as being that of one who comments, observes, makes meaning, or works toward a consciously preconceived goal, such as trying to enhance the other's experience of self. In addition to these functions, I also see the necessity of the therapist and supervisor being able to live out and express what they are immediately experiencing in a way that never may be interpreted or commented upon, or which was never a part of a conscious goal.

The use of the primary mode of experience in therapy and supervision, as I have thus far described it, is obviously a delicate issue and cannot be employed indiscriminately. Before outlining some guidelines for working in this way, which will be illustrated later through some supervisory vignettes, I would like to discuss what I believe to be the importance of "living out" the primary experiential mode in supervision and treatment. If secondary process/observation enables us to know what we are doing, to interpret what something means, to have an overall direction and purpose in our work, to bind psychic energy in the service of building up psychological structure, to make the unconscious conscious, and to have our relationships with others make sense and to eliminate distortions from them, the model I am proposing enables us to not know what we are doing, so that we may do something that exceeds what we already know. It allows us to live and be guided by deeper, unconscious psychic forces, to release psychic energy in a way that cannot be consciously channelled and, perhaps, biased beforehand, to make what is conscious unconscious, to open up new pathways of interpersonal interchange and expression, and to approach the edge of present unconscious resistances and patterns. Finally, functioning within this mode may place us in a position whereby we may trust, not only another or what we already know, but the deep psychic processes that inform us as well, as, for example, Groddeck (1977) has written about them.

The image that comes to mind is that of an interpersonal ecosystem, in which all experience that passes through the minds of both participants can be made explicit. The crucial criterion for experience in this mode is that one does not feel like the author of these experiences. It is what comes to the supervisor or supervisee rather than what they volitionally and rationally think and construct. The latter falls within the traditional model of boundaried, rational, and interpretable experience and discourse. Here, discrete things can be given discrete meanings. In the primary experiential mode, psychic experience, whether it be ideas, feelings, fantasies, or physical sensations, simply occurs and may lead to other such experiences. The second experience may, in turn, be succeeded by a third, and so on. The questions that begin to emerge here are what such experiences may lead to, the effects they may have on the participants involved (e.g., their level of energy, feelings of relatedness to one another, etc.), and whether there will be any connections between such experience and the mode of meaning.

The caveat in employing the primary mode of experience is that to search initially for meaning eliminates such experience or breaks the existing chain of successive primary experiences. As with Heisenberg's uncertainty principle in physics, one can measure either the location of an electron or its momentum; both cannot be determined at the same time. Similarly, a supervisor may have either to "go with" an experience or to try to find out what it means. The breaking of the chain of experiences in the now observer's mind causes the chain to cease to exist phenomenally. Contrariwise, to allow primary experience to continue is not to concern oneself with authorship of such experience, and to live instead in the medium of such experiences—to be participant to them. This view differs from Lacan's formulations regarding a chain of signifiers, which experience is for Lacan (Wilden, 1973). In contrast, I am not suggesting that there need even be within the primary mode signified experiences that these experiences are pointing to. What is important instead is the psychological context that such experience creates. Meaning and primary experience may, at times, coincide, but one does not begin by searching for meaning.

Daniel Stern's (1985) concept of attunement is relevant. According to Stern, it is necessary for a mother to resonate with her infant's energy level. The mother is pulled along by the feel and excitement created by the child and extends it through her own feeling and actions, which, in turn, help to further move the child along, and so on. The meaning of the actions themselves are not what is central; rather it is the openness of new possibilities in action and experience that such attunement affords that matters most.

Except in cases of paranoid or extremely rigid schizoid and obsessional character structures, the possibilities for working directly from the primary mode of experience are greater in supervision than they are in therapy, since defenses and core issues are usually not addressed as directly. What is necessary is that supervisee and supervisor be interested enough and open to the autonomous movement of their own psychic processes to enable them to set aside their concern for what things mean, and to be willing to risk having their present meanings turned around. Engler's (1984) work on going beyond one's sense of individual self in psychotherapy and meditation, and my paper on participatory experience (Wilner, 1987), which explicates various issues related to the use of the primary mode in treatment, explore this matter further.

Significant for the supervisory relationship is the supervisor's cognizance of the importance of the therapist living out, in a real and attuned way with the patient, the latter's immediate psychological dilemma. As the following supervisory vignettes will illustrate, the patient places the therapist in a position whereby the latter will have to struggle with the self-same issues that the patient is presently undergoing. Furthermore, the suggestion is that the therapist will have to satisfactorily resolve within his or her own psychology whatever issue is at hand before the patient will be able to risk his or her own deeper immersion in the corresponding issue. The therapist thus goes first in "modeling" for the patient how it is to be done, while exemplifying the courage necessary to do so. In the true interpersonal nature of the psychotherapeutic and supervisory process, why should patients or supervisees be willing to engage in what their own therapist or supervisor is not willing to undergo? At the level of facing one's real fears or making real change, a corresponding willingness on the part of the other participant in the process is likely to be necessary.

What is being described is not necessarily related to therapists or supervisors divulging personal information about themselves, since the engagement I am referring to occurs largely unconsciously, and few of the issues involved are made fully explicit at the time. To attempt to first observe what is happening before becoming a participant in it, usually, as indicated above, aborts the "real" aspects of the process. The issues then would be discussed "as if" they were going on, but, in fact, would presently not actually be occurring. Knowledge may result, but without a real experience of self that is actually undergoing change. Khan (1972) describes quite clearly the importance of the patient having to recreate the actual context of his or her psychological struggle in the treatment relationship so that change which is *not out of context* can occur. This paraphrasing of Khan's position is further supported by Noy's (1969) formulation that actual changes in self-experience are related to the concrete nature of primary process. In contrast, concepts such as transference and countertransference are usually dealt with clinically within the secondary process interpretive mode.

I have discussed (Wilner, 1987) how it may be possible for work to go on in the interpretive and secondary process/meaning mode while real change occurs in the primary mode, with the experience of both modes entering awareness at once. But suffice it to state here, engagement within one mode to the exclusion of the other leads either to an "as if" adaptation, along the lines of Wolstein's (1974) formulations concerning the consequences of invoking a primary ego/consensual validation orientation in treatment, or an empty-of-meaning result, which is part of too great an emphasis on the individual self. Here, enactment, acting out, and catharsis tend to occur but without deeply rooted change.

I am, therefore, not advocating a supervisory or psychotherapeutic position that eschews secondary process, interpretation, and meaning. In fact, the living out of primary experience is often employed by the borderline individual as a defense against the awareness of a rationally ordered and essentially predictable world, which such patients experience to be both a dangerous trap that subjects them to the possibilities of annihilation, as well as limiting the immediate expression of their impulses and feelings, which they have little tolerance for containing. In my view, one should be both an attuned participant as well as a rationally interpretive observer, while remaining aware of how an exclusive immersion in one of these modes may be a defense against the emergence of the other. From another perspective, either of these modes may serve as a psychological context out of which the other draws from and develops within (Wilner, 1989).

It follows that the crucial distinction supervisor and therapist must make is when the focus on meaning, for example, is being utilized as a defense against the living out of real experience and when it is being employed as a necessary context out of which primary experience may later emerge. I believe that this distinction can only be made phenomenologically. The supervisor, in the present instance, can intervene only with what is experientially available to him or her at that moment. As I hold the primary mode to manifest itself largely as a flow or stream of experience, one should express that which in one's mind appears to have a life of its own, and to then see whether this leads to other such experiences in the supervisor's own mind or in the supervisee's. In contrast, a discrete experience is more likely to appear slower moving and of one's own making, though there are exceptions to this, as in the arising of a sudden and singular insight. But here, the emergence of the insight appears involuntary. Experiences which are more static and voluntary, on the other hand, are naturally better suited to be weighed within a context of meaning.

One should not, I believe, search for a stream of experiences or try to invoke one. Such experience will rather present itself as such, just as one finds oneself searching for meaning within a "meaningful" psychological context. The caution is to avoid trying to make meaning out of primary experience, and to attempt not to generate primary experience out of meaning. The error that is made is usually the former, owing to our essentially cognitive orientation within Western societies. It, in fact, actually appears unnatural to try to generate primary experience in a voluntary way, without the use of drugs and techniques that aim toward creating regressive and/or mind-expanding experiences. I believe that the two modes will "present themselves" to us in their own ways and will "find" their own natural points of intersection. Arieti (1967) has written about such nexes as tertiary processes. But they may also be viewed in this context as the fortuitous or, perhaps, determined overlapping of contexts to a mind disposed to experiencing their convergence with one another.

Case Examples

The following four supervisory vignettes illustrate various points made in the above discussion.

In the first example, the therapist stated, "I am going to present this patient in a seminar tonight, and I don't feel that I understand her. This is the patient who said to me, 'You should be living with my mother!' The specific problem I'm having right now is how to handle the patient's having told me that she can no longer come at her regular Monday hour because she just got a new job. I was angry with her for presenting me with the problem in this way, like I'm supposed to take care of it. I can't see her later on that same evening. I already have my 9:00 hour filled. The only alternative is a Saturday morning although I told her that there will be a few Saturdays I will have to miss. I had wanted to keep those Saturday hours open for doing testing, consultations, and to make up sessions. She once told me that I worked too hard, with regard to a Saturday morning appointment we once had. Now she's making me work hard again."

This is a therapist with an obsessional style who needs to be in control. I commented that the patient had her off balance with her request, and that she sounded as though she felt more upset than actually angry with the patient for making it. I pointed out that she seemed trapped by her own need to take care of all situations, and felt guilty that she couldn't. She couldn't be a good enough "mother" to this patient—a borderline woman who remains forever angry with her own mother. The patient has actually placed the therapist in a position of needing mothering or help herself, rather than being able to remain the objective handler of things, which she has always tried to be. The patient, in fact, sounds as though she is acting like her own mother, with the therapist becoming the daughter. Thus, the therapist is, in a sense, now actually living at home with the patient's mother—feeling both that she should do everything for her now mother-patient, while resenting it at the same time.

I also was put in the position of being asked to help her with a specific problem, as the therapist was with the patient. However, the solution to the problem lay first in not trying to comply with the literal request, and instead becoming aware of the transferential and countertransferential implications that it brought about. Furthermore, I explored with the therapist what this implied about the therapist's own character structure: how her obsessive-compulsiveness could be viewed as a defense against less than firm boundaries of her own, a possible borderline problem, since she so readily shifted positions with the patient, and also how this tendency could be utilized therapeutically in helping her to identify better with certain patients. I referred to this problem as being potentially in the service of expanding her countertransferential potential. I communicated to the therapist that her focus on the issue of giving the patient a new appointment time might be a substitute for the feeling that she did not have enough of her own psyche available to her to give to the patient therapeutically, felt the strain that the patient was placing on her unexplored psychic reserves, and therefore focused on the appointment issue instead.

A second therapist wanted to discuss a patient whom she said is more than borderline. I commented that the patient then went over the line, to which the therapist responded that she didn't even know where the line was with this patient. The latter is close to 300 pounds, addicted to Valium, which she has taken regularly for almost 25 years, and has developed an intense homosexual transference to the therapist. I initially said that the therapist would have to draw the line herself with the patient, which I later amended to the therapist as having to note and hold the patient to the lines that the latter herself inadvertently drew.

As the therapist was referring to the "weighty" problems that this patient posed, I found myself becoming indifferent to what she was saying, and becoming interested instead in just relaxing, of which I informed the therapist. The therapist took this as a possible attitude to adopt with the patient, since the latter regularly sabotages any efforts made to help her. If one makes less of an effort, the prospect of sabotage is lessened. Such a task of providing the patient with a different actual experience in treatment may be necessary in those instances when the behavior and experience in question are so entrenched and gratifying that they prove refractory to change by ordinary analytical approaches.

Apropos of the issue of drawing the line, I said that if the patient talks about wanting to be the therapist's lover, the latter might ask her what kind of lover did she think she would make for her, and did she think that she would be satisfying to the therapist. If she didn't, the therapist could then ask why she would want to make the life of one she loved miserable.

I advised the therapist to use the patient's own articulations as the line which she would have to hold to as a way of resolving the gross split in the patient's experience between the good therapist, who was actually suffering in the sessions, and the bad patient, who did not appear to be in such distress. In the meantime, the therapist, in a more relaxed way, could ask the patient about her culture, for example, which is different than the therapist's, and more objective things about herself. I also suggested that the therapist be wary of anything the patient might do to try to please her; indifference for instance, might serve to evoke the patient's anger and self-directedness.

In the third example, the patient, a rabbi's daughter, is described by her therapist as having been raised in an obsessional style, and as being difficult to work with. The patient was away for two weeks recently. While the therapist said that she missed her, in a sense, she hesitantly added that she also didn't, suggesting that she was glad to be rid of her during this time. I said that the therapist seemed to experience the patient to be a pain-in-the-ass.

The therapist, who is obsessional herself, said that she is concerned about making an ass of herself. She finds the patient intimidating and is afraid that she will not know how to treat her. I experience the patient as not really being a patient yet, and think that I wouldn't like to treat her. The therapist believes that the patient can be worked with, and I ask how. She replies, "Through osmosis—to get in through her pores." I tell her that it seemed she might be able to treat this patient, whereas I didn't think I could.

The therapist couldn't indicate specifically how she would actually get into the patient. I suggested, upon thinking once again of the patient as a pain-in-the-ass, "You can get into her by first letting her get into you—into your own ass or under your skin, so to speak." The therapist felt uncomfortable about this, and I suggested that one might be able to keep one's dignity even while making a fool of oneself. Apropos of these reversals, I reiterated that the therapist might be able to treat the patient better than I could, for all my talk about letting patients get to me, I might remain closed with this patient and consider her to be untreatable. I might do this rather than be willing to run the risk of feeling the insecurity and discomfort of working with her. In contrast, the therapist, who felt openly insecure, might try harder and in more imaginative ways.

The issue that the therapist originally presented for discussion was whether she should put the patient on the couch at this time. I replied that the time didn't seem right for this. The therapist said that she tries to give the patient room, doesn't press her. However, occasionally, the patient, who is interested in the field of psychology, will come in and say, "I've been feeling borderline or schizoid today," or use some other technical term. The therapist has treated these offerings as garbage, and tells her, "Well, you know what we can do with these terms; put them right there in the wastepaper basket." I commented that using these terms might be the patient's way of getting into her. I suggested that she ask the patient what she specifically means by these expressions, rather than simply discarding them. It may be possible the patient knows what they mean and be able to apply them better than the therapist.

The therapist said that she would be embarrassed were this to happen. She quoted a teacher who said that when he feels the desire to get into a debate with a patient, he feels he's lost the patient. I nevertheless followed up by raising the possibility that were she to permit herself to challenge the patient as to what the latter meant by these terms, in effect to compete with her, and be able to accept gracefully the possibility either of defeat or victory, this stubborn and obsessional patient might be able to feel less afraid of being defeated, overpowered, and embarrassed herself. She also might be better able to let the therapist in, not to mention allowing her own defended-against thoughts and feelings through.

But the therapist would have to undergo this experience first, as in the first two examples cited. The first therapist had to experience her own need to be taken care of in the immediate relationship with the patient before the latter could. The second had to first acknowledge the patient's own line and stick to it, while permitting herself to relax with less weighty and charged issues before the patient could engage her own line. In addition, she might now herself be able to enjoy a whimsical psychotic-like pseudologic with the patient—a departure from her previous stance of being masochistic food for her patient's sadistic cannibalistic cravings.

In the present supervision, with the establishment of the pattern of reversals, and of the authority figure letting herself be penetrated and defeated by the individual in the lesser position of authority, an inquiry could be undertaken into how the patient may have remained stubborn and closed because a significant figure in her own life, perhaps her rabbi father, could not allow the patient to reach and possibly defeat him. Thus, the therapist would have to bare her own potential inadequacies first. Interestingly, since the specific issue presented was the use of the couch, the issue of baring one's metaphoric "behind" was further elucidated, in that this would have the therapist actually sitting behind the patient. The therapist may therefore have to be prepared to accept her own inadequacies before she could literally assume the position to accept tolerantly the patient's, which the patient may sense.

With a fourth therapist, my supervisory emphasis was different. I made a more conscious and deliberate effort to loosen his wordy and ponderously obsessional style, while helping him to avail himself more imaginatively of his interest in words. Previously frozen into a stilted therapeutic relationship with his "sad sack" patient, whose incessant complaints the therapist dutifully listened to, and upon whom he could make few demands, not even for the money that the patient owed him, the supervisee said that I had jolted him in our previous meeting. I had in this session confronted him with his fear of the patient, the anger that the patient elicited in him, and with how bound up and guilt-ridden he was—a now abused helper, or "sad sack" therapist himself.

True to the therapist's obsessional style, and in contrast to his hysterical patient, who kept presenting him with messes to clean up, the therapist wanted to have the full picture about things before he would act. I later took this to be a metaphoric message about his wanting to be offered something by the patient without having to work or ask for it, since the patient does actually paint pictures. As I later came to experience and formulate it, the therapist had all the words, but was having difficulty making them come alive and dance.

I began to experience, and further worked to bring about, a looseness in the meanings and associations of the words we were using to discuss the case. This followed my starting to feel impatient, bored, and angry. When I began to find myself wanting to end the session early, I knew it was time to "mess things up," albeit while still remaining within a loose but coherent structure. I thus behaved more hysterically myself, like the patient, but within a context of meaning, which the therapist depended upon. In essence, I became a bridge between the two.

For example, when the therapist spoke about wanting to get the picture, I suggested he think about Mussorgsky's "Pictures at an Exhibition" when he needed to do this. He said he had forgotten how this piece went, and I told him that I didn't have "the picture" now either, but he could think of the name anyhow. We laughed about this, but I sensed he was beginning to get angry.

When the therapist spoke about the patient *recounting* something that had happened to him, I mentioned the Count of Monte Cristo. The therapist then thought about dueling with his patient, to which I offered *dualing* instead, in the sense of dual psyches, each evoking the other. This led to a discussion of how both the anal *counter* and the phallic Count are necessary treatment styles.

When the therapist said that the patient *recoiled* from something the therapist said, I mentioned "like a coiled snake about to attack." I said that the therapist would have to risk the patient's attack, which he himself recoiled from, and which I was now risking with the therapist, before the patient would be willing to extend himself fully, or phallically, if you will. I then said that once the patient had showed himself in this way, it would be possible to catch him in the "sad sack"—either the patient's own or the therapist's. The therapist then reported for the first time how the patient had ordered his girl friend around in an authoritarian manner, as though he were a feudal lord. We then discussed the therapeutic possibilities of exploiting this contradiction between the patient's tyrannical nature and poor-me image.

Finally, we explored how the therapist might overcome his queasiness about being firmer with the patient, which might actually help to lift the latter's depression by getting him to uncoil. I used the example of kicking the patient while he was down or, to extend the previous metaphor, while he was in a recoiled position; in other words, to challenge rather than to comply with the patient's demands while he was complaining and depressed. This might be an incentive for the patient to get up from his depression, and be up for the therapy, which he hasn't been.

Summary

I have illustrated a bi-modal approach to supervision. My position has been that as we try in a secondary way to formulate meaningfully our experience, we are in a primary, concrete way being formed by the experience we are undergoing. Furthermore, I have stressed the importance of reporting to the supervisee the flow of the supervisor's own primary experience as the means of creating a context whereby the possibilities for undergoing real change and feeling are maximized, even as the supervisor continues to deal with supervisory issues in a meaningful and interpretive manner. It is the latter modality that enables us to be aware of the existence of parallel processes and of our compulsion to repeat, whereas the quality of being able to just "happen upon" things, carried by the primary mode, sensitizes us to what is vivid and sharp, and can experientially carry our more organized minds to places they may have never been.

References

Arieti, S. (1967). *The intrapsychic self.* New York: Basic Books.

Engler, J. (1984). Therapeutic aims in psychotherapy and meditation: Developmental stages in the representation of self. *Journal of Transpersonal Psychology, 16,* 25–62.

Groddeck, G. (1977). *The meaning of illness.* New York: International Universities Press.

Khan, M. (1972). The finding and becoming of self. In *Privacy of the self* (pp. 294–305). New York: International Universities Press, 1974.

Levenson, E. A. (1972). *The fallacy of understanding.* New York: Basic Books.

MacMurray, J. (1957). *The self as agent.* London: Faber & Faber.

Modell, A. H. (1975). The ego and the id: Fifty years later. *International Journal of Psycho-Analysis, 56,* 57–68.

* Noy, P. (1969). A revision of the psychoanalytic theory of the primary process. *International Journal of Psycho-Analysis, 50,* 155–178.

Stern, D. (1985). *The interpersonal world of the infant.* New York: Basic Books.

Wilden, A. (1973). On Lacan: Psychoanalysis, language, and communication. *Contemporary Psychoanalysis, 9,* 445–470.

* Wilner, W. (1989). Experiential confinement as a condition of psychological change. *American Journal of Psychoanalysis, 49,* 51–66.

* Wilner, W. (1987). Participatory experience: The participant-observer paradox. *American Journal of Psycho-Analysis, 47,* 342–357.

Wolstein, B. (1974). Individuality and identity. *Contemporary Psychoanalysis, 10,* 1–14.

Some Remembrances of Supervisory Sessions with Erich Fromm

George D. Goldman, Ph.D.

The following is an account of a case presented to Erich Fromm for supervision in July 1958. I had recently graduated from the William Alanson White Institute and was anxious to work on a case with Dr. Fromm.

Dr. Fromm was seen in his New York home on Riverside Drive. He was on a long visit from his permanent residence in Mexico. He was very open and did not display any strong need for anonymity and neutrality. Sessions would extend through his lunch hour. He would have his maid bring his lunch during our session, and he would casually eat, with neither apology or explanation, nor allow extra time. He would also answer telephone calls during our session. Two other details stand out in my memory. He was quite casual in attitude and dress; at no time did he wear a jacket. The other detail concerned my awareness of his experiencing physical (stomach) discomfort at times during the sessions and verbalizing about it.

First my overview of his theoretical framework for treatment: He felt if the real person, YOU, could make contact in reality with the core of the real OTHER, then and only then could therapy take place. Timing, theoretical frame of reference, developmental theory, one's readiness to hear, the potential of your confrontation, stirring up resistance were all dismissed. If you know something about the patient, you don't keep it secret. The patient is more often than not ready to hear it. The countertransferential acting-out dangers seemed to be minimized by him, although he did focus a lot on the therapist.

Perhaps I realized with bitterness that some of the bad habits, like answering the phone during sessions, I have exhibited in the past

71

I learned from him. I justified them by saying that if this authority on "exploitation" did not consider what he did to be exploitation, why should I? I have fought my own tendencies to act-out as he did during supervision since then and have, I hope, controlled them.

The Case

The patient was a 28-year-old, single, white Jewish male, born and raised in a nearby metropolitan area. He was employed as a marketing consultant for a Madison Avenue management firm. He has an older, married sister, age 30, and a younger, single brother, age 24. The patient's father is described as a small man, lacking in ambition, initiative, and responsibility. His one asset is that he is a warm person. The patient's mother is the stronger parent. She is gregarious, active in the synagogue sisterhood and in local politics, and the one who made the family decisions.

The following interpersonal events, which the patient had labeled as the "white bread incident" and the "towel incident," were presented to Dr. Fromm with the above brief history. The white bread incident occurred when the patient was 13 years old. He was sent to the store on a Sunday night to buy a rye bread. The bakery did not have any rye bread; the delicatessen next door did not either. He brought back a white bread. The patient's mother then "blew her top," telling him he was stupid, inept, and in general berated him for bringing white bread when he knew the family never ate white bread. The story was supposed to illustrate how his mother never gave him a chance to use his own judgment but tried instead to dominate him completely.

The second incident occurred when the patient was 23 years old and living at home. He asked his mother for a large bath towel to wash his car. She said a small one would be sufficient. He again asked for a large one. She came all the way out to the car with the large towel but, before handing it to him, tore it in half and gave him the two smaller pieces, saying she was sure this would be enough.

The case was presented to Dr. Fromm to help clarify what could be done with long-term dependency.

Dr. Fromm said, "Why would the patient call these 'incidents'? They seem to be ordinary life experiences. He seems to be collecting further proof that he is innocent. Saying, 'See it's all my mother's fault. If you can help, OK, but what can one do?' This historical exploitation is a nice rationalization to continue his lack of responsibility. It reminds me of Freud's life. When he was 7 years old, he wet the rug in his parents' room. His father said to him that he was a no-good boy who would never amount to anything. Freud then used this 'trauma' to explain his ambition. But looking back to the time when Freud was 2 years old, there was an earlier experience where Freud, the very young child, wet his father's bed and when admonished said, 'Don't worry, when I am older and wealthy, I will buy a new big, red bed? So the father's wrath at Freud, age 7, was only a secondary reaction to his son's contempt. Freud was the complete favorite of his mother. He was not a harmless little boy, but a little dictator.

"Analysts can be much too uncritical of their patients. Why didn't the boy bring home rye bread? Could it really be possible that there was no rye bread available in town? He knew the family did not eat white bread. What was he trying to do by so innocently bringing white bread? This is nonsense.

"This boy is tied and was tied to his mother. He was her favorite, the crown prince who roared for the reins of government. The weak father protest is not the case.

"Be careful in assessing the infant: (a) Were the parents so bad? (b) Was the patient so innocent? (c) Were these incidents so traumatic? What lies behind them?

"The patient and analyst should never enter into a gentlemen's agreement that says to the patient, 'you are right and you are a fine young man.' The patient will feel safe, feeling his parents were wrong, since he, then, does not have to take responsibilities. The behavior of the patient could be provoked.

"In analyzing present behavior, the analyst should ask himself: Why is this behavior still continuing? Present behavior can be a repetition of childhood traumas, but often many things have changed. This patient has succeeded in talking of his mother all the time."

Dr. Fromm didn't believe that this was the patient's real problem (that the mother was so controlling). "The patient had the idea he had to be the greatest hero in the world. Then his mother's 'promise' would be fulfilled. This and his competition with men (tied in with his contempt for his father) are the sources of his great ambition. He sets ambition to be everything. When he does this, his relations with others can only have this driven quality. But this doesn't explain why he has been sick all this time. He holds on by his continued talking. He hates anyone who stands in his way on the path to the good life that was 'promised.'

"The historical method is fine for pinning down the patient's anger. But you can best feel the peculiar quality of it in the present. Watch for what in the patient's story is tricky. What is he hiding? The patient is not so innocent. He did not live up to his obligations. He still doesn't. He pleads his innocence through many incidents. He fooled you. He wanted to. But he also wants to get well. He resents it terribly that you could be fooled. He will not forgive you."

I asked Dr. Fromm about tracing back the "pattern" of fooling a significant authority. Dr. Fromm said, "The patient succeeded in fooling you. That is enough. That is a fact. Why go back? It is also a fact that while he did all he could to seduce you, he resents it that he could. This is a very frequent situation that I see as I supervise analysts. They enter into a secret gentlemen's agreement with their patients. Both fool the other. Both pretend that all is going well until one of the two explodes."

I discussed my theory of psychoanalysis. This, in summary, is: No child is born bad, mean, etc. Behavior that is now uncomfortable and getting the patient into difficulties with people was learned in order to cope with a situation that once existed for this patient. If one can delineate what the patient is doing, what he learned it for, and with whom, it can be seen to be unnecessary. Then, as the situation which called it forth no longer exists, the patient with courage to change can, with help, evolve a new pattern.

Dr. Fromm agreed in general with this, but added, "If after 5 years the patient is still in treatment, the method is not being successful. You should ask yourself, 'What is this patient really after?' He wants admiration, to be superior to other men; he wants to find people who will cater to him, feed him, follow his every whim. He tries to manipulate people into this role. Aside from being pampered, he wants very little. To accomplish this, he is charming but utterly insincere. He doesn't really give a damn for anyone else. He isn't so innocent. He is tricky. It comes out in his story of the incidents. To do what he did, he has to be tricky."

Dr. Fromm suggested that if the patient calls me a fool, I should say, "I have been a fool, but where do we go from here? You have been splendidly manipulative. It must have been more important to prove me a fool than to get better." Dr. Fromm felt this is part of the patient's pattern of showing up men: "In her 'promise' that she would protect him when ill or weak, understand him when he was troubled, etc., the mothering one gave to the young child, she was also asking him to be everything for her. The father would be seen as ineffectual if he did not protect his son from a mother like this. This boy was under her power and today continues to fall under the power of a woman. He wants to be better than other men so that he will be keeping his part of the bargain. If he succeeds, he will find someone who will be glad to take care of him. He does try for this through trickery and charm, but he is utterly unrelated. Everything is by bluff. Then what is the reason? Is it that his mother was so strict? This is nonsense. He and his mother, both, probably worked well in belittling the father. She didn't do enough for the patient, he felt. You fell for the patient's sob story. What a tragedy it is to be 28 years old and tell of this as illustration of your life. This might be something to tell the patient." Dr. Fromm felt that if this was said, the patient would have to come to grips with his problems: "Now the patient is making a lot out of nothing. All I see in the 'incidents' is the patient and his mother arguing about who is right about the triviality of who is right. You as an analyst should ask yourself, 'Why should a man of his age spend his time with all this bullshit?'"

The first dream of the patient was presented: "I walked into a room and two men were wrestling on the floor. Suddenly, one man got on top of the other and took a knife and slit the other man from crotch to belly button. I yelled, 'What is happening?' The man underneath said, 'Don't worry, we are only playing.' Then I noticed he didn't have a penis."

The patient's associations were that the man underneath was the husband of a woman with whom he had had an affair. The knife was one his mother had when the patient was 5 years old and naughty and she threatened to kill him with the knife.

The patient and I agreed that the dream demonstrated the patient's competition with men and need to belittle them, transforming them into women, being contemptuous of them so he could feel superior.

Dr. Fromm said, "The theme is his competition with other men. To sleep with a married woman is always a sign of a deep competitiveness with other men. He always had the desire to be superior to other men. He made the other man small by making him into a woman.

"In analyzing his dream, the patient starts with the realistic present situation (the affair with the married woman). He then associates to his mother and the knife. This is the family situation. The mother and he are allies. Again, there is a different slant on his relationship with his mother. What has gone on is a deep alliance between this boy and his mother. Yet when she did not give him enough (all that he wanted), he felt cheated. This is the opposite of what he gives consciously.

"One other important factor. This is all play—yet one man is mutilated in a gruesome way. This is life for this man. There is a great fear of reality breaking in. This is the main fear of people who have not detached themselves from their mothers. Life is still the child's world. Nothing that happens will not be taken care of by the mother of the child if the child keeps his promise and is what his mother 'wanted him' to be. Many of these mother-dependent people keep this attitude throughout life. Life remains a charmed world. Nothing is really serious. 'Life cannot touch me' is their attitude. They have never really thought of questions of their powerlessness and help-lessness in terms of the inevitability of death, etc. Their only feeling is that they will be protected if they are 'good.' They do not ever take the responsibility of being adults. Sometimes, the only time that reality ever breaks in is when something real comes up that cannot be averted by this fantasy world, such as a girl they love leaving them, inevitable illness, or death. This shows the patient how unpro-tected he is and can become a really positive event. This seems to have happened when his girl left him.

"Analysis can, if one is not aware of what is happening, increase this sense of unreality (in these mother-dependent people). The analyst now protects him from reality. In father-centered people, there is more reality orientation because of the father's role as the disciplinarian. If they do well, they are praised; if they do poorly, they are punished.

"In reality, this boy was the apple of his mother's eye. She wanted him to be a success so she could be proud of him. Because of her 'promise' of protection, he has never left the closed shelter of his unreal world. For such a person, when reality breaks in, the mother could not protect him. With all his charm, he cannot change this. Then is when he felt his first real panic.

"As an analyst, you should never participate in this protective atmosphere. If after analyzing a patient such as this for 1 year, you see that nothing happens, you tell him of this quite bluntly and then say if no progress is seen at the end of a second year you will quit. The patient must accept responsibility for change. This is reality.

"If you could have said all of this to the patient after his dream, since he was aware that reality could break in, the patient could change. Under the threat of reality breaking in, a patient can change considerably. Analysts often make the mistake that great changes don't take place unless there is a great inner change. In reality, a great threat can make for great change.

"This person, regardless of his age, had protected himself from reality all his life. Everything in life had gone according to his charming manipulations. Panic for him is the feeling: 'I am on my own and utterly unable to handle it.' This is so often true in mother-attached people. For them, no feeling is real; happy or sad, life remains unreal."

Dr. Fromm asked me a question about the patient's ex-girlfriend. I could not answer it fully. Dr. Fromm said, "If you hear a story, provided you listen at all, the story should become as clear as if you had been there. You should never be left with the feeling that you don't fully understand anything the patient says. If you don't, there will just be a lot of accumulated misunderstandings. You should keep this as a basic rule. Do not fail to question unless, in listening, it becomes so clear that you feel you were actually there."

The patient had the following dream three months before: "I dreamed that I was dreaming about having intercourse with my girlfriend. (This made me sexy the next day.) In my dream's dream, I had satisfactory intercourse, and in the dream, I had a nocturnal emission. My father came into the room. (In reality, when I lived at home, my father would be the one to awaken me.) To do this, he tried to take the covers off. I didn't want him to see the wet pajamas. He grabbed the blankets and pulled. I screamed, 'Daddy, don't.' I woke, but went back to sleep and continued dreaming. My mother then came in. Although she was curious about what was going on underneath, she didn't pull the covers off."

The patient's associations were: "The dream's meaning is obvious. Sex is bad. I'm ashamed, guilty. I see my parents coming in as a fear of being caught."

Dr. Fromm asked to hear all about the patient's girlfriend and the patient's relationship with her. He wanted to know her social class, religion, background, and appearance. He then said, "I have heard his associations, and it is all trash, just words. Why not say this to him? The main problem is to engage the patient, to listen and really react, to get into a situation where he cannot kid himself. Say to him, 'You say your mother did not respect you. You have no self-respect. How can anyone respect you?' Wake him up to a reality instead of prolonging the fiction. 'Sure you have no self-respect, but it is not because of your mother.' One engages oneself, and one sees. We do not know what will be the outcome. The analyst must feel faith in this man becoming alive. If you believe this, you must engage him. Force him by your attitude to talk of something real, in a way that is real. That is all I know when I am analyzing someone. I don't know if I will cure him, or what will come next. I am as utterly real as I can be. I forget I am an analyst. I am like him, a person. I talk with authority because I talk with myself being expressed. I talk of my own reactions. If the patient talks with this very intelligent talk, we are not engaging one another. Try to engage him by making real comments, by reacting to him. It doesn't matter if you are right or wrong as long as it is the real you reacting.

78   *Psychoanalytic Approaches to Supervision*

"I feel the dream means: He says that he is afraid of sex, that it is evil. He says he is afraid his folks will expose him, that his father is worse. This doesn't fit.

"They are showing him he is still a little boy. 'You are a little boy who still wets the bed.' He sees himself not as a man. His father has been rougher. He wants to eliminate the father. The mother is much more understanding. She would say that it is all right to sleep with a girl as long as you do not love her. Actually, his problem with his girlfriend is that he acted like a demanding pampered little boy. In the dream, he senses he is a little boy, and so when he has an affair he can only act like a little boy. This is much more than 'sex is evil.'

"If the analyst can't feel what the patient is feeling, the patient can't feel him. If the analyst talks, then it is he, the authority, talking *to,* not talking *about* the patient. An analyst is the opposite of a mechanic working on a car. You are not the doctor and he the patient. You are not normal and he the patient. You are both people. An analyst can be as crazy as hell, but he must have the faith that people (he and the patient) can emerge.

"We are in the only field where an experienced and well-trained doctor like yourself can legitimately say that he has never, and does not know of anyone who has been, really cured by the method he uses. This puts an analyst in a fraudulent and guilty position. Thus, in turn, it makes for the analyst being encouraging or 'hopeful.' It is not any wonder that a patient feels better with this encouragement.

"An analyst must feel for and with, without identifying with a patient. One must participate vividly in the other's life, feel and see the patient as someone real. But do not identify with them. We are them, and still ourselves. We are all exactly like everyone else, yet perfectly unique.

"I would like to make a few general remarks on man. For an animal, life is no problem; life is automatically regulated by instinct. Man is different. Life poses the question: 'What can an animal do who can reason?' Man must overcome his sense of powerlessness, weakness, and apartness. If he does not: insanity. How can we answer these problems? 1) Regressively. 2) Progressively.

"Regressively—we can return to mother's hand or womb, or father's bed. This attempt would end up in tragedy. Being born as a man, you must progress.

"Progressively—develop one's independence, love actively, develop. Be oneself, yet related. This latter is the ideal of mental health.

"In the history of man, you can find relations of a regressive type. Man worshiping trees, animals, trying to return to nature and primitivity. Or of a progressive type, where man moves forward toward being himself, such as Zen Buddhism.

"The sick man of our day is afraid to move forward. Unfortunately, in our society man can move regressively and still find happiness in social acceptance. Resistance is a violent defense against leaving the charmed land of certainty and moving into the world of reality. This is a great fear.

"The analyst has to see every person as a hero of a drama. If we see a patient in terms of one problem—like his girlfriend left him—you could become bored. But if you see him as a human being, he becomes like the hero of a Shakespearean drama. This person becomes part of the drama of life, struggling for physical and spiritual survival. This, in itself, is exciting, although the person may not be doing great things. If you can feel this, you will be able to make the patient exciting to himself. If you can see the patient like this, and the patient can also, then he can have an exciting interest in himself as a human being struggling along. The life of an individual is as exciting as the history of man. We cannot see man as, first, someone with symptoms trying to get adjusted. Psychoanalysis must be a study of existence. In the history of man, there are only five or six plots possible, but the exciting thing is to discover the plot, the drama, what has become of this piece of life? What was this man meant to be, and what of this has he used? Questions every analyst must ask himself regarding every patient."

I asked Dr. Fromm what he meant by his concept of "meant to be." He said, "The physical and psychic are always together. The facial expression or the whole body tells us something of this man. We are born with much more potential, personality-wise, than Kretschmer or Sheldon ever thought. We, as analysts, start out with the idea that all a person is is due to his experiences in childhood. But, we have to realize that these are not experiences on a blank sheet, but on a specific person. We, therefore, must say, 'What was the person meant to be?' Then we can see how circumstances affected this child. For example, a baby born timid and sensitive could develop into a man who is a poet or an artist. But if this child had an aggressive, domineering mother, one strong possibility would be that this baby would be squelched. On the other hand, if this mother had an aggressive baby, the baby's aggression would be accentuated, and the adult would be quite different.

"To get well is to find out what your patient was meant to be biologically, not just psychologically. A person can be born lusty, gutsy, strong and hungry for life. Another can be born quite aesthetic.

They should develop, if given the opportunity, into quite different adults. One cannot say that one is better than the other; one must, for his patients' sake, help them find what they were meant to be.

"I used to feel that this emphasis on the constitution was defeatist and reactionary, but I now feel it is important. Temperament leaves open both positive and negative values. Some people are born with congenital goodness or congenital badness or destructiveness."

I questioned the validity of this statement. Dr. Fromm said, "If as a psychologist, you can accept a trait like intelligence having limits placed upon it by heredity, why not the same thing for goodness or badness? Analysts can do something for their patients if they recognize this and channelize their patients' energies along the proper lines."

I felt this point was very unclear. Dr. Fromm said, "With this patient, you fan the patient out of just talking and into living. By this time, you two pretty well know each other's moves (the gentlemen's agreement). The analyst must break through this complacency and move the patient.

"Your patient says he doesn't know what an adult is in this session you've just read to me. I would say to him, and I would be very sarcastic, 'and how would you know?'

"He would then say, 'What do you mean?' I'd say, 'You are not part adult.' Bang! Now it would be up to him to react. The analyst with a patient who has been in analysis for this long a time, with this type of deep dependency especially, must get into the arena. You must use an approach of directness."

The patient's recent hour was characterized by what I felt was extremely hysterical, histrionic, unreal behavior. The patient talked during this hour of wanting to "fuck" his mother, of fantasizing doing it during the hour, and vividly described his mother playing with his penis and, after it was all over, slapping him in the face.

I treated this fantasy as though the patient were acting out something in the transference that was unclear, and kept the focus on the present analyst-patient relationship to find out what the patient was saying symbolically.

Dr. Fromm said, "You have to decide: Is he real or not? I feel he is real, or at least a good deal of it is. He cannot forgive his mother or any other girl for not being very close and everything to him. If this was not an act, you would have deprived him of a very meaningful experience if you treated it as such. You have the patient on the couch. You encourage him to be free and say anything that comes to mind, and then, when deep unconscious material comes out, you don't deal with it."

I asked, "What do you do with it?" Dr. Fromm answered, "The sexual fantasy with his mother was a defense against his deep passive needs for his mother. He became aware of her 'promise' and how desperately he wanted to be taken care of. He could give in to it and regress back to infancy. If he did, he would go crazy. He is 2 or 3 years old and expressing his sexuality to fight his dependency. Yet, he is expressing this within the framework of the mother relationship. The treatment has regressed him back to this point. You wanted to do this. Why is this story insincere? It fits the dynamics. Does it frighten you because it is too Freudian? This would be mutual insincerity.

"Remember the mother could not have given him all he wants unless she was crazy. The primary fear is of dependency. Why fear the sexual act then? If he fucks his mother, in his fantasy, he destroys her as the all-powerful mother and makes her into just any other woman. He was on the verge of being sucked into complete dependency, and, for the sake of his continued sanity, he had to destroy her image. For him, inasmuch as mother is mother, sex is not sex, but is feeding. His interest is not to satisfy and love the woman, but to get relief from his tension.

"This patient has said he wants a strong father. A person who has a weak father wants a strong father. To say his father is weak and you are his mother is to say you are weak. This boy, who suffered so from having a weak father, is very angry that you haven't been strong enough. He has all the fury of his disappointment. A boy threatened by the smothering mother, who would desire to sleep with her so she would possess him completely, wants a strong father, who could have made a man out of him by putting mother in her place. He must have a great deal of resentment and fury towards his father for not having saved him from his mother.

"The patient feels that you let him pull the wool over your eyes, and he feels resentful, for you too are therefore weak. This to me is the main point. Analysts go on fishing expeditions with their patients too often. You make a remark that is a legitimate and correct psychoanalytic interpretation, but wherever the patient has thrown the ball, you have gone. You don't seem to have any goal as to where you felt the ball should have gone that hour. I hear the patient say, 'You are a weak father, and I want a strong one.' I say to myself, 'Any boy would want a strong father to save him from such a mother.' You have disappointed him the same as his father did. I know that this is the important thing that he is saying that has to be opened up.

"You, as his analyst, must say what you know is going on unconsciously, not just say what it might be and just hope that this is relevant. In the seminars that I give, I so often hear analysts ask something, hoping that the patient will say something relevant. Analysts should be a step ahead of their patients and should know and direct patients to that which is important."

I asked about letting patients use their associations, and see where these lead. Dr. Fromm said, "Free association leading to 'the answers' is a myth. One must understand the use of resistance to see this. You must give the patient a lead, one that cannot be misunderstood. For as soon as the patient hears the right thing, he will know. The analyst has the aim of getting at what is in the patient by leading him there. When I say the analyst must lead the patient to the answer, I always mean the answer that is within the patient. Often I hear analysts asking patients a question. I ask the analyst what he expects the answer to be. Quite often the analyst says that he doesn't know. I feel that the analyst should so empathize with a patient that he would know anywhere from one to three possible reactions or answers to any questions. I would not ask the question, for after all, I am a step ahead of him. I should know. If I don't know, he certainly doesn't know. It is, therefore, useless to ask a question, if I do not know the answer. In line with this, the analyst should be more active, not in talking, but in knowing what is happening. This patient needs guidance, he needs a good father.

"The analyst should be like a guide on a mountain-climbing expedition. You cannot carry the patient. You should guide him and, if necessary, should even physically assist him. A good mother's role, just being there, is not enough. This is especially true with mother-dependence."

I asked Dr. Fromm how all of this would apply to the mother-dependent woman. Dr. Fromm said, "With a girl, the problem is, in one way, very much the same. I have seen women with terrifically strong mother fixations, where it works the same. With a boy, identification with the mother is dangerous; it destroys the sex role. With a girl, she is not thrown off the track, but the danger of being absorbed is still there. I'm not clear, not sure at all of this. I feel one's own sex comes in here. I feel a man can experience what a man can experience, and he can't do this as well with what a woman experiences. Girls who did not have a loving mother try to get a man to be a mother to them. This becomes terrifically frustrating all around. If he is not a man, it will be frustrating to both, no matter what her initial unconscious need. I almost feel men should analyze men. In a girl, if she becomes the man, she can handle the mother and keep from being engulfed.

"In regard to being supportive with this patient, yes, be kind. Prevent suffering that is not necessary, but remember to reach your goal. There is often suffering. This is inevitable for life. For this patient, the basic situation is one of utter valuelessness and help-lessness. How does he then establish his manliness? He must, or he would soon be crazy. He does it, in part, by stabbing out and getting back at every man. By even small defiances, he establishes himself as a man. By defying you and his boss, by being even five minutes late, it is a small ease, a compromise.

"To be a man, then, in summary, he: 1) fucks a girl; 2) makes a fool of other men. But for him, it must always be a hit-and-run affair (his premature ejaculation). Your job is that you must show him that he feels like vermin, dirt. He does this, rebelling, to establish his sense of power and manliness. He has a tremendous need for strong men, as he doesn't and hasn't taken his own responsibilities in his relationship with his mother. He would want a strong father (and you) to help him with his mother. So, because both have failed, he hates you and his father.

"This aggression to you has two sources: 1) he hates all men, as a carry-out of his mother's contempt; 2) he hates his father for failing him. To see what responsibilities he has to assume is a surface step, a small one, though a step in the right direction.

"To get better, this patient must see himself as a vermin or a louse. You must really be in contact with the patient when you say this. You must say it when you feel intimate and loving. If you feel this about him yourself, do not say it to him, then. He must know this self-perception eventually.

"He must see how with feelings like this, no one could live. He must, therefore, reestablish himself: 1) by fucking; 2) by attacking every man. These have been his reactions to the anxiety of any self-awareness. Lastly, he must see how much he would have wanted his father to be a strong father and not a kind mother. If all of this is more than theory, and he and you both know it, then he really will make progress. He must feel it strongly.

"Without recrimination, he must feel his need of women (mother) being the breast of the world and men (father) being the strong one."

Thus the supervisory sessions ended. It was an interesting and invaluable experience.

Supervision in Psychotherapy and Psychoanalysis

Edith Schwartz, Ph.D.

This paper addresses the ways in which supervision of psychoanalysis differs from supervision of psychoanalytically oriented psychotherapy when conducted under the auspices of an analytic training institute. Theories of psychoanalysis deal with the nature, origin, and resolution of mental conflict. Gill (1954) defined psychoanalysis as the establishment of a regressive transference neurosis by means of interpretation, carried out by the analyst from a position of technical neutrality. Fancher (1987) defined psychoanalytic psychotherapy as all psychotherapies based exclusively on psychoanalytic theory, but utilizing deviations in technique, including reduced frequency, sitting up, suggestion, and various supportive or ego-building techniques. There is little agreement in contemporary literature on how these two treatment modes differ significantly, where they may overlap, and for whom each is the therapy of choice.

Some authors claim that a healthier, better structured person can use psychotherapy. Others claim that for the more disturbed, characterologically disordered person, psychotherapy is the proper treatment. In the past, there has been agreement that psychoanalysis had been developed as a treatment for neurosis and that preoedipal patients lack the strength to endure a long, autonomous process. Today there is a deplorable tendency to define psychoanalysis in terms of session frequency or use of the couch and to regard

The author thanks Ernestine R. Haight of Boulder, Colorado for her perceptive reading of this paper and her many helpful suggestions, which enhanced the final product.

psychotherapy as a process in which the therapist intervenes frequently and freely, and is a "real person" to the patient. There is an underlying understanding that the same phenomena are seen in both forms of therapy but at different levels. The same goals (symptom reduction, conflict resolution, making the unconscious conscious, strengthening of ego functions, especially reality testing, attainment of separateness and autonomy, replacing destructive patterns of relating with healthier and more adaptive ways of functioning) operate, but as stated, at different levels and at a different pace. The patient's treatment goals (not life goals) are paramount in each therapy. Frequently, psychotherapy begins when the patient is in a critical situation and is only anticipating a focused resolution.

Whether we concern ourselves with psychoanalysis or psychotherapy, we view the patient as having organized his or her personality in relation to current objects as repetitions of the themes of his or her prototypic relationships. How much we deal directly with them is dictated by the type of therapy undertaken. The most marked difference between psychotherapy and psychoanalysis lies in the handling of the transference. In psychoanalysis, the goal is to bring about the resolution of the transference neurosis so that the patient comes to regard, understand, and relate to the analyst as a real person, and thus freed from the patient's transference projections, distortions, and idealizations. In the psychoanalytically oriented psychotherapies, the centrality of the transference is the underlying dynamic of the therapeutic relationship, and techniques of clarification, confrontation, and interpretation are utilized. In psychotherapy, it is frequently more therapeutic (or possibly just customary) to leave untouched a selection of the patient's projections and idealizations of the therapist, since they can help to maintain the person's stability, even though some magical thinking may be involved.

The other obvious difference in the two modes of treatment is that over the years, progression in psychoanalytic process has been well documented in various papers and books on techniques, beginning with Freud, (1905, 1912, 1913) and extending to Fenichel (1941), Glover (1958), Waelder (1939, 1962) and Greenson (1967). While there are differences stemming from the analyst's personality and character, psychoanalytic procedures are well defined and theoretically clear. There is some degree of consensus on the "developmental" stages through which the typical psychoanalysis progresses. Many authors have written about psychotherapy with preoedipal or borderline patients, such as Kernberg (1975), Kohut (1971), Frosch (1970), and Giovacchini (1979), but there is little agreement on technique and successive stages of treatment. Since psychotherapy usually begins in the middle of the patient's unpredictable, unanticipatable, and idiosyncratic psychic state, it is unlikely that a developmental progression can be charted for psychotherapy. Without a method of treatment based on an expectable treatment progression, the practice of psychotherapy, of necessity, remains an art which requires of the practitioner extensive knowledge, intuition, sensitivity, tact, skill, and the ability to tolerate primitive and bizarre material and outbursts of rage. Most psychoanalytically trained therapists regard the practice of psychotherapy as more difficult than that of psychoanalysis, and for good reason.

Hence, the supervision of psychoanalysis might be expected to be more systematic than that of psychotherapy. When supervising a young analyst, one looks with him or her at diagnosis, resistances, transferences, countertransferences, what to address at a given moment, and the various character traits of the analyst such as a desire to make "brilliant" interpretations, a preference to talk rather than remain silent, a tendency to teach and explain, an unconscious wish to give advice and to take care of the patient, an inability to abandon one's own values, and a need to deny part of the material presented. All of these things can be dealt with handily in a systematic, educative process.

When supervising psychotherapy, understanding the patient and his or her possible diagnosis is a puzzle from the beginning. The therapist must learn to have heightened observational powers and use his or her own intuition and own unconscious. This is very difficult to teach. The supervisor cannot be certain that what he or she is told is accurate, because any number of problems could intervene, including the fact that reporting to a supervisor does influence listening and memory. With the more disturbed patient, there may be changes between sessions in his or her life situation, in ego states, moods, in what he or she talks about, and the young therapist may find this hard to follow. Both the therapist and the supervisor have a lot of speculative, exploratory work to do together, and the supervisor must sense whether the material is tolerable to the therapist. Countertransference problems are often of a very different nature than those that arise in psychoanalytic treatment of a less disturbed personality.

The triad of learning in psychoanalysis has been personal analysis, taking courses at an institute, and supervision. Freud did not feel that psychoanalysis could be learned didactically, but rather only through a preceptor process. Classes are necessary for absorption and articulation of the learning and readings, and primarily to develop ownership of ideas—for the student to make them his or her own. Also, the student knows him- or herself and his or her limited number of cases, but needs broader knowledge, which can only come through training in classes and, additionally, work in supervision.

What happens in supervision? The candidate comes to understand the dynamics and technical issues of the case, which stem from a deep understanding of both the unfolding and covering up processes of the patient. This leads to an understanding of when and when not to be silent, and some formulations to guide in making these interventions. Intertwined in this is the candidate's response, conscious or unconscious, articulated or hidden, to the supervision, including theory, style of interaction, and the personality of the supervisor.

A supervisor must constantly differentiate a "dumb" spot from a "blind" spot. When the supervisee does not know something, it can be from lack of training and knowledge, or it could stem from neurotic inhibition. For instance, there is a situation which might be called "compulsive inexperience," in which the student continuously presents himself as not knowing. The ability of the supervisor to assess the spot accurately, depends on how free from narcissism he is, because there are times that he must be able to tolerate an unknowing or blocked supervisee. The supervisor is in a position to help the candidate discover his blind spots. A supervisee said, "I need help in evaluating my own work." I viewed this as a professionally mature comment in which she was mindful of her learning needs. A determinative aspect is whether or not the supervisee is currently in analysis. There have been analysts who have refused to do control work with a candidate who is not currently in treatment. The thinking here is that the patient's material is a stimulus to which the therapist must be open, and at times may need help in processing.

The student presents the unfolding of interaction between the patient and him- or herself, which the supervisor and the student process jointly. There are endless loopholes and problems that can occur in this process, including both or either the supervisor or student converting this process into a hidden psychotherapy, or too personal a relationship.

There is a question about the theoretical responsibilities of the supervisor. Is it the supervisor's responsibility to integrate or to explain the various approaches to phenomena such as drive theory, object relations, ego psychology, or self psychology? Is this an institute responsibility?

The supervisor is concerned with how the candidate enables the process to take place and looks with the supervisee at what has happened. The conceptualization of what structural changes have taken place needs to be articulated in the supervisory process. The role model in psychoanalysis is the way in which we listen; in psychotherapy, the focus is on what has to be accomplished. This difference would be reflected in the stance of the supervisor.

The supervisor of any type of therapeutic process has the potential for being an auxiliary observing ego (Windholtz, 1970). This means that the supervisor has to be seen as an ally, and internalized in a positive mode. If internalized negatively, the supervisee might take recourse to evasion, noncommunication, or other forms of resistance. Positive mode implies an assumption of respect for differences, and an understanding that the differences are negotiable, and usable. Both supervisor and supervisee contribute to the development of positive or negative mode.

Learning does not take place by being lectured, awed, or dazzled by examples from the supervisor, or even the written word. Does the supervisor create iatrogenic learning problems for the candidate? Does the supervisor assume that all learning difficulties come from the student? Does the student prefer to see it that way, too? The literature speaks to the notion that students can have problems in this area.

The relationship between the supervisor and the supervisee can be influenced by any number of factors. Does either one hide behind his or her role? Is the predominant tone collegial, trusting, competitive, accepting, belligerent, false? This complicated relationship has been described by Ekstein and Wallerstein (1958) as a rhombus—patient, therapist, supervisor, and administrator (or institute).

In the early stages of training, the young analyst lacks clarity of his or her work ego and psychoanalytic ego ideal. I think that this is furthered in the supervisory process more by indirection than by the declarative statements. I think the supervisee reads the real attitudes of the training analyst.

The control analyst has to help the student analyst deal with the slow pace, the gradual accretions, the microinternalizations of the patient in the analytic process. To some extent, the student in control analysis must be able to regress to a state of mind equivalent to the patient in free association. How this correlates or does not with the student's own analysis is something with which the student must contend. Reading Mary Dick's (1987) description of this is a beautiful experience. In psychoanalytically oriented psychotherapy the interaction is different. The question of the correct focus of the material arises. There is concern if the focusing or the interpretation is too late to be effective, or too early, so that it feels peremptory and perhaps distorted to the patient.

The psychoanalytic process is slow. There is difficulty when either a supervisor or candidate psychologically needs each insight to be a "eureka" experience. Of course, the supervisor does invest his or her feelings about being a supervisor in the relationship with the supervisee. This encompasses feelings about his or her own experience at the institute, and unresolved personal problems, particularly those having to do with the needs for power and narcissistic gratification. When the supervisor misses countertransference issues, we would assume that his or her own analysis has been incomplete.

What effect is there on both the control analyst and the candidate when a defined transference neurosis is not achieved in the therapy? The statements of the training committee of each institute are relevant here, as well as the theoretical stance of the supervisor. It may also be quite important whether or not it is a first or second control case for the candidate. For some institutes, the analytic comprehension of the patient's dynamics and an understanding of why a transference neurosis did not coalesce are sufficient. Falsification of a transference neurosis could only occur out of collusion. In any event, the pressures of these questions and expectations do not burden the supervisory process in psychotherapy.

In supervision, the pedagogic responsibilities take ascendance over the student's characterological or clinical difficulties, but the interactions between supervisor and student are not exclusively didactic. Supervisors vary in their capacity for cognitive explanation of dynamics, process, and technique, and in how strongly they exert a particular direction on a student. I have said, on occasion, "If this were my patient I would do such and such," and then explained my rationale, which then becomes an avenue of discussion. If supervision is pedagogy and not therapy, what does the supervisor do if he or she notes particular problems, evasions, or gaps? I feel that one should draw attention to these problems in the case material and suggest that further exploration take place elsewhere—in the analysis. More students lean toward a confessional approach than toward an educational posture in their relations with the supervisor. Each student needs a different frame of reference in order to learn, and that could even include one-upmanship, spite, or oppositionalism.

There is the question of how long to remain in supervision,

despite any institute requirement. One person in control analysis said that she had been advised by her analyst to stay "briefly" in any supervision so that she could be exposed to a variety of theoretical positions. Another person said that supervision was a potential threat to her transference, and she could not remain in supervision. Many candidates advise other candidates to shop around for another supervisor. One resolution to some of the questions raised is to participate in peer group supervision, which removes the role of an authority figure. Sometimes this is handled by forming a study group with an acknowledged leader in the field.

Both supervisor and supervisee are influenced by the fact that their interaction is taking place under the auspices of an institute. This weighs heavily on the candidate who is being evaluated, and whose progress through the institute can be influenced by this experience. The control analyst has the power to affect the candidate's progress in the institute, and this has an impact on every aspect of the relationship. Also the supervisor is compared to the analyst of the candidate, for better or worse. Further, the supervisor is the recipient of the candidate's transference to the institute. There are many complications in the candidate-supervisor relationship. Several students have spoken about the fact that they feel more "under the gun" in control analysis than when they were in supervision with their psychotherapy cases. In the latter, they knew that their progress through the institute would not be affected by their supervision, and they therefore felt freer and better able to develop their own style.

The supervisor also can be affected by how closely he or she feels the student's progress or lack of progress is a reflection of his/her ability, and what this might do to his/her prestige among colleagues. The relative isolation of the supervisor in the consulting room, and not making the opportunity for the interchange of ideas and corroboration of his findings from colleagues, calcifies his way of working and teaching candidates. There are students (individual cases) to whom the control analyst may react negatively. There may be a personality clash, or the control analyst may not want to be responsible for a particular student's work. In such cases, it would be best for the control analyst to help the student find another supervisor. Also, if the student does not find the proper learning ambience with a particular supervisor, a change may be indicated.

The fact of the matter is, although statistics are just being accumulated about this hidden area, many analysts have a dual practice of psychoanalysis and psychotherapy. There are fewer and fewer analysts who report that they have a full-time analytic practice, seeing analysands four or five times weekly. The professional issues must be addressed in an open and sharing manner. For instance, how much modification of the treatment process can take place and have the treatment referred to as psychoanalysis? On the other hand, psychotherapists, and maybe some analysts as well, have once and twice weekly psychotherapy patients on the couch.

One of the key differences between psychoanalytically oriented psychotherapy and psychoanalysis is the degree of regression induced in the patient. The control analyst must deal with his or her own and the student's anxiety, distortions, and particular reactions to the regression. Also, infantile material and fantasy are focused on in analysis. The interaction between supervisor and supervisee effects, both in subtle and direct ways, how freely the patient communicates with the therapist. The communications between the patient and therapist have to be received, understood, and used by the candidate in a well-timed manner.

The focus in psychoanalytically oriented psychotherapy is much more toward reality, reinforcement of ego strengths, and reconstructions. An uncovering process is not sought to the same degree and regression is dosaged. When doing psychoanalytically oriented psychotherapy, the therapist should know what should or should not be done, or approached, based on an understanding of the underlying dynamics and a clear assessment of what the patient is capable of handling.

The control analyst who sees psychoanalysis as magical, pure, satisfying to the elitist, may regard the supervision of psychotherapy as a watered down version of psychoanalysis. This might make psychotherapy an obscure and demeaned practice, which could lead to the employment of inappropriate techniques. There can be trouble in the other direction, in assuming that psychotherapy has no restrictions, which could lead to impulsive activity, rapid confrontation with the patient, rationalized and quick interpretations, or advising excessive passivity.

The supervisor's primary goal is the facilitation of the student's understanding of the therapeutic process in psychoanalytically oriented psychotherapy or psychoanalysis, and his or her eventual self-supervision. Supervisory skills refer to the ability to present ideas and to remain empathic and intuitive with the student. The ability of the supervisor to do this derives from his or her own clinical skills and ability to teach. The teaching of supervisory skills is currently absent from the curricula of institutes. Somehow it has been expected that, like Athena, it will burst forth full-blown, from the head of anyone who chooses to supervise. This lack of training needs to be rectified. There could be supervisory seminars in which there would be didactic training in articulating dynamics and process, the sharing of clinical material, questions about case handling in terms of candidates' needs, and discussion of supervisory processes that exemplify early attunement to student problems. Hopefully, an ambience would be created to help the supervisor reach his or her true feelings and problems in relation to supervising, and also help in the recognition of countertransference difficulties.

I suggest that there should be some teaching of the psychotherapy process in the beginning of institute training. It should be more in the direction of what not to do, what to stay away from, when deeper understanding should not be shared with the patient. At an advanced stage of training, classes in theory and technique should be offered in psychotherapy training, after the candidate has an understanding of psychoanalysis, including theory and technique as a body of knowledge, and has had some clinical experience. Then the differences between psychoanalysis and psychotherapy can be observed and understood. In other words, I think the student should first learn what is not analysis, then what is analysis, and thirdly, what is psychotherapy. Then students can make a clearer assessment of the effectiveness, limitations, advantages, and disadvantages of psychoanalytically oriented psychotherapy. This will also help the students' clinical judgment in consultation. Are the two treatment modes clearly dichotomous or do they shade off one into the other? Professional efforts have to be made to clarify distinctions between the two treatment modes' thinking, in both the institute and supervision.

Psychoanalytic psychotherapy does not mean that there is neglect of uncovering work nor enhancement of internal changes. The emphasis is on making defenses more effective and adaptive. At the far end of the scale, namely, crisis intervention or brief therapy, the therapist may use concrete and/or cognitive approaches. Here again there are divergent views, some stating that brief therapy is appropriate for patients who are well focused, mature, have a limited problem, and are capable of using confrontation without debilitating defensiveness. Leo Stone (1982) even wonders whether psychoanalytically oriented psychotherapy should be used first, to see whether it could suffice instead of psychoanalysis.

Summary

The time has come for the institutes to give courses in both psychotherapy and supervision as part of their training programs. Also, the conversion of psychotherapy to psychoanalysis needs to be addressed, most probably in the techniques courses. Vicissitudes in our field are a constant, but we cannot ignore the responsibility for discussion, implementation, training, and theoretical understanding of these changes, as well as the corollary techniques for clinical work.

References

Dick, M. (1987). Contribution. In P. A. Dewald (Ed.), *Learning process in psychoanalytic supervision: Complexities and challenges*, pp. 448–471. New York: International Universities Press.

Ekstein, R. & Wallerstein, R. (1958). *The teaching and learning of psychotherapy.* New York: International Universities Press.

Fancher, E. (1987). The issue of training analysis for psychoanalytic psychotherapists. Personal communication.

Fenichel, O. (1941). *Problems of psychoanalytic technique.* New York: *Psychoanalytic Quarterly.*

Freud, S. (1905). On psychotherapy. *Standard Edition, 7,* 257–268. London: Hogarth Press, 1953.

Freud, S. (1912). The dynamics of transference. *Standard Edition, 12,* 99–108. London: Hogarth Press, 1958.

Freud, S. (1913). On beginning the treatment. *Standard Edition, 12,* 121–149. London: Hogarth Press, 1958.

Frosch, J. (1970). Psychoanalytic considerations of the psychotic character. *Journal of the American Psychoanalytic Association, 18,* 24–50.

Gill, M. (1954). Psychoanalysis and exploratory psychotherapy. *Journal of the American Psychoanalytic Association, 2,* 771–797.

Giovacchini, P. (1979). *Treatment of primitive mental states.* New York: Jason Aronson.

Glover, E. (1958). *The technique of psychoanalysis.* New York: International Universities Press.

Greenson, R. (1967). *The technique and practice of psychoanalysis.* New York: International Universities Press.

Kernberg, O. (1975). *Borderline conditions and pathological narcissism.* New York: Jason Aronson.

Kohut, H. (1971). *The analysis of self.* New York: International Universities Press.

Stone, L. (1982). The influence of the practice and theory of psychotherapy on education in psychoanalysis. In E. D. Joseph & R. S. Wallerstein (Eds.), *Psychotherapy: Impact on psychoanalytic training* (pp. 75–118). New York: International Universities Press.

Waelder, R. (1939). The criteria of interpretation. In S. Guttman (Ed.), *Psychoanalysis: Observation, theory, application* (pp. 189–199). New York: International Universities Press, 1976.

Waelder, R. (1962). Psychoanalysis, scientific method and philosophy. In S. Guttman (Ed.), *Psychoanalysis: Observation, theory, application* (pp. 248–274). New York: International Universities Press, 1976.

Windholtz, E. (1970). The theory of supervision in psychoanalytic education. *International Journal of Psychoanalysis, 51,* 393–406.

The Parallel Process Phenomenon Revisited: Some Additional Thoughts About the Supervisory Process

Fred Wolkenfeld, Ph.D.

It is fitting that a discussion of parallel process phenomenon be included in a monograph on supervision. For there remains something baffling and intriguing about this phenomenon, with enormous complexities which cut across many aspects of the supervisory process with which teacher and student must contend. It is my thesis that any supervisory situation of dynamic psychotherapy—individual or group, on a one-to-one basis, or in a continuous case seminar—will provide the necessary conditions for the *inevitable* emergence of parallel reenactments. This is particularly true for the supervision of psychoanalysis and, I should emphasize, the supervision of supervision. It is also my experience that simply being informed of the existence of the parallel process phenomenon is sufficient to predicate that supervisors and/or supervisees who previously were unfamiliar with this experience will become conscious of their direct participation in it. The emergence into consciousness of what has been occurring all along will render the experience uncanny, as the familiar but unknown becomes known and unfamiliar (*unheimlich*).

In this chapter, I will summarize some of the highlights of a paper written by Helen Gediman and myself, "The Parallelism Phenomenon in Psychoanalysis and Supervision: Its Reconsideration as a Triadic System," which was published in the *Psychoanalytic Quarterly* in 1980.

95

I will add some points not made in that paper, so this presentation will not be entirely familiar.

A Working Definition and Three Clinical Examples

Parallel process phenomenon is a multidirectional representational system in which major psychic events, including complex behavioral patterns, affects, and conflicts, occurring in one dyadic situation—analysis or supervision—are repeated in the other.

A First Example. Arlow (1963) writes of supervising an analytic candidate who was treating a young, male homosexual patient. The patient was described as submissive and ingratiating, particularly in relationship to perceived strong men, whom he admired and whose prowess he wished to grasp in the act of fellatio. The psychodynamics of the case and the nature of the transference became clearer in a dream the patient had, which the therapist reported during a supervisory hour. In the dream the patient saw himself lying on the couch, turning around to face his analyst and then offering him a cigarette. "At this point in the supervisory session," Arlow writes, "The therapist reached for a pack of cigarettes, took one for himself, and although he knew very well that I do not smoke, extended the pack to me and asked, 'Do you want a cigarette?'" (p. 580).

A Second Example. A supervisor looked forward to her sessions with a particularly gifted analytic student, who with regularity anticipated all the issues that crossed the supervisor's mind and came to similar conclusions. The experience was heartwarming to the supervisor and also a source of deep gratification that such an harmonious "supervisory alliance" had been established. It was this very harmony, however, that alerted the supervisor to the apparent absence of any resistance on the part of the patient about whom the supervisee was reporting. In fact, the patient was described as rare and gifted, with a talent for analytic self-exploration. The patient had developed a working alliance quickly and had a talent for independently arriving at the very interpretations that the analyst had in mind. It seemed that the analyst needed only to be available as a facilitating object for the treatment to take off. Once the supervisor became aware of the parallel process, she learned from the student analyst that her patient disguised his rage in a previous treatment by saying exactly the thing the therapist wanted to hear, thereby "psyching him out." It seemed as if all three—patient, analyst, and supervisor—were colluding to avoid competitive and angry feelings via maintaining a harmonious pseudoalliance.

  A Final Example.   A supervisee found herself temporarily reporting on one case to two different supervisors because of administrative factors which she had partially brought about. In both supervisions she focused primarily on her adolescent patient's anxieties about loyalty conflicts toward her estranged parents. The patient feared leaking secrets from one parent to another and felt that confiding in the therapist was tantamount to a betrayal of her mother. The therapist seemed unaware of the similarities to her own personal situation even as she approached the program director, in a manner that closely approximated a state of libidinized anxiety, for advice about whether she might be hurting the feelings of Supervisor A, who was leaving the institute in two weeks time, if she reported on the case to Supervisor B, who was the senior of the two and who was taking over the supervision. The first supervisor also contacted the program director, who became aware of feeling uncomfortably like a middleman in the whole affair.

  Regarding this last example, Gediman and I (1980) point out how the echoes of the patient's chief complaint seem to be reverberating dramatically throughout an administrative hierarchy; we then raise the question of whether it is not the other way around. Perhaps the patient was sensitized to certain unresolved conflicts in the therapist? Perhaps the therapist was reenacting certain unresolved tensions within the administrative structure of the training institution? Perhaps the therapist was particularly sensitized to those tensions in the program and in her patient because of her own unresolved conflicts over loyalty? Perhaps the program director made the tensions within the institution concrete by assigning the therapist to two supervisors on one case in the first place? And so on go the combinations and permutations. Can we really identify a set point of origin for these parallels in the patient, or in the therapist, or in the supervisor—or in the supervisor of the supervisor, for that matter? Our thesis, which I am reviewing here, is that we emphatically cannot!

  It is perhaps no surprise that papers on parallel process phenomena written by supervisors are replete with examples that place the reenactment in the supervisory situation and identify its source in the treatment process. Freud's (1914) observation that what is not remembered is repeated through enactment provides the background for most hypotheses offered. Differences exist about the nature of the therapist's identification with his or her patient (whether neurotic or otherwise), its place in the supervisory situation (informative or disruptive), and even whether it is phase-specific (essentially restricted to the beginning of a treatment process or throughout). Searles (1955), for example, views parallel-isms as a "reflection process," whereby the therapist enacts an as yet not understood conflict of the patient for his/her supervisor, *whatever its specific content*. Others emphasize shared conflicts between analyst and patient, which are then repeated in the supervisory situation.

From the structural point of view, Arlow (1963) writes of shared fantasies (id impulses), anxieties and defenses (ego), and ideals and values (ego-ideal and superego), which serve as potential contributors to parallel reenactments. He also refers to the oscillating level of ego functioning during the reporting process in both analysis and supervision—objective reporting of data and enacting the experience of the analysis parallels the therapist's oscillation between observing the patient and identifying with him or her, which, in turn, is similar to the patient's shifts from free association to the use of the observing ego. Reenacting in supervision what has occurred in treatment is seen as a regression in the service of the ego which characterizes both situations. Arlow says nothing about similar shifts in cognitive functioning by the supervisor!

Sachs and Shapiro (1976) believe that parallel reenactments occur primarily in initial treatment phases as new patients seek help from novice therapists who are just beginning to seek help in supervision. Treatment difficulties, resistances, and impasses elicit strong feelings of inadequacy, which are reenacted with the supervisor. Lederman (1982) characterizes the student-analyst position as one of enormous conflict and ambivalence, given his/her dependent role as trainee, on the one hand, and authority as analyst, on the other hand. He sees the demands of switching roles from analyst to patient to student as extremely taxing, leading to identification with patients' resistances, negative transference reactions, and acting-out behavior, which are repeated in the supervisory situation. Ekstein and Wallerstein (1958) have elaborated the role of shared parallel learning problems and parallel ways of seeking help and of helping in therapy and supervision.

Even though Ekstein and Wallerstein (1958) and Searles (1955, 1962) seem to be aware of multidirectionality, only Doehrman (1976), not a supervisor but, at the time, a doctoral candidate who re-searched the supervisory process for her dissertation, specifically states that it is not always clear which way the mirror is facing. In every case she studied, she found that the therapists enacted in the treatment situation, either in the same way or the opposite way, what they experienced as the supervisors' behavior with them—enacting or reacting against their supervisors' core neurotic problems. While she honors multidirectionality in spirit, perhaps it is only fair to balance the story as a nonsupervisor to fix the source of parallel reenactments in the supervisor and the supervisory situation.

In our original paper, Gediman and I (1980) argue that theories based on the neurotic identification of the analyst with his or her patient, which is then reflected in supervision, beg the question more than they illuminate the issue, and, indeed, that hypotheses offered in the literature to date lack sufficient explanatory power to account for the following observations:

1) Parallel reenactments are ubiquitous and inevitable and show a remarkable degree of specificity;
2) Parallel reenactments are multidirectional with no clear set point of origin;
3) Parallel reenactments are not limited to beginning analysts but include senior clinicians and supervising psychoanalysts, who have themselves presumably undergone a thorough analysis;
4) Parallel reenactments are not pathognomonic of neurosis but run the full range from normal to pathological.

Similarities Between Psychoanalysis and Supervision

Our position emphasized the structural and dynamic similarities between analysis and supervision, which link patient, analyst, and supervisor in a highly charged, complex representational system of interaction. These shared dynamics pursuant to and congruent with the structural similarities provide the fertile soil for the inevitable emergence of parallelisms (see Gediman & Wolkenfeld, 1980, p. 246).

The major structural and dynamic features overlap one with the other in a variety of ways, but for expository purposes we high-lighted the following:

1) "Both psychoanalysis and supervision are helping processes;

2) Both psychoanalysis and supervision require the involvement of
   the self;
3) Both psychoanalysis and supervision rely heavily for effectiveness on multiple identificatory processes" (p. 246).

Helping Processes

Gediman and I identified the helping process as the structural
feature that is most important for understanding parallelisms, and
how the need *for* help, shared by patient and analyst, places one in a
subordinate position for which the parent-child relationship serves
as the universal prototype. Thus, tensions surrounding the giving-
receiving situations, which may trigger drive derivatives from any
psychosexual stage of development, and the permanent struggles
over the wish for authoritative guidance and anxiety over influence
are pervasive and characteristic of both psychoanalysis and supervision.

I would like to emphasize a less publicized aspect of the
therapeutic and supervisory process, namely, conflicts surrounding
the need to help—shared by both analyst and supervisor. Consider
for a moment the "backtrack interpretation"—and what analyst has
not used it? An analytic candidate discusses his patient's dream in
supervision and emerges with a deep understanding of its meaning.
In his session with his patient the next day, the analyst finds himself
searching hard for an opportunity to share this new insight with the
patient, even though a week has passed since the dream was first
reported. Such a session generally goes something like this: The
analyst seizes upon some peripheral remark of the patient to say,
"You know I've been thinking about the dream you had last week, you
know the one about . . . and it occurred to me that . . ." And the
interpretation is given with almost complete disregard for its
relevance at the moment.

Certainly a need to reestablish a narcissistic sense of adequacy
and maybe even an attempt to impress his patient with his brilliance,
albeit borrowed, are involved here. But what may also be prominently implicated here is the need to help. Help in analysis requires
the inhibition and sublimation of prototypical forms of help: feeding,
holding, soothing, reassuring, advising, informing, answering, and so
on, in the service of structural change. In analysis help is provided
through interpretation within the context of a position of neutrality
and a profound concern for the patient's autonomy. Timing and tact,
therefore, do not refer exclusively to issues relating to resistance and

narcissistic vulnerabilities, but also to autonomy. Interpretations given by an oracle do not lead to insight and change, but are rendered ineffectual because of the patient's resistances, and perhaps harmful because they reinforce unconscious magical beliefs, increase the idealization of the analyst, fuel dependency wishes, and undermine the achievement of autonomous functioning. Thus, even interpretations, which are the major vehicle for the analyst helping another human being, must be tempered by numerous technical and therapeutic concerns. It is a difficult struggle to hold back our understanding, as we are personally committed to helping a suffering patient. The student-analyst above was compelled to share his understanding despite its temporal irrelevance under the pressures of a need to help.

Consider now another example, which I believe is also reminiscent. A supervisee reports on the major developments in the treatment of his patient, including shifts in the transference and resistances, since the last supervisory hour. The supervisor interjected, "You may remember that we discussed this last week and actually we anticipated this development." While there are frequently good pedagogical reasons for reminding the supervisee of a prediction made, the remark can also be seen as a gratuitous interruption and perhaps an expression of narcissistic exhibitionism. The shared "we," then, is really a cover for the royal "we," as the supervisor reminds his student and himself of his talents. However, like the vignette above, I wonder whether this example is not more prominently a derivative of the need to help and a reminder of the supervisor's helpfulness.

Involvement of Self

Under the second category, involvement of the self, Gediman and I (1980) described how self-exposure is an integral and absolute requirement for *both* analysis and supervision, which, in turn, generates narcissistic concerns and issues relating to the maintenance of the integrity of the work-ego on the part of all three participants. The scope of the exposure of the self and, therefore, the degree of narcissistic vulnerability differs from patient to analyst to supervisor, of course, but it is not necessarily less profound. Without elaborating on the self-esteem problems each participant faces in the respective dyads, I do want to point out that supervisors, too, are not immune to the need for approval from their supervisees and from colleagues in the community. Under the impact of writing this paper, for example, I discovered that analysts under my supervision rarely had time to complete reporting the sessions of the previous week, regardless of the number of hours the patients were seen that particular week—two, three, or four times. It was as if I had arranged unconsciously (with help) that the candidates would remain in a state of need, so as to bolster my work-ego and reassure their return for more supervision the next week.

Most significantly, but still subsumed under the category of the involvement of the self, Gediman and I (1980) likened supervision to analysis in that it, too, is a dynamic process, which has as its ideal goal the transformation of the novice therapist into what Isakower (1957) calls an "analyzing instrument." The teaching of technical skills and theoretical formulations are, thus, necessary but not sufficient. The capacity for independent learning, the use of one's own unconscious, the freedom to attend in a relaxed fashion, and the tolerance for ambiguity are all critical objectives of the supervisory process, as they are in the analytic process. The supervisor must resist the temptation of molding the student in the supervisor's image and recognize imitation and compliance for what they are, an initial phase in learning and a potential defense against further, more meaningful change.

Consider the common situation of the student analyst who seeks quick understanding, paralleling his or her patient's need for premature knowledge as a defense against the process. The pressure to know and its counterpart, the intolerance for ambiguity and even temporary confusion, are particularly strong in beginning analysts because of the particular insecurity of their position, but are by no means limited to them. Knowledge is power with which to impress themselves and their patients with their adequacy (and, as we have already said, fulfill the need to help). Supervisors often become aware of this phenomenon by getting in touch with a developing need within *themselves* for quick understanding and for proving *their* competence to the student (and again to fulfill the need to help).

Regardless of what the supervisor does, the overriding guiding principle must be the facilitation of the transformation of the student into an analyst, which carries with it a whole series of values which must be internalized. The supervisor conveys these values by personifying them, not by articulating them. We can imagine, for example, a supervisor elaborating with considerable brilliance on the meanings of the analyst's need for quick answers in relationship to what is going on in the treatment, thus giving the analyst insight into the process while inadvertently reinforcing the analyst's feelings of inadequacy and compensatory need for quick solutions. DeBell (1963) reminds us that supervisors are eminently seducible by students, and that supervisory monologues about a case under the guise of a dialogue between supervisor and supervisee are not that rare.

Identification Processes

Finally, in our third category linking supervision and analysis Gediman and I (1980) agreed with other writers that the essential mechanism of parallelism is identification, but elaborated on how all three principals of the triad—patient, analyst, and supervisor alike— are involved in multiple identificatory processes because a variety of identifications are *required* for the unfolding of the analysis and supervision. These identifications fall under two broad categories: the working/supervisory alliance and empathy. Let me say a few words about each.

Psychoanalysis is a cognitive-affective experience which requires an identification of the patient with the analyst's "analytic attitude" (Schafer, 1983) to sustain the relationship through the numerous emotional turmoils and negative transference reactions. These identifications and internalizations, with their intrapsychic representations, are intrinsic to the analytic process and constitute what Greenson (1965) calls the "working alliance."* Its successful achievement, in fact, can be considered a major criterion for termination of the analysis.

Likewise, the achievement of a truly collaborative effort, which goes beyond a mechanistic, technical approach and maximizes openness and the sharing of doubts and ignorance and countertransference reactions, requires an identification and internalization of the supervisor's analytic attitude. Fleming and Benedek (1966) refer to this as the "learning alliance" and as essentially equivalent to the therapeutic or working alliance.

Turning the mirror the other way, Schlesinger (1981) describes supervision as an "enabling process." He says, "It is the function of

---

*For the purpose of this paper I have retained the concept of the working alliance even though I side with the increasing skepticism regarding its usefulness. In this connection it should be noted that the working alliance is not equivalent to the therapeutic alliance and that Schafer's description of the analytic attitude is far more comprehensive than Greenson's concept of the working alliance. None of this, however, changes the arguments in this paper.

the supervisor to facilitate this process of combined personal and professional growth in the candidate . . . the activity of the supervisor must be governed by his understanding of what the candidate needs to know at any given time and what sorts of clinical experiences will permit him to learn what he needs to know in optimal fashion" (p. 30). Later in the same chapter, he writes how "the goal [of supervision] is not only to facilitate the acquiring of a piece of information but also to enhance the capacity to become an independent learner" (p.33). He argues for a "diagnostic" point of view toward the supervisee's learning process.

While the term "diagnostic" carries with it the implication of objective assessments and classifications, such as years of training, progress of personal analysis, knowledge of theory, talent, and so on, there is no question that what is inherent in the "enabling process" is the notion of creative change of the student into an analyst. In the charged atmosphere of the supervisory relationship, with its own set of ambiguities and uncertainties, empathic identification of the supervisor with the candidate and perhaps even with the candidate's patient is required. Oscillating between observing and experiencing on the part of the supervisor is as central to supervision as are the fluctuations implied in "evenly hovering attention." Furthermore, in both analysis and supervision, the analysand and the analyst occupy the unique position of reporters of events, even as each participates in the event. It is again through empathic resonance that the ambiguities inherent in reported and enacted experiences are apprehended.

It is no surprise, therefore, as Gediman and I (1980) pointed out, that supervisors so often slip in referring to their supervisees as patients. It could hardly be otherwise, given the focus, under optimal conditions, on the personality nuances and temperaments of their students in the context of a helping process. The principal point, however, is that parallel reenactments occur because multiple identifications are *required* by all three participants for the unfolding and success of the analytic process and the supervisory process— processes that share the significant structural and dynamic features of being helping situations in which self-exposure and self as instrument are centrally involved.

Psychic Reality

I would like to digress for a few moments and discuss briefly a topic critically involved in the doing and teaching of psychoanalysis—the concept of psychic reality.

Throughout his writings and with increasing prominence, Freud distinguished between external, material, and objective reality, on the one hand, and psychic reality, on the other. As early as 1895 in the "Project for a Scientific Psychology," he wrote, "Indications of discharge through speech are also in a certain sense indications of reality—but of thought-reality not of external reality" (p. 373). Further elaborations can be found in "Totem and Taboo" (1913), "The Interpretation of Dreams" (1900), "The Introductory Lectures" (1916–17), and "The 'Uncanny'" (1919). For example, in the last sentence of "The Interpretation of Dreams," added in 1914, Freud wrote, "If we look at unconscious wishes reduced to their most fundamental and truest shape, we shall have to conclude, no doubt, that psychical reality is a particular form of existence not to be confused with material reality" (p. 620). Most pertinent for our discussion, Freud wrote in "The Introductory Lectures" (1916–17) regarding the analysand, "It will be a long time before he can take in our proposal that we should equate phantasy and reality and not bother to begin with whether the childhood experience under examination is the one or the other . . . the phantasies possess *psychical* as contrasted with *material* reality, and we gradually learn that in the world of neuroses it is psychical reality which is the decisive kind" (p. 368).

Finally, in "Moses and Monotheism" (1939), he distinguished between "internal psychical reality over the reality of the external world" (p. 76). It is of some interest to me that in his final statement of the subject, Freud returns to the same designation, "external reality," he used in his first remarks some 40-odd years earlier. For it still remains unclear whether Freud essentially restricted the notion of psychic reality to the "world of neurosis" and neurotic functioning, or whether he conceptualized psychic reality as the proper field of study of psychology with its own order of reality and scientific law, or whether it is a general principle of mental life which encompasses everything that takes the form of reality for the subject (see Laplanche & Pontalis, 1968). I am suggesting that by returning to the designation "external," rather than "material" or "objective," Freud is focusing on the locus of stimuli and minimizing the epistemological difference between so-called objective reality and psychic reality.

A similar ambivalence I am tempted to say, resides in the concept of transference, that is, whether transference is restricted to neurotic distortions in the analytic situation, which Szasz (1963) says is like defining microbes as little objects appearing under a microscope, or whether it is a universal phenomenon—an ego function and maybe even a talent, as Bird (1972) suggests. I hope it is apparent that insofar as the concepts of psychic reality and transference approximate universal prototypes, distinctions between objective "facts" and distortions become less meaningful.

Be that as it may, my main point here is that it is the emphasis on psychic reality, particularly as manifested in the transference neurotic reactions, that distinguishes psychoanalysis from other forms of therapy. As analysts, we are not concerned with defining reality, or pursuing the literal truth of the patient's perceptions, whatever that means, or even directly with the patient's life. Rather, our focus is on the immediate drive derivatives and defenses operative, the intrapsychic specificities of the patient-analyst interactions, and the functioning of the patient's mind. We are more concerned with the analysand's honesty of reporting and associating than with the reality testing of his or her external life.

We know well with how much resistance this mode of viewing phenomena is met by our patients. It is a "proposal," to use Freud's word, hard won on the battlefield of analysis, as we, analyst and patient together, thread the pieces of the patient's psychoanalytic biography into an internally consistent, cohesive, and, I would say, aesthetically pleasing tapestry—the patient's image with all its colors and variations, the *patient's* narrative truths.

Patients are satisfied with far less than the full development of a transference neurosis and comprehensive exploration and understanding of the functioning of their minds. They tempt us constantly through a variety of means, including the very process of analysis itself, into shifting the focus to the patient's life, to the control of the patient's behavior, to the testing of the patient's reality, and even to interpreting the behavior of significant others. We are tempted away from the immediate psychic events to more distant phenomena because of the constant struggle surrounding the need to help and what really constitutes help in analysis and the anxieties inherent in the emotionally laden, aim-inhibited intimacies of the analytic relationship.

Loewald (1960) has written brilliantly on how the analyst is co-actor in the therapeutic process and how through interpretation he makes himself available for a new object relationship. It is the internalization of the interaction between analyst and patient, not simply of an object, Loewald argues, that accounts for the resumption of ego development in analysis. Schafer (1983), too, in his description of the analytic second self and the conditions for loving, describes transference as a new form of experience for the analysand, despite its relationship to unconscious, repetitious experiences. We err, he says, when we think "that the analysand's love, respect, and gratitude are simply and only blind repetitions and therefore entirely unearned" (p. 57). McLaughlin (1981) describes how the relationship itself may be the carrier of the analytic process and places the analyst and his/her reality on an equal footing with the patient and his/her reality.

Finally, Schwaber (1983a, 1983b), in a series of beautiful papers, places the analyst within the psychic world of the patient. She emphasizes how the listening perspective of the analyst as an "observer within the experiential world of the observed" (p. 527) yields much more understanding than the hierarchical reality view of the analyst as arbiter of whether distortion has or has not taken place. She writes, "The challenge, then, for us as analysts and therapists, is to find a way, from deep within ourselves, to come to terms with the idea that we do not know one more 'true' reality and that the patient's view, even about us, is as real as the one we believe about ourselves" (1983b, p. 390).

We bite the bait of certain knowledge and familiar notions of reality in order to place ourselves and/or our patients outside the immediate situation. In this way we defend against our centrality to the experience, prevent further regression on the part of the patient, and defuse transference neurotic reactions, particularly those dealing with envy, hate, murder, sadism, death—negative transference in its fullest meaning. Ultimately, our concern is that in crossing the boundaries to understand our patients, we risk losing ourselves and fusing the boundaries.

The view of the supervisor as the dispassionate mentor, whose advantage it is to be positioned outside the patient-analyst interaction, may serve a similar protective function for the supervisor in the supervisory relationship. In this way, envy and competition can be denied, despite our looking in the face of our replaceability, and our real power over students minimized in order to sustain the fiction of benign neutrality.

Internalization of the Psychoanalytic Attitude

I now come to the major undercurrent of this paper, namely that psychoanalytic education, particularly supervision, has as its main objective, not the teaching of technique and theory, critical as they are, but rather the ever-increasing refinement of the supervisee's psychoanalytic mode of listening—the enhancement of him- or herself as instrument, the internalization of the "psychoanalytic attitude." It is essentially this objective that constitutes one of the major similarities between analysis and supervision—both have as their goal creative, internal change. As supervisors we understand that our supervisees, in reporting analytic sessions, have absorbed much more than they can readily verbalize. It is through our own analytic mode of listening, with our musings, suspension of judgment, tolerance for ambiguity, and rejection of the illusion of certain knowledge (even though we must give up our student's awe for us) that we can grasp to some greater degree what has transpired psychically between patient and analyst.

It is very likely that parallel reenactments are the examples par excellence of the abiding influence of unconscious processes, as each of us, patient, analyst, and supervisor, in our overlapping fashions are both reporting and enacting, observing and experiencing. The supervisee is the central person in this triad, but his or her centrality to parallelism is more apparent than real. As Gediman and I (1980) note, we need only place the supervisor in a similar situation, such as a continuous case supervision seminar, for him/her to become the apparent main figure in the repetition of psychic events. The feeling of the uncanny when we, as supervisors, are confronted by a parallel reenactment is due to the reminder that the unconscious has no regard for time, place, or seniority.

References

Arlow, J. A. (1963). The supervisory situation. *Journal of the American Psychoanalytic Association, 11,* 576–594.

Bird, B. (1972). Notes on transference: Universal phenomenon and hardest part of analysis. *Journal of the American Psychoanalytic Association, 20,* 267–301.

DeBell, D. C. (1963). A critical digest of the literature on psychoanalytic supervision. *Journal of the American Psychoanalytic Association, 11,* 546–575.

Doehrman, M. J. G. (1976). Parallel processes in supervision and psychotherapy. *Bulletin of the Menninger Clinic, 40,* 9–110.

Ekstein, R. & Wallerstein, R. S. (1958). *The teaching and learning of psychotherapy.* New York: Basic Books.

Fleming, J., & Benedek, T. F. (1966). *Psychoanalytic supervision: A method of clinical teaching.* New York: Grune & Stratton.

Freud, S. (1895). Project for a scientific psychology. *Standard Edition, 1,* 295–401.

Freud, S. (1900). The interpretation of dreams. *Standard Edition, 5,* 339–630.

Freud, S. (1913). Totem and taboo. *Standard Edition, 13,* 1–100.

Freud, S. (1914). Papers on technique. Remembering, repeating and working through. *Standard Edition, 12,* 147–156.

Freud, S. (1916–17). Introductory lectures on psychoanalysis. The path to the formation of symptoms. *Standard Edition, 16,* 358–377.

Freud, S. (1919). The "uncanny." *Standard Edition, 17,* 217–256.

Freud, S. (1939). Moses and monotheism. *Standard Edition, 23,* 7–140.

Gediman, H. K., & Wolkenfeld, F. (1980). The parallelism phenomenon in psychoanalysis and supervision: Its reconsideration as a triadic system. *Psychoanalytic Quarterly, 49,* 234–255.

Greenson, R. R. (1965). The working alliance and the transference neurosis. *Psychoanalytic Quarterly, 34,* 155–181.

Isakower, O. (1957). Report to the curriculum committee, New York Psychoanalytic Institute. Mimeographed.

Laplanche, J., & Pontalis, J. B. (1968). Fantasy and the origins of sexuality, *International Journal of Psychoanalysis, 49,* 1–18.

Lederman, S. (1982). Theoretical and clinical aspects of supervision. Paper presented at the Department of Psychology, Bronx Psychiatric Center.

Loewald, H. (1960). On the therapeutic action of psychoanalysis. *International Journal of Psychoanalysis, 41,* 16–33.

McLaughlin, J. T. (1981). Transference, psychic reality, and counter-transference. *Psychoanalytic Quarterly, 50,* 639–664.

Sachs, D. M., & Shapiro, S. H. (1976). On parallel processes in therapy and teaching. *Psychoanalytic Quarterly, 45,* 394–415.

Schafer, R. (1983). *The analytic attitude.* New York: Basic Books.

Schlesinger, H. J. (1981): General principles of psychoanalytic supervision. In R. S. Wallerstein (Ed.), *Becoming a psychoanalyst: A study of psychoanalytic supervision.* New York: International Universities Press.

Schwaber, E. (1983a). A particular perspective on analytic listening. *Psychoanalytic Study of the Child, 38,* 519–546.

Schwaber, E. (1983b). Psychoanalytic listening and psychic reality. *International Review of Psychoanalysis, 10,* 379–392.

Searles, H. (1955). The informational value of the supervisor's emotional experiences. In *Collected papers on schizophrenia and related subjects* (pp. 157–176). New York: International Universities Press, 1965.

Searles, E. (1962). Problems of psycho-analytic supervision. In *Collected papers on schizophrenia and related subjects* (pp. 584–604). New York: International Universities Press, 1965.

Szasz, T. (1963). The concept of transference. *International Journal of Psychoanalysis, 44,* 432–443.

Symposium

*Gender Issues in
Psychoanalytic
Supervision*

Introductory Remarks

Jeanne M. Safer, Ph.D.

This symposium explores the role of gender in psychoanalytic supervision. Until recently, the impact on supervision on both the conscious and unconscious dimension of gender has not been sufficiently recognized or examined. These effects are pervasive, and often subtle, and they contribute significantly to the complex of transferences which determine the utility and effectiveness of any supervisory relationship.

Our objective is to identify the specific contributions of gender to the supervision process, in order to elucidate how it interacts with individual personality characteristics and other factors such as age and experiences of authority. Rarely is gender alone the determining factor in a successful supervisory outcome (as defined by both participants). Rather, it is here conceptualized as a variable whose weight depends on its place in the representational worlds of the participants and the resulting intersubjective context. The meaning of male and female authority and a variety of conscious and unconscious needs and conflicts in both participants affect their relationship.

Symposium presented at the Postgraduate Center for Mental Health, April 1, 1987, New York. Participants: Dale Mendell, Ph.D. (Speaker); Jeanne M. Safer, Ph.D. (Moderator); Anna Duran, Ph.D., Wilma Cohen Lewis, Ph.D., Arnold Rachman, Ph.D., and Steven Schiff, Ph.D. (Discussants).

Cross-Gender Supervision of Cross-Gender Therapy

Dale Mendell, Ph.D.

In this paper, the recent interest in the effect of gender on the analytic process is expanded into an exploration of the salience of gender for the supervisory experience. A long-standing tradition within psychoanalysis, which asserts that the sex of the analyst vis-à-vis the patient is unimportant, as major transferential configurations will be reenacted regardless of analyst gender, has been questioned by a number of authors (Liebert, 1986; Meyers, 1986; Moldawsky, 1986; Person, 1983). Their findings that transferential sequences and manifestations appear to be influenced by the sex of the analyst need not surprise us, as gender is probably the most salient aspect of the analyst as a real object.

The patient's gender-based feelings and expectations about the analyst are complemented by the analyst's culturally sanctioned conscious and unconscious stereotypes about gender. In order to fully hear, understand, and be available to their patients, student analysts face the task of revising these stereotypes, which can be particularly pervasive and intrusive when patient and therapist are of the opposite sex. In my view, a supervisor of the same sex as that of the patient is uniquely qualified to help the cross-sex therapist to recognize and modify biases based on culturally sanctioned defensive patterns.

As a female supervisor, I have been particularly aware of the dynamics involved in the triad of female supervisor, male candidate, and female patient. (Near the end of this paper, I will include some brief comments on the triad of male supervisor, female candidate, and male patient.) In particular, I've noted therapist resistance to recognizing the female patient's preoedipal maternal transference and to becoming aware of the patient's rage.

Liebert (1986) and Moldawsky (1986), while recognizing the attraction the mothering aspects of the therapeutic encounter have for men, also stress the discomfort implicit for a man in being viewed transferentially as a woman, as it unconsciously raises issues such as passive homosexual longings and questions of genital intactness. Such issues, with their connotation of regression to identification with the early mother, form the basis for the difficulties male therapists tend to experience in acknowledging a preoedipal maternal countertransference. In addition, both the castrating and annihilating aspects of a female patient's rage tend to make a male therapist, particularly an inexperienced one, anxious; a not unusual reaction is that of attempting to deny or neutralize the patient's anger. These culturally normative anxieties are reflected in the stereotypic postures women tend to display toward men, that is, behaving in a charming, ingratiating, and nonaggressive manner. Thus, a therapeutic collusion can occur in which the patient's dissembling or maintaining a fixed erotic transference is unconsciously welcomed by a male therapist who is reluctant to open a "Pandora's box."

These powerful unconscious dynamics—difficulties in acknowledging the preoedipal maternal countertransference and the patient's rage—figure prominently in the following examples from my supervisory experience.

A lack of therapeutic movement was the problem brought to supervision by a scholarly, responsible therapist. The patient, who was about to be divorced, presented herself as increasingly helpless, fragile, and unable to stand up for herself. While her therapist empathized with her timidly expressed feelings of anger, he never connected them with her feelings of helplessness. "It was necessary for me to point out to him that an interpretation which ascribed her feelings of helplessness to her rage at being abandoned and which attributed the function of helplessness to a furious demand for restitution was in order. Interestingly, although the therapist acknowledged the validity of the interpretation, he found it difficult to utilize, especially transferentially. He mistook his patient's stubborn silence for evidence that the interpretation was 'too hard on her.' Not until she produced a dream in which she was driving a car that had stopped with smoke coming from the engine did he recognize that the therapeutic impasse was ending as the patient accepted the linkage between her helplessness and her rage and, not so incidentally, her therapist's newfound ability to accept this" (Mendell, 1986, p. 272).

The second candidate's patient, a former call girl, wished to alter her conscious perception of men as cruel and sexually exploitative; she was less aware of her sadistic wishes to retaliate for her own abandonment by her father and completely unaware of the underlying rage toward the preoedipal mother. The analyst, a superior candidate in many ways, nevertheless used both isolation and denial to defend against his preconscious awareness of his patient's primitive dependency longings.

As the patient's attachment to her analyst grew, she requested a change from three to four sessions per week. As he reported the manner in which he refused, I was struck by his subtly triumphant and rejecting tone. It took some time for him to acknowledge that he was pushing the patient away due to his fear and anger. At a later point, the patient expressed sexual feelings for the analyst which were markedly different from her feelings as a call girl; the analyst referred to her as a prostitute and was surprised at her shock and indignation. Once again I had to point out that he had pushed her away because he feared the intensity of his own response.

While a male supervisor would no doubt note and correct the therapeutic errors described above, I believe there are added dimensions for the male candidate in discussing a female patient with a female supervisor. To begin with, the experience of being female tends to sensitize the supervisor to the subtle adaptations female patients make to empathic failure on the part of a male therapist. I was, for example, quickly aware of the subtly triumphant tone in which my supervisee spoke to his patient and her immediate masochistic response of "begging" for a fourth session. Most importantly, the supervisee internalizes certain qualities of the supervisor (Wallerstein, 1981). "If successful, a male candidate's identification with his female supervisor will result in an expansion of empathic capacities through allowing the feminine aspects of his personality to emerge. Through sharing the fearsome experience of a female patient's rage and neediness in the relative safety of a positive relationship with a female supervisor, each of my male students became able to react in a less fixed and stereotypically male style. Each of them was able to feel less threatened by the necessity of partial regression to an archaic position with his patient, and less endangered by the patient's anger, with which he now felt more empathy" (Mendell, 1986, p. 274).

Turning to the triad of male supervisor, female candidate, and male patient, which has similar potentialities in promoting therapist growth (Alonso & Rutan, 1978), I will briefly touch upon two factors that commonly contribute to female therapist's inhibitions in exploration with their male patients. First, the therapist may be conflicted about identifying with the phallic assertive qualities of her father, which would result in discomfort about actively entering the "inner space" of her male patient. A positive relationship with a male supervisor can result in an identification with his "male elements" in their clinical manifestations, integrating these aspects into her identity as a professional woman.

Second, as reported by Wayne (1987), the female supervisee "may feel a sense of dread" about her patient's size, strength, and ability to overpower her aggressively and sexually. Wayne continues: "Fears of genital-narcissistic injury can become pronounced, and several supervisees have reported being able to approach the patient with a greater sense of confidence because I am a male supervisor." An unconscious splitting of the paternal imago into the phallic-aggressive father (patient) and the rescuing, powerful father (supervisor) whose strength the supervisee borrows to prepare herself for the necessary exploration of the patient's strongly guarded inner space is posited.

Analytic training is truly a crucible for personal change. This paper has focused upon one important area of reorganization: developmentally determined and culturally sanctioned defensive patterns utilized in dealing with the opposite sex. It is suggested that cross-gender supervision is uniquely suited to assisting in these necessary changes.

References

Alonso, A., & Rutan, S. (1978). Cross-sex supervision for cross-sex therapy. *American Journal of Psychiatry, 135*(8), 928–931.

Liebert, R. (1986). Transference and countertransference issues in the treatment of women by a male analyst. In H. Meyers (Ed.), *Between analyst and patient: New dimensions.* Hillsdale, NJ: Analytic Press.

Mendell, D. (1986). Cross-gender supervision of cross-gender therapy: Female supervisor, male candidate, female patient. *American Journal of Psycho-analysis, 46*(3), 270–275.

Meyers, H. (1986). Analytic work with women: The complexity and the challenge. In H. Meyers (Ed.), *Between analyst and patient: New dimensions*. Hillsdale, NJ: Analytic Press.

Moldawsky, S. (1986). When men are therapists to women: Beyond the oedipal pale. In T. Bernay & D. Cantor (Eds.), *The psychology of today's woman: New psychoanalytic visions*. Hillsdale, NJ: Analytic Press.

Person, E. (1983). Women in therapy: Therapist gender as a variable. *International Review of Psychoanalysis, 10,* 193–204.

Wallerstein, R. (1981). *Becoming a psychoanalyst: A study of psychoanalytic supervision*. New York: International Universities Press.

Wayne, M. (1987). The male supervisor, the female therapist, the male patient: Supervisory and treatment dynamics. Paper presented at Workshop Series of the Postgraduate Center for Mental Health.

Response and Commentary

Jeanne M. Safer, Ph.D.

Dr. Mendell's paper demonstrates the value of cross-sex supervision as a technique for broadening the analyst's perspective by calling attention to unconscious attitudes toward the opposite-sex patient. An opposite-sex supervisor, she argues, is especially attuned to such issues and, therefore, is in a particularly good position to point them out. This deepens the therapist's ability to empathize with and understand the patient's experience.

Certainly it is important for a training institute to insure that candidates have the widest possible exposure to the perspectives of both male and female supervisors, as well as to alternative theoretical points of view.

While it is essential to recognize and to specify the special understanding which cross-sex supervision can bring to the analytic enterprise, it is also important not to jump to the conclusion that only a woman can understand another woman or a man a man. Our patients often raise this with us when they ask, "How can you understand me if you are/are not married, homosexual, a mother, a Catholic, etc." We answer, of course, that the ability to empathize and understand another person's experience, fortunately, does not require that it be identical to our own.

We must also guard against the assumption that there is a uniquely "feminine" or "masculine" style of supervision—or of analysis—or that a same-sex or opposite-sex supervisory dyad has an identifiable quality independent of the personalities of the participants. There is an extraordinary range of such qualities within each sex. The Jungians take this far too concretely, in my opinion, when they require that all candidates in training have two analyses, one with an analyst of each sex; one could have the bad luck to have two analysts of opposite sex with exactly the same personalities!

I feel that the nature of the interaction between the personalities of the participants, of which gender is only a feature, is the principal determinant of the supervisory atmosphere. Personal sexual identity, the significance of the opposite sex and of authority figures in the individual representational worlds of both participants, and how these are manifested in the relationship they create, are the crucial factors.

I recall a striking example of such an interaction in an experience I had with a supervisee. She was a woman about my age, articulate and intuitive, who was in the difficult position of simultaneously holding a responsible position in a related field at the same time as she was a beginning student in analytic training. We discussed quite candidly how hard this was, how critical she was of herself for not knowing what she felt she ought to know or what she thought others thought she ought to know, and things seemed to be going fine. Her work was excellent, and I let her know it.

Evidently she felt comfortable enough to confide in me that she was having trouble with another supervisor, also a woman, who happened to supervise her on the site of her job. She felt this woman to be highly critical and judgmental. This surprised me, since I knew her supervisor intimately, and she seemed like the last person who might be seen that way. I encouraged her to talk it over, and happily the problem was solved.

The year went by. She continued to do well, and I was thoroughly enjoying our work together. Toward the end, I sent her a patient and wrote her an excellent evaluation.

Imagine my astonishment when she told me during our last session of the year that she had been amazed that I sent her the patient, that despite my comments she had been convinced throughout that I thought she was hopeless and her work terrible. How did she explain my praise? I was humoring her. Had she not been uncomfortable? No, because she realized that I liked her, and because she had accepted that I couldn't do anything for her. It turned out that the tables had now turned. The other supervisor, who had originally been the bad one, had switched roles with me in her mind. I should add that the other supervisor had the same analyst and supervisor as I and is strikingly like me in style and theoretical orientation. As we were discussing this, the student suddenly realized the real reason for projecting such criticality on me despite the evidence: I physically resembled her mother to an amazing degree—height, coloring, haircut, and clothes.

What I found fascinating about this encounter was that here two rather similar supervisors, both women, were experienced in alternating opposite ways. The alternation was based on a split maternal transference, which was virtually unrelated to the actions of either of us, but which ended up projected onto me because of a chance physical resemblance. This ultimately determined the supervisee's interpretation of our relationship. On the basis of this sobering experience I gained a healthy respect for the complexities of the interaction of gender, personality, and the unconscious of both participants.

One, Two, Three Strikes, You're Out

A baseball metaphor describing a
potentially disastrous supervisory experience

Arnold Wm. Rachman, Ph.D.

When I was a first-year candidate at the Postgraduate Center for Mental Health, I had a disturbing yet interesting supervisory experience, which illustrates some of the gender issues inherent in the supervisory process.

The supervisor was a female psychiatrist who had a reputation of being eccentric and very difficult. I came fresh from my humanistic training at the Counseling and Psychotherapy Center founded by Carl Rogers at the University of Chicago.

Dr. H took over the session as soon as I sat down and asked me to discuss my session in a spontaneous way. I began to describe one of my first attempts to conduct a psychotherapy session at the Postgraduate Center. After I had talked for about five minutes, Dr. H suddenly exclaimed, "That's strike one!" I did a double take. I continued on with my description of the session, beginning to wonder what I had done wrong and assuming that I was not acting like an analyst. After about another minute I heard a still louder exclamation of "That's strike two!" emanating from somewhere in the direction of Dr. H. I was beginning to show some signs of anxiety, as I experienced her voice detaching itself from her body, and I wasn't sure she was talking to me. But, since there was no one else in the room but the two of us, I realized that I was beginning to move into the twilight zone of depersonalization.

Perhaps my experience of feeling the ego strength of recently receiving my doctorate and integrating my positive supervisory experiences at Chicago allowed me to find the strength to confront the situation rather than fade away completely. So I said to myself, "Arnold, you've got to do something or this supervision is going to blow up in your face." I took a deep breath and directed my remarks directly into the eyes of Dr. H, saying, "Apparently I've gotten two strikes on me. Before I get the third strike and strike out, could you tell me what game we're playing?"

It was like a magical intervention, the kind we all dream we will make one day in an analytic session, which opens up the door to self-disclosure. She laughed, changed her hostile, confrontative manner and revealed her negative feelings about male psychologists. She said the male psychologists she had supervised were usually very intellectual, but emotionally inhibited. They knew how to think, but not how to feel. She thought she heard me being the intellectual in my initial presentation. I appreciated her disclosure, although, I must admit, it upset me that she had such a negative prejudicial view of male psychologists. I told her that it might be true that psychologists could intellectualize, but I hoped she wouldn't place me in that box, because I had come from a tradition that valued the experiential, emotional component in the relationship.

We had a very positive, freer, less tense interaction for the rest of the session. Actually, the supervision turned out to be a nurturing, empathic learning experience for me. What is more, a personal relationship developed from this contact.

The experience highlighted for me, early in my training, the psychodynamics of gender issues as they are interwoven in the fabric of personality. It was fortunate for me, that I could react to what was a negative experience of being perceived as an emotionally inhibited male psychologist with a positive sense of myself and an ability to confront the supervisor. She was able to respond to my intervention, and we formed an empathic bond which nurtured me during my formative years as a neophyte psychoanalyst.

Transference Issues in Cross-Sex Supervision

Wilma Cohen Lewis, Ph.D.

I am going to approach the topic of transference issues in cross-sex supervision from the point of view of the learner, the supervisee. The position that I am taking is that what appear on the surface to be gender issues are on a deeper level transference issues: transference projections and displacements, both positive and negative. These transference issues may be triggered by the sex of the supervisor, a salient dimension, as well as by age and other concrete factors.

I believe that the sex of the supervisor has the potential to have as great an effect in supervision as in treatment, but that the way in which the supervisor handles the issues and potentialities will determine their impact, as well as the success of the supervision.

The sex of the supervisor may serve as the point of departure for transference phenomena in supervision as well as in analysis. The difference between analysis and supervision, and it is a critical difference, is that in analysis the transference is encouraged to expand; in treatment, transference is the vehicle of cure. In supervision, however, intense transferences can become obstacles to learning. The success of supervision in facilitating learning will depend upon avoidance of intense transference, particularly the negative transference.

As Berk (1977) has pointed out, most supervisees approach supervision with a great deal of anxiety about their performance. In their anxiety about living up to their ego ideal, supervisees may defensively project their own punitive superego onto the supervisor. The supervisor is then expected to be critical, judgmental, and punitive.

124

I find this particularly true in analytic training, where every candidate is already a fully qualified professional with experience. Some are even experts in their fields—university faculty members, heads of departments. Each now has to be a learner of psychoanalysis. The fear of exposure is great.

The successful supervisor is able to allay the anxiety and avoid the development of negative transference, thereby removing obstacles to the learning; whereas, the unsuccessful supervisor either fails to recognize this dynamic or is incapable of neutralizing the negative transference.

Here are two anecdotes from my own experience as a learner:

Experience Number 1. I began supervision in my first year of analytic training with a male supervisor, who provoked the most intense anxiety in me. Had he been younger, I would have related to him more as a peer. Had he been older, my transference would have been more grandfatherly and more benevolent. But he was of the age that triggered the most intense anxiety in me about male authority figures. The combination of gender plus age is loaded with transference potential.

I anticipated criticism. I anticipated rejection. I anticipated that he would find me inadequate and wanting.

My supervisor was actually fairly anonymous. He shared a few experiences but never mistakes or messes. He was cool and not particularly open. He would sit silently and watch me as I struggled to find words to express myself. He did not praise, support, or encourage. My anxiety mounted.

When I got up the courage to talk about how anxious I felt with him, he handled it analytically. He asked whether there was anything he had done or said. I said, "No," and began to tell him that I did not have these feelings about the chairman of my department in graduate school. He interrupted and told me to save my associations for my analyst. It was my problem.

My anxiety intensified. My negative superego projections intensified. Now it was no longer criticism that I anticipated—it had been confirmed by him. In the silences that grew longer when I would struggle to find words to express my thoughts, he would sit silently and look at me impassively. At times I was so anxious that I could not get the words out of my mouth. As far as the learning was concerned, I might as well have not been there. It was excruciating.

Was this gender? This could only have been provoked by a male supervisor around his age.

Experience Number 2.   Here is another experience I had in supervision—same components, a very different outcome.

Several years later, I went into private supervision with a male supervisor about the same age who is known and highly respected for his theoretical knowledge and clinical skill. Here I had gender, age, and reputation, the most loaded of all for me in its potential to provoke anxiety and intense transference reactions. The situation was further complicated because I was already a graduate of this institute. I knew the supervisor, and I knew that he thought well of me. In addition, here I had something to lose: his good opinion. "What if he finds out that I am not as good as he thought I was?" This in addition to other negative superego projections.

With all this anxiety, you might well wonder why I went into supervision with him. I had actually put off the wish for years. I did it because I would no longer avoid it. I knew what I needed to learn, and he was the best person I knew.

My anxiety and defensive negative superego projections were rampant at the beginning of this supervision. But he was warm. He talked. He shared. He was encouraging. He talked to me like a colleague. He praised. He expressed confidence in me. He shared his own experiences with patients, sometimes mistakes. He shared his questions and his doubts. At times he even shared aspects of his own psychodynamics to make a point. He listened, respected me, and was available as a mentor. When I told him at the beginning that I was anxious and had avoided this supervisor for a long time, he shrugged and said, "You have some transference." Normal, natural, no big deal. Even this was handled in a nonjudgmental and noncritical way. He allayed my anxiety and diluted and neutralized my negative superego projections. In this supervision, I was open. I was relaxed. I was eager and excited about learning. We tackled clinical questions. We tackled theoretical questions. My clinical work and my own work as a supervisor improved. I did not have nearly enough time for all I wanted to talk about. I even wondered, "Can you go to supervision twice a week?"

Same psyche. Same trigger or point of departure: gender. Same potential. Very different outcomes.

It could be argued that in the first case, it was a father transference, and in the second case, perhaps a mother transference. However, it is important to note that, in each case, I began with the same transference.

Was this gender? In each case, these intense reactions could only have been triggered by a male supervisor around this age.

In conclusion, in my opinion, what appear on the surface to be gender issues are, on a deeper level, transference issues—potential, nascent transference projections and displacements. These reactions may be triggered by the sex of the supervisor, a salient dimension, as well as by other factors.

Whether these intense transference reactions continue, are reinforced, and become obstacles to learning, or are diluted and neutralized, will depend upon the personality of the supervisor as well as his or her conscious or unconscious insight into this dynamic.

References

Berk, R. (1977). Reported by B. Fielding, The supervisor—facilitating and/or hindering learning in a psychoanalytically oriented training center. *Postgraduate Center Colloquium, 1,* 34–38.

Cross-Gender Supervision Problems: Reality, Social Fictions or Unconscious Processes?

Anna Duran, Ph.D.

Supervision, like psychotherapy and psychoanalysis, is not a value-free process. Supervision is an interpersonal process in that both trainee and supervisor possess concepts about the social world that include society's view of roles and behaviors appropriate for women and men. These social concepts are reflected in the language habits and communication processes of each person as demonstrated in how he or she describes and explains supervisory goals, processes, and expectations. Specifically, the content of these communications involve certain parameters, such as who in the relationship can hypothesize, the extent of question-answer behavior, the expression of curiosity, the range of emotions that can be displayed, and whether the relationship can tolerate disagreement and yet promote exploration of clinical material. Each person comes into the relationship with experiences in terms of each of these communication sequences. How these elements are negotiated, whether consciously or unconsciously, will play a part in determining the comfort, trust, and the quality of the atmosphere for learning that is created.

Since each of these elements of the communication process between supervisor and supervisee is already complex, it can be a simple matter to ignore the role that cross-gender supervision plays in the parameter setting issues noted above. However, the teaching-learning atmosphere can be severely impaired if, in a cross-gender supervisory relationship, these elements of the communication process are not acknowledged as areas where gender and cultural differences may emerge. The outcome of not acknowledging these realities could give permission for the supervisor's unconscious wishes and fears, which can be enacted through the creation of biased judgments and evaluations of the supervisee, hence, producing a false reality or social fiction about the supervisory process and the participants.

An additional area that can be impacted by differing social concepts and values concerns the characterization of various social interaction sequences, namely, the interpretation of clinical information (such as what occurs between patient and analyst) and inferences about a patient's psychology will be at times subject to debate and negotiation. For example, Schafer (1984) found gender differences in clinicians' tracing of a storyline in their understanding of a patient's problem. The theme of pursuing failure is relatively more conspicuous in analytic work with men, while the theme of idealization of unhappiness is relatively more observable in analytic work with women.

Overall, the supervisor's training goals, his or her social concepts about gender, and the trainee's level of comfort with the expression of differences in opinion will contribute to the level of empathy achieved during the supervisory process. However, as pointed out by Dale Mendell's article, empathy can vary in cross-gender supervision, that is, gender sometimes makes a difference and sometimes it does not. Given that we need to consider that cross-gender supervision problems are occasionally a reality, it becomes important to consider several questions:

1) When gender is an issue, what kind of errors in empathy can occur?
2) What are the unconscious and conscious attitudes about gender differences that can affect the supervisory process?
3) When are cross-gender supervision problems social realities, and when are they social fictions that are assumed to be a part of unconscious processes?

The research literature on the role of clinicians' perceptions of expected behaviors and attitudes toward women supports the viewpoint that there are some commonly held social notions about women that have a negative impact on listening and clinical inferences (Denmark, 1980). For example, there is intolerance of the expression of anger or hostility by women. And societal stereotypes of masculinity and femininity, whether conscious or unconscious, have elicited a double standard of mental health for men and women.

The role of social concepts regarding the expectations of the behaviors of men also need to be considered (Abend, 1982). Studies that have focused on men have found that the expression of distress may be more accepted in females than males (Lorr et al., 1960), and that males who deviate from their prescribed gender role may be judged more harshly than females (Carlson, 1981). Also, male patients' opinions or perceptions may go unquestioned by female clinicians who are anxious about the feminine role prohibition against exercising authority over men (Ambramowitz et al., 1976).

Overall, these conclusions demonstrate that social concepts can have an impact on the therapeutic process. Because the business of supervision is to examine elements of process and the organization of the patient's issues, the role of social concepts is likely to impinge upon the supervisory process of an analyst in training as well.

In terms of unconscious and conscious attitudes that can affect the supervisory process, personally held notions concerning the experience of difference, especially when a person's gender is experienced as a salient feature in a social episode, need to be articulated with greater specificity. In an exploratory study on personal experiences with difference (Duran, 1988), patterns of how gender differences are thought about seemed apparent. These patterns varied in level of cognitive engagement. Each pattern suggests that the extent to which individuals can understand their personal emotional experiences in social episodes where they experience being noticed because of their gender, or they feel different because of their gender, will influence how they focus their attention on the experiences of others. These patterns, it would seem, could influence the supervisory process as well, in that the level of cognitive engagement with respect to gender differences will determine the course of cross-gender supervision.

In summary, both conscious attitudes, as reflected in social concepts held by analysts, supervisors, and trainees, and unconscious social predispositions, unless monitored and managed, can create cross-gender supervision problems. The supervisor, in particular, needs to be aware of his or her thoughts about differences and the etiology of the emotional content that support their existence and use. Pursuing themes solely in the name of unresolved unconscious conflicts without wondering if a contrary storyline applies and without asking if there is the possibility of gender bias, circumvents a training opportunity to encourage the development of emotional richness and intellectual depth of the trainee in service of the patient.

References

Abend, S. A. (1982). Sexism and psychotherapists: The relationship between sex of therapists, their level of training and their sex-role stereotyping. *Dissertation Abstracts International, 42,* 13, 4A.

Ambramowitz, C. N., Abramowitz, S. I., & Weitz, L. J. (1976). Are men therapists soft on empathy? Two studies in feminine understanding. *Journal of Clinical Psychology, 32,* 434–437.

Carlson, N. (1981). Male client-female therapist. *Personnel and Guidance Journal, 60,* 228–231.

Denmark, F. L. (1980). Psyche: From rocking the cradle to rocking the boat. *American Psychologist, 35,* 1057–1065.

Duran, A. (1988). Subjective experiences with being different. Unpublished manuscript.

Lorr, M., O'Connor, J. P., & Stafford, J. W. (1960). The psychotic reaction profile. *Journal of Clinical Psychology, 16,* 241–245.

Schafer, R. (1984). The pursuit of failure and the idealization of unhappiness. *American Psychologist, 39,* 398–405.

Gender Issues and the Art of Psychoanalysis

Stephen M. Schiff, Ph.D.

To examine the contribution of cross-sex supervision to the development of the analytic candidate, it would be useful to keep in mind the task of the analyst. Loewald (1980) states that the analyst, like a sculptor, must possess the ability to see the "core" of the patient in order to bring out the particular patient's innate capabilities. In doing this, the analyst needs to be able to see correctly the patient's current developmental level plus maintain a sense of perspective encompassing the patient's potential development. In doing so, the analyst needs to avoid molding the patient in his/her own image or imposing on the patient his/her own concept of what the patient is to become.

Differences between the analyst and the patient, such as those of gender, have the potential to enhance the treatment or, conversely, may serve as an obstacle to the analyst's ability to perceive accurately the patient's "core." To cope with such differences, the analyst needs an accurate intellectual understanding of the patient, an emotional attunement and responsivity to the particular patient's potentialities, and an ability to sort out his/her own countertransference reactions. The latter could be sorted out into those that signal the analyst's biases and those that carry useful information about the patient.

Applying Loewald's ideas to the supervisory process, we may view the supervisor's task as that of helping the analyst to see accurately each patient's innate capacities and the resistances to their further development. With this in mind, the female supervisor may have a unique contribution to make when working with a male analyst/female patient pairing. The female supervisor may be able to provide a more complete, objective understanding of female development. In addition, she is probably better able to understand and communicate to the male supervisee the subjective experience of the female patient than would a male supervisor.

Reference

Loewald, H. W. (1980). On the therapeutic action of psychoanalysis. In *Papers on psychoanalysis*. New Haven: Yale University Press.

Symposium

*Psychoanalysis
versus Psychotherapy:
Different Approaches in
Supervising Graduate
Clinical Students*

Introduction

Ruth Ochroch, Ph.D.

Efforts to distinguish psychoanalysis from psychoanalytically oriented psychotherapy emerged almost at the beginning of the psychoanalytic movement and continue to the present. The near synonymous use of "psychoanalysis" with "psychoanalytic therapy" and "psychoanalytic therapy" with "psychoanalytically oriented psychotherapy" have been decried in the writings of Fromm-Reichman (1959), Waelder (1960), and others. Efforts at the differentiation of psychoanalysis from psychoanalytically oriented psychotherapy and of conceptual and methodological differences have continued to concern writers in the field.

Brenner (1982), Kohut (1984), Singer (1970), and others have focused on definitions of psychoanalysis. They, plus such authors as Gill (1982), Kernberg (1984), and Spiegel (1984), have defined the psychoanalytic method. The conceptual basis of differing psychoanalytic theories as an arena of present day interest is reflected in the recent works of Greenberg and Mitchell (1983), Kohut (1984), Masterson (1985), and Pine (1985). The applicability and effectiveness of psychoanalysis versus psychoanalytically oriented psychotherapy have been addressed by such writers as Basch (1980), Langs (1973), and others. An examination of the essential principles, the method or process and the goals of psychoanalysis and psychoanalytically oriented psychotherapy reveal a wide range of general similarities.

Symposium presented at the American Psychological Association Convention, August 31, 1987, New York. Participants: Ruth Ochroch, Ph.D. (Chair); Suzanne M. Gassner, Ph.D., Bertram P. Karon, Ph.D., and Joseph W. Newirth, Ph.D. (Speakers); and Jerome L. Singer, Ph.D. (Discussant).

Despite these similarities, the writings of such authorities as Brenner (1984), Gill (1982), and McDougall (1985) contend that psychoanalysis is a deeper, more systematic, and technically different method of personality exploration and change. Other authorities, such as Crowley (1984) and Paolino (1981), feel that such differences are invalid and represent different points on a continuum with much overlap. Both sets of authorities, plus Chrzanowski (1984), Kohut (1984), E. Singer (1970), and J. L. Singer (1985), deal with the differences among techniques and the variant or invariant nature of the techniques. They debate the efficacy of reliance on free association, the use of the couch, the frequency of sessions, the passive encouragement of a regressive transference neurosis, and the achievement of structural personality change and healthier adaptation through the resolution of the transference neurosis.

Training in psychotherapy in a psychodynamic/psychoanalytically oriented clinical program is one of the crucial paths for doctoral students to achieve professional status. There are obvious differences in the patients accepted for treatment in clinics staffed by doctoral clinical students and the patients accepted for treatment by analytic candidates in analytic training institutes. There may also be differences in frequency of sessions, as in many psychodynamic/psychoanalytically oriented doctoral programs patients are usually seen twice a week. Psychoanalytic training institutes may see patients from two to four times a week. In view of the overlaps between dynamic psychotherapy and psychoanalysis, questions are frequently raised as to how differently and toward what end are supervisors training clinical doctoral students in psychotherapy compared to candidates for psychoanalysis. Levenson (1984) and Spiegel (1984) represent the emphasis on the differences in the supervision process, while Crowley (1984), Paolino (1981), and Singer (1970) represent a minimization of differences.

The following papers in this symposium include the positions of three analytically trained supervisors at different clinical doctoral programs as to their own differentiations between psychoanalysis and psychodynamically oriented psychotherapy in their supervision of psychotherapy, and a discussion of the three papers.

References

Basch, M. F. (1980). *Doing psychotherapy.* New York: Basic Books.
Bienvenu, J. P., Piper, W. E., Debbane, E. G., & De Carufel, F. (1986). On the concept of psychoanalytic work. *American Journal of Psychotherapy, 11,* 277–289.

Brenner, C. (1982). *The mind in conflict.* New York: International Universities Press.

Chrzanowski, G. (1984). Can psychoanalysis be taught? In L. Caligor, P. M. Bromberg, & J. D. Meltzer (Eds.), *Clinical perspectives on the supervision of psychoanalysis and psychotherapy.* New York: Plenum Press.

Crowley, R. M. (1984). Being and doing in continuous consultation for psychoanalytic education. In L. Caligor, P. M. Bromberg, & J. D. Meltzer (Eds.), *Clinical perspectives on the supervision of psychoanalysis and psychotherapy.* New York: Plenum Press.

Fromm-Reichman, F. (1959). *Psychoanalysis and psychotherapy: Selected papers of Frieda Fromm-Reichman* (D. M. Bullard, ed.). Chicago: University of Chicago Press.

Gill, M. M. (1982). Psychoanalysis and psychotherapy: A revision. *International Review of Psychoanalysis, 11,* 158–165.

Greenberg, J. & Mitchell, S. (1983). *Object relations in psychoanalytic theory.* Cambridge, MA: Harvard University Press.

Kernberg, O. F. (1984). *Severe personality disorders.* New Haven: Yale University Press.

Kohut, H. (1984). *How does analysis cure?* Chicago: University of Chicago Press.

Langs, R. (1973). *The technique of psychoanalytic psychotherapy.* New York: Jason Aronson.

Levenson, E. A. (1984). Follow the fox. In L. Caligor, P. M. Bromberg, J. D. Meltzer (Eds.), *Clinical perspectives on the supervision of psychoanalysis and psychotherapy.* New York: Plenum Press.

Masterson, J. F. (1985). *The real self: A developmental, self and object relations approach.* New York: Brunner/Mazel.

McDougall, J. (1985). *Theatres of the mind.* New York: Basic Books.

Paolino, T. J. (1981). *Psychoanalytic psychotherapy.* New York: Brunner/Mazel.

Pine, F. (1985). *Developmental theory and clinical process.* New Haven: Yale University Press.

Singer, E. (1970). *Key concepts in psychotherapy.* New York: Basic Books.

Singer, J. L. (1985). Transference and the human condition: A cognitive-affective perspective. *Psychoanalytic psychology, 2,* 189–220.

Spiegel, R. (1984). Communication and the use of the couch within the psychoanalytic situation: A supervisory perspective. In L. Caligor, P. M. Bromberg, & J. D. Meltzer (Eds.), *Clinical perspectives on the supervision of psychoanalysis and psychotherapy.* New York: Plenum Press.

Waelder, R. (1960). *Basic theory of psychoanalysis.* New York: International Universities Press.

The Implications of "Control-Mastery Theory" for Supervision

Suzanne M. Gassner, Ph.D.

During the last 12 years I have been a member of the Mount Zion Psychotherapy Research Group, headed by Drs. Harold Sampson and Joseph Weiss. Our group has been studying the empirical evidence for a new psychoanalytic theory, developed by Dr. Weiss and informally referred to by our group as "control-mastery" theory.* My own use of this theoretical point of view and many years of supervision with Drs. Sampson and Weiss have very much influenced my own work as supervisor of graduate students in clinical psychology at the University of California at Berkeley.

My goals as a psychoanalytically oriented psychotherapy supervisor are to help students learn:

1) how to use the first few treatment sessions to develop a fairly specific case formulation;
2) how to evaluate the accuracy of the case formulation and, where necessary, revise it, by studying whether or not the formulation can successfully predict what kinds of therapist interventions promote or impede patient progress; and

---

*The "control" portion of the term refers to the hypothesis that patients can exercise some control over their unconscious mental life. The "mastery" portion of the term refers to the hypothesis that psychotherapy patients are motivated to master their problems in treatment.

3) how to apply the case formulation and the information contained in the on-going therapy hours to arrive at case-specific guidelines for the therapist's clinical technique.

In order to further explain how I conceptualize the supervisory task, it will be necessary for me to describe briefly what Weiss's theory proposes. I offer this sketchy summary of "control-mastery" theory in order to clarify how I teach psychodynamically oriented students to think about clinical process. This summary, however, may misinform, because it is an oversimplification of a complex and rich psychoanalytic perspective. A comprehensive presentation of the theory and supporting research data are available in *The Psychoanalytic Process: Theory, Clinical Observations and Empirical Research* (Weiss, et al., 1986).

Weiss's theory emphasizes the importance of trauma in the etiology of all forms of psychopathology. By "trauma," we mean primarily any experience or ongoing life circumstance that leads an individual to believe that an important goal, be it an instinctual wish or an ego striving, must be given up in order to avoid the interrelated dangers of damaging one's love objects or being damaged by them. Patients enter treatment consciously and unconsciously motivated to achieve important goals by mastering the traumas that had made these goals too dangerous to pursue.

In keeping with Freud's (1926) signal theory of anxiety, "control-mastery" theory assumes that following a traumatic occurrence, anxiety will be experienced whenever an individual unconsciously anticipates that there might be a danger of being retraumatized. Guided by unconscious memories of childhood traumas, people form unconscious beliefs about what constitutes situations of danger and use these beliefs to calculate the potential consequences of gratifying a particular impulse or pursuing a particular goal. We refer to these beliefs as "pathogenic beliefs." Pathogenic beliefs can take the form of powerful, unconscious commands, which compel an individual to behave in certain ways or which prohibit other kinds of behavior. This is to say that compulsions and inhibitions can be understood as efforts to avoid the dangers foretold by pathogenic beliefs.

Typically, pathogenic beliefs involve irrational explanations about how one's behavior caused the trauma to occur. Sometimes these convictions develop at a later time, when the patient reconstructs what had happened earlier. Often the patient has overgeneralized from the traumatic experience. Such patients believe that they must govern their behavior in accordance with these false causal explanations, not only in the setting in which the trauma occurred, but more generally in the world at large.

The irrational ideas to which a patient subscribes may stem from a number of sources. They may result from the distorting influences of early childhood cognition. They may result from an identification with the parents' pathogenic beliefs. They may also result from the child's compliance with the parents' interpretation of reality.

In our view, patients, be they in psychotherapy or psychoanalysis, are strongly motivated, both consciously and unconsciously, to gain insight into and work through their neurotic conflicts in a fundamental way, in order to master their problems. Weiss's theory assumes that patients are capable of working constructively to master their problems and that they attempt to enlist the therapist's help in their efforts to achieve this mastery.

We believe that patients develop "unconscious plans" for how to overcome their problems in treatment. Broadly speaking, unconscious plans are ways of achieving therapeutic goals by mastering the effects of childhood traumas and thereby overcoming internal obstructions that interfere with the pursuit of those goals. Unconscious plans contain therapeutic goals as well as unconscious strategies for attempting to achieve these goals. Patients' therapeutic strategies are not fixed or blindly followed, but rather are tentative and conditional, that is, they are modified and revised as the patient attempts to do the therapeutic work.

Unconscious strategies include, as a key component, various ways to "test" the therapist in an effort to disconfirm the pathogenic beliefs and the associated dangers that prevent patients from pursuing or achieving their goals. Testing is the most effective means by which patients can reevaluate the reality basis for the dangers predicted by their pathogenic beliefs. Patients test in order to ascertain if the conditions of safety exist for making conscious their pathogenic beliefs and attempting to master the childhood traumas from which they arose.

There are two ways in which patients test the therapist. One is that patients unconsciously turn passive into active. In this process, patients treat the therapist in the very ways in which they felt themselves to have been treated and which they found traumatic as children. Unconsciously, they hope that the therapist will not be traumatized as they were, but will instead be able to maintain a therapeutic stance.

The other way that patients test is through transference repetitions. Patients relate to the therapist by repeating patterns that characterized their behavior with their parents. They especially repeat those behaviors they believe were the provocations that led to their being traumatized. Through transference, patients unconsciously attempt to disconfirm a pathogenic belief by testing to see whether the therapist, like the parents, will respond in a manner they found traumatic as children.

Passed tests help patients challenge their convictions about the reality of the dangers their pathogenic beliefs predict. As patients discover that the therapist does not reenact with them the traumas they experienced with other family members, they feel safer to lift their defenses and to begin working through their childhood traumatic experiences. We expect that when a therapist passes a test, the patient typically will become more relaxed, bold, and insightful. Often the patient will also bring out new information and, sometimes, warded-off memories. It should be noted, however, that while a test is in progress, patients may express negative feelings about the very therapist behaviors they unconsciously find reassuring.

In addition to passing patients' tests, the therapist helps them by making "pro-plan" interpretations, whose import is to make conscious and implicitly disconfirm some aspects of the patients' pathogenic beliefs, or otherwise to assist patients in moving toward their therapeutic goals. When the therapist provides patients with insights into their pathogenic beliefs, it increases their conscious control over the effects of those beliefs as well as their capacity to reality-test the dangers predicted by those beliefs. When the therapist fails a test, or makes interpretations that confirm patients' pathogenic beliefs, we expect that patients will experience an increased sense of danger and become more beleaguered, resistant, and uninsightful. Often, following a failed test or an "anti-plan" interpretation, patients will give the therapist additional tests or easier tests, with the unconscious hope that this will help the two of them get back on track.

In supervision, we work with the first few treatment hours to infer what the patient's unconscious plan is likely to be. The plan formulation contains the following components:

1) We try to determine the patient's treatment goals. These goals are the capacities the patient wishes to achieve through mastering childhood traumas.
2) We try to infer what the obstructions are that interfere with the patient's ability to achieve these goals. These obstructions are conceptualized as unconscious pathogenic beliefs. They involve

the patient's irrational fear that pursuing these goals will expose the patient or someone the patient cares for to painful experiences of guilt, shame, humiliation, or anxiety.

3) We infer, based on the nature of the traumas, how the patient is likely to behave if he or she tests the therapist by turning passive into active or by transference.

4) We formulate the kinds of insights the patient will unconsciously experience as pro-plan or anti-plan interpretations.

Weiss's theory provides specific empirical criteria for evaluating the effectiveness of the treatment process. Our research group has conducted several studies (Weiss et al., 1986) whose purpose was to ascertain whether the predicted correspondence actually existed between the analyst's passing tests or making pro-plan interventions and the patient's becoming more insightful and making analytic progress. In a successful treatment, patients creatively and boldly test the therapist in ways that have a potential of disconfirming their pathogenic beliefs. As patients feel increasingly safe with the therapist, they are able to lift their defenses, bring into consciousness their warded-off strivings, feelings and memories, and reflect insightfully upon them. In a successful treatment, therapists are able to pass many of the patient's tests, make corrections for failed tests, and make pro-plan interpretations that increase the patient's insight and diminish the patient's unconscious sense of danger. When the therapeutic process has these characteristics, patients are able to make progress in disconfirming their pathogenic beliefs and, thereby, to emancipate themselves from the constraining effects of their traumatic experiences.

Thus it is that the effectiveness of the student's treatment interventions can be studied on the basis of the demonstrated effect they have on the patient's work. I ask students to pay close attention to when it is that the patient's work becomes more progressive, that is, the patient becomes more insightful, bold, provides new information, or perhaps expresses a previously warded-off memory, idea, or affect. Likewise, I ask students to be alert to what has been happening in the treatment process at those times when patients retreat or become more defensive, anxious, or distant from their own experience and the experience of the therapy relationship. Another way that we learn how better to work with a given patient is to identify times in the treatment when the patient is being particularly insightful and bold. We try then to reconstruct what events in the treatment and/or in the patient's external life seem to have contributed to the patient's increased freedom to work progressively. These moments allow us to make additional inferences about what experiences increase the patient's unconscious sense of safety.

Therapy supervision, therefore, can be a process in which both supervisor and supervisee form hypotheses about the kinds of therapist interventions that lead to demonstrable patient progress and the kinds of interventions that impede the patient in his or her work. It is possible to supervise students using this theoretical framework, regardless of the particular clinical intuitions or theoretical perspectives the student brings to supervision. Studying sequences of the therapy process becomes the basis for confirming, disconfirming, or revising hypotheses about the patient's unconscious plan.

The "control-mastery" theory is equally applicable to my work with psychotherapy patients and with analysands. Although I have not supervised any psychoanalysts, were I to do so, my approach to studying the treatment process would be essentially the same. Weiss developed many of his ideas by studying the process notes from his work with patients in psychoanalysis (Weiss et al., 1986). He was particularly curious about those sequences of events that did not fit his own preconceptions, based on his own analytic training, of how the treatment process works. After he developed his theory, the Mount Zion Psychotherapy Research Group tested many of his ideas using the process notes and transcripts from short-term therapy cases, as well as from a completed psychoanalysis conducted by a psychoanalyst from a distant city (Weiss et al., 1986). This analyst was unfamiliar with the "control-mastery" perspective. Our research has shown that the same principles apply in short-term psychotherapy and in psychoanalysis.

I would also like to discuss how I try to help students in supervision make use of their own subjective reactions to their patients. I start with the premise that unless there is clear-cut evidence to the contrary, a supervisee's emotional reactions to the patient inform us about some aspect of how the patient is working in treatment. "Control-mastery" theory assumes that when a therapist is having a strong emotional reaction to the patient, usually the patient has turned passive into active. Often our patients cannot tell us directly about their memories of traumatic events. Therefore, patients will often reenact with their therapist those kinds of interchanges that as children they found to be traumatic. We expect that oftentimes, patients who are highly traumatized will for years primarily test the therapist by turning passive into active. I should add that at times, when a supervisee is feeling overwhelmed by a patient, he or she may treat the supervisor in a way similar to how the patient is treating the supervisee.

I find that it is very relieving to beginning therapists to discover that there is much information about the patient contained in their own affective responses to the patient. Beginning therapists often fear that they will be judged harshly if they do not like their patient or are upset by something the patient is doing. As supervisees learn about the importance of passive-into-active tests, they become more interested and feel safer to attend to their own subjective reactions, and thereby bring more data about the therapist-patient relationship into the treatment. Most of the students I have supervised have begun some psychotherapy for themselves. This also makes it easier to concentrate on the data about the supervisee's reactions to the patient for the sole purpose of understanding more about what that reaction tells us about the patient's history and the pathogenic beliefs the patient is testing by inducing certain feeling states into the therapist.

References

Freud, S. (1926). Inhibitions, symptoms and anxiety. *Standard Edition, 20,* 77–175. London: Hogarth Press, 1959.

Weiss, J., Sampson, H., & the Mount Zion Psychotherapy Group (1986). *The psychoanalytic process: Theory, clinical observation and empirical research.* New York: Guilford Press.

Psychoanalysis, Psychoanalytic Therapy, and the Process of Supervision

Bertram P. Karon, Ph.D.

Since the 1940s psychoanalytic therapy has been distinguished from psychoanalysis proper. In the earlier literature (e.g., Sterba, 1935), "psychoanalytic therapy" was used simply to indicate that what was being discussed was psychoanalysis as therapy, or its therapeutic action.

Freud, while decrying "wild analysis" (1910), was not rigid as to the technique he utilized, as evidenced by his case histories, for example, the "Rat Man" (1909), or the techniques he accepted in his students and colleagues (e.g., Aichhorn, 1936).

One of my early psychoanalytic instructors defined psychoanalytic therapy as being as much like psychoanalysis as the defenses of the patient, the time available, and the skill of the therapist permit. That has always seemed to me a proper definition.

The continuity that is implied is real. As my students have pointed out, I am apt to use the phrase "real treatment" to mean "psychoanalysis or psychoanalytic therapy," as in the sentence, "After years of medication, behavior modification, cognitive therapy, and so forth, the patient finally began real treatment."

Any psychoanalysis which is not good therapy cannot be good psychoanalysis. Psychoanalytic theories provide the basis for proper technique, whether standard or modified. Suitable modifications, or parameters, of psychoanalysis and psychoanalytic therapy are always used by competent clinicians, as required by the defenses of the patient.

147

"Parameter-phobia" among analysts is the result of an internalized punitive psychoanalytic superego based on experiences with one's real psychoanalytic supervisors fused with remnants of the preexisting primitive sadistic superego. It should not be necessary to say, but it is necessary to say, that the concept of "parameters" does not refer to crimes, but to consciously conceptualizing the rationale for technical procedures, so that you can consciously evaluate their effectiveness and keep track of the inevitable countertransference distortions.

Where the dividing line between psychoanalysis and psychoanalytic therapy is drawn varies from writer to writer. It may be that psychoanalysis is "any investigation that takes seriously the unconscious and repression, resistance and transference," or any technique that consists of doing what needs to be done, to the best of your ability, on the basis of a psychoanalytic understanding of the patient and the treatment process. Or only if the patient is seen at least three, four, five, or six days a week, on a couch, facing away from the analyst, and suffers from neurotic or certain characterological problems. Or only if structural change is produced, or only if a full "transference neurosis" occurs and is resolved, or only if the sole therapeutic agent is interpretation, narrowly defined. It really makes no difference in treatment where you draw the line, as long as the technique used, whether called psychoanalysis or psychoanalytic therapy, is appropriate to the defenses of the patient, in the best judgment of the analyst or therapist.

Thoma and Kachele (1987) point out how difficult such criteria are to use scientifically, and the clear continuity between various psychoanalytic therapies and psychoanalysis, and how everything that is learned about the psychoanalytic therapies illuminates the process of psychoanalysis proper, and that what is learned in psychoanalysis is relevant to understanding the psychoanalytic therapies.

For any therapy with any patient, it is my experience that the more time available, the easier it is for both patient and therapist. Unfortunately, the therapist's schedule, the patient's schedule, the need to charge a fee, and the limited financial resources available all lead to briefer therapy, both in time and in number of sessions per week. Every genuine therapist feels the conflict between wanting to help as many people as possible and wanting to do a therapy that is thorough and helpful, and we know best how to do that in ways that take time. Every genuine therapist also knows the conflict between wanting to be available to everyone irrespective of financial status and wanting to live in the way that a decent income permits, or, if part of an agency, the need to maintain the fiscal solvency of the agency, particularly if the agency provides real help.

There is, as far as I know, no systematic research on the effects of number of sessions per week per se on the nature and content of the hour or on the course of the treatment. The nearest to a systematic study was the report of Alexander and French (1946) that reducing the number of sessions per week seemed more compatible with effective treatment than cutting down the calendar time. Technically, they suggested that in once or twice per week therapy, more of the transference reactions outside the therapy hour had to be analyzed as opposed to analyzing the transference neurosis itself.

Certainly, under even the most stringent institutional restrictions, I would recommend strongly that the first week of treatment for psychotic individuals should be five sessions, although the length of the session may be shortened to half an hour. Even if the treatment is going to be continued on a once per week basis, the patient needs to know you are there, the therapeutic alliance needs to be established, and the therapist and patient need to have a chance for the transference and countertransference dynamics to begin to be apparent.

It is not uncommon to hear fears that too intensive a frequency will cause too much regression, particularly for borderline patients. But it is not the frequency per se which is disabling but the character of the sessions. In particular, it is essential that the therapist or analyst be willing to provide as much structure and support as the defenses of the patient require. This is not a one-time diagnostic judgment, but a reaction in each hour to the patients as they experience that therapy hour, so that the patients' ability to cope with the anxieties aroused by their memories and transference reactions are not exceeded. Again, it is not uncommon to hear that too few sessions are so unhinging that the patient had better not be treated psychotherapeutically at all, but medicated, punished, advised, or left alone. Again, the problem is the character of the session. The greatest danger is that nothing of importance will happen with too low a frequency, although it is true that with a low frequency, it is harder for the therapist to obtain the necessary information about the therapy to guide the process optimally.

Sometimes the low frequency is forced by the defenses of the patient, however. One psychotic depressive patient moved to her parents' house instead of to a hospital. They lived some 40 miles away and could only bring her once a week. This turned out to be an advantage. Like many psychotic depressives, this lady was very irritating. It was possible for her to have a reasonable, kind, but active therapist once a week, although by the end of her hour my countertransference was such that I usually felt enraged at her. By the next week, however, she once more had a rational and kind therapist for most of her hour. The treatment progressed to a very satisfactory outcome—not only did her psychosis remit, but she handled her five children more appropriately, had a better relationship with her husband, including a better sexual relationship, and held a part-time job successfully for the first time in her marriage. In part because of their better relationship, her husband became more effective and was able to earn more money, which was important for their way of life. But given the intensity of my emotional reaction, it is questionable that such a benign outcome would have been possible if she had been seen more frequently, particularly at the beginning.

One ambulatory depressive of 20 years standing was told that he should be seen a minimum of three times a week, and that while no firm estimate could be made, he would need to be in treatment at least two or three years. He was irate: "You are just trying to run a bill on me. I know. I have friends who work in an HMO. They treat people in 16 sessions. That's all anyone needs. And I'm not coming in more than once a week." He was told that, while I disagreed, I would certainly do what I could for him in the time he allowed.

At the tenth session, I reminded him that he had only six more sessions, and asked how he felt about it. He was furious that I would not see him more than 16 sessions. After he berated me, he was told that if he felt that strongly, I would continue treating him. Shortly thereafter he became furious that I refused to see him more than once a week. After allowing him to berate me, I again conceded to his wish to be seen twice a week. After a few months he became furious that I refused to see him more than twice a week. Again, after allowing his rage, I agreed with his demand for three times a week. The analytic treatment then proceeded with the difficulties usual for severely depressed, hostile patients.

An ambulatory paranoid patient, with a delusion that there was a rumor that he was a homosexual, was unable to work. Previous therapy had enabled him to finish schooling and embark on a professional career (not in the psychological professions). This rumor had followed him, however, from city to city. Despite offers to cut his fee, he insisted on being seen not more than half an hour once per week because he "could not afford any more." He would sit in the furthest corner of the room, and stated that he had no thoughts, what did the therapist want to talk about? It was possible nonetheless to help him, in the minimal time he permitted, to be able to work, to relate to friends, and to date without the "rumor" recurring. While the treatment was terminated prematurely by the therapist's standards, with many neurotic traits remaining and far short of our analytic ideal, the treatment was a success by the patient's standards, was well worth the time involved, and has led to stable functioning for years (as of now).

Most people who think about the issue of the ideal training of a psychoanalytic therapist recommend that the novice should first experience a thorough personal psychoanalysis, then conduct traditional psychoanalyses under supervision, and then be trained in briefer psychoanalytic therapies. Thus, the therapist will really understand, from his or her own analysis, what therapy is about, learn from supervised analyses what would come to the surface if there were sufficient time, and then be able to utilize this in briefer psychoanalytic therapy.

Almost nobody goes through the sequence of training in that rational order. For example, no graduate student in our program practices psychoanalysis, in the narrow sense. The only practitioners I supervise in psychoanalysis are psychologists and social workers in the community, who are in private practice or community agencies, have been analyzed, and have taken seminars in analytic technique and wish eventually to be trained as psychoanalysts. Graduate students, often without any prior personal therapy, begin by doing brief psychoanalytic therapy. Most of the competent ones obtain some personal psychotherapy before they finish graduate school, but do not begin personal psychoanalysis until they are out in the field, primarily for financial reasons.

Before we despair, however, we should note that the first generation of psychoanalysts, whose contributions display a level of insight, creativity, and therapeutic competence far above what is usual today, went through what we would consider haphazard training. Of course, these were bright, creative, highly motivated individuals, who lived psychoanalysis. They learned as much as possible about psychoanalysis in the broadest possible sense. You may argue, as Robert Knight (1954, pp. 24–25) has, that they were less well-adjusted than the present generation, but better analysts. Knight argues that his generation of candidates was motivated to learn as little as possible about psychoanalysis and get through their training, and this led to the proliferation of explicit requirements. But this very proliferation of explicit requirements appeals to that kind of candidate he deplores, while discouraging the creative individuals to whom psychoanalysis appealed earlier.

Many of our current creative psychoanalysts have gone through unusual routes in their training. The question is: does the irrational route that we have created in graduate school make any sense at all?

I have found it useful to supervise only students (or professionals) who choose to be supervised by me. This is now a general rule in our Psychological Clinic. Those who choose to be supervised by me already have a strong interest in psychoanalysis. Obviously, I expect even the most inexperienced student to have read Freud's *Introductory Lectures* (1916–1917) and *New Introductory Lectures* (1933), his papers on technique (1963), and at least one paper of mine. I then require them to read Fromm-Reichmann's *Principles of Intensive Psychotherapy* (1960), if they have not already done so, and David Malan's book on brief therapy, *Individual Psychotherapy and the Science of Psychodynamics* (1979). I have never had a novice therapist who did not get enthusiastic about that book. Indeed, graduate students uniformly object, "Why did you make us read Fenichel? It's all in here anyway, only much clearer."

Any other reading will be based on the individual case. If the patient has psychotic features, obviously I assign my book (Karon & VandenBos, 1981).

I stress the continuity between psychoanalysis and psychoanalytic therapy. I like the kinds of clinicians, students or the more experienced, who get themselves into the dilemma: "I think I can help this patient, but my colleagues/supervisors/setting says that it should be interrupted or can't be done, and I think they are wrong, but I need supervision from someone experienced. Maybe I'm wrong (although I don't think so), or maybe I'm getting in over my head, but this patient is treatable, and they are not going to treat him or her, if I don't. You are the only one I know who would encourage me to treat this patient."

Since I believe in self-selection, I tell prospective student trainees that I expect them to see any patient I supervise at least twice a week. Moreover, since my own patients rarely see me for less than two years, I require that students I supervise make a commitment to be available to the patient for a minimum of two years, even though that is not the academic requirement. In addition to being a reasonable requirement, it weeds out those who are not highly motivated. (One bright student asked me if it was all right if he saw a patient five days a week, and did a brilliant job of psychoanalytic therapy with a severe borderline.)

There are many disagreements about the philosophies and techniques of supervision. In particular, how much of the student's dynamics do you delve into, how much is it didactic, how much do you focus only on the patient, should you use audiovisual aids or observe the actual interview?

But far more important than the technique of supervision is whether the supervisor has anything to teach. You cannot teach what you do not know. You cannot supervise what you do not practice. If you are not a competent clinical psychoanalyst, you cannot supervise psychoanalysis adequately. If you do not practice psychoanalytic therapy well, you cannot supervise psychoanalytic therapy adequately. No supervisory technique will work if the supervisor is teaching what he or she does not know, and any technique is likely to be helpful to the novice if the supervisor is knowledgeable.

In supervision, particularly with early students, the supervisor is a safety net. The student has the security that there is backup for any crisis. The supervisor, however, does not take over the case. Students cannot possibly communicate everything they know about a case. And it is the students' responsibility to act on their own best clinical judgment, even if they are wrong. What the supervisor provides is: "This is what I hear, what I might do, and if you cannot do any better, you can always do or say what I would have. And, of course, I expect you to review everything you do."

The supervisor is not the student's therapist. While the anxieties involved in doing psychoanalytic therapy are contained by the supervisor, the supervisor does not delve into the student's dynamics. The opposite stance is experienced by the student as intrusive, punitive, and scary. It is useful to say, "I wonder if there is a personal issue here, that you might want to discuss with your therapist. Think about it and you decide. You don't need to discuss it with me." For a student not in therapy: "I wonder if this isn't making you anxious. This is very difficult material (or this is a very difficult person). This might be a good time to start your own therapy. You don't need to discuss your personal issues with me, but think about it."

The injunction "you don't need to discuss it with me" allows students the privacy and maturity they need and allows them to discuss freely some aspects of it if they choose. They usually do choose to discuss what seems most pertinent.

Supervisees identify with supervisors. If they are treated kindly and supportively, they tend to treat their patients kindly and supportively. If their difficulties and pain as therapists are shared, they can share the patients' pain and difficulties. If the supervisor is cold or punitive, students become cold or punitive. If the supervisor is curious, accepting of the human condition, sees the value in "mistakes," is comfortable with the unconscious, and expects students to be first-rate, then the students tend to value their curiosity, learn from their mistakes, learn about the unconscious, and become first-rate.

I recall my first supervisory hour with Richard Sterba. It was my second control case. After driving 100 miles on a Sunday, feeling both anxious and excited, I presented the case material. His first supervisory comment was, "Do you mind if I make a suggestion?" And he waited for an answer.

I was startled. "Of course. Please."

He then said, "I would have said it differently," and proceeded to suggest a far more therapeutic phrasing of the interpretation.

But in that first supervisory intervention, before he communicated specific information, he communicated a feeling of respect for the other person, which hopefully I internalized.

Even the novice students in our program who are supervised by me have done some counseling or psychotherapy, and so it is my job to reach them where they are and broaden and deepen their knowledge and technique. This is, of course, true no matter at what stage they are in their training. For professionals in private practice who seek me out, I find I have to encourage them to consider seeing the patient more intensively, or using a couch when it is appropriate. Just as there is a resistance in some therapists to using "parameters" appropriate to the defenses of the patient, there is also a resistance in others to using classical technique when it would obviously be helpful.

Of course, one must also serve as a kindly superego and parent figure. Supervisees need to know that if a crisis occurs that they cannot handle, they have immediate access to someone who will be there. Even when their handling of the crisis is appropriate, they need a kindly superego who will tell them so and allow them to tolerate their anxiety (and even learn from it about themselves and the patient). Indeed, experienced professionals sometimes need that kind of sharing. In the face of difficult resistances, and the pessimism of colleagues, supervisees need the optimism of the supervisor that if one does as reasonable a job as one can, the odds are the patient will respond. Supervisees also need to know that their experience of the treatment as difficult occurs because it is difficult work, and the pessimism and alarmism of colleagues is a function of the latter's experience of working, as most mental health professionals do, with inadequate training. If supervisees are treating the kind of patient whose defenses do not permit him or her to communicate that the therapist is being helpful, the support and evaluation of an experienced supervisor becomes essential. Supervisees need to be reminded that most appropriately treated patients benefit greatly, that the patient cannot give the feedback you would like, but that the procedures and interpretations seem appropriate and should be continued or should be modified in specific ways.

Once a supervisee has continued the treatment of a difficult patient, about whom other professionals have been pessimistic, until the patient has palpably improved, this serves as a benign trauma from whose effects the supervisee never recovers.

I rarely use mechanical aids. In my project in treating schizophrenics with psychoanalytic therapy, the early hours of both the experienced therapists and the trainees were viewed on videotape and discussed for training purposes. That was initially useful. It was also reassuring to the novice in dealing with unpredictable patients that the sessions were being simultaneously watched by colleagues who could intervene if necessary.

The students then, and the students at the university, did not find the discussion of their tapes remarkably helpful, but do report observing my tapes as helpful. The model of correct interventions helps, but even more, they notice that I am sometimes tired, distracted, insensitive, and have countertransference reactions, and despite that, even very difficult patients obviously improve. Therefore, it cannot be a trick that only some gifted, superbly trained individual can practice, but something that intelligent human beings who want to be helpful can learn to do.

It is my experience that the traditional supervision hour, with the student recounting from notes is best. I request that the notes be written after the hour, as Freud (1912) recommended, not during it. What the students bring up is what is puzzling to them, and then anything you say has an effect in changing their understanding and technique. Your insights meet their need, help resolve their anxieties or curiosities. When you bring up something from a tape, it does not have the same effect in facilitating their learning, because it does not meet their needs. It must be admitted that one psychopathic student was able to lie to me successfully in ordinary supervision hours. But supervision is not police work. For the bulk of students this is the optimal way to go. One cannot corrupt the teaching process because one liar can take advantage of you.

In supervision of psychoanalysis, the supervisee is more experienced, so less time need be spent on basic mechanics. More time is available to listen to the subtle aspects of the fantasy material, which is more available, and the supervisee is more sensitive to the transference and countertransference issues. Most often experienced supervisees are held back by one formulation of the material, including the transference and countertransference, which has prevented them from hearing a different, more relevant formulation. But the difference in supervision is one of degree.

As Richard Sterba has pointed out (personal communication), supervision is easier than psychotherapy because the supervisee's unconscious almost always organizes the material so that only the addition of the last link is needed, even though the supervisee seemingly does not consciously understand it.

Bruno Bettelheim (1983) once said, "If you treat the patient with common courtesy, and treat the patient the way you would want to be treated, you will almost always do the right thing." And I would add, "If you treat the supervisee with common courtesy, and treat them the way you would want to be treated, both you and they will almost always do the right thing."

References

Aichhorn, A. (1936). *Wayward youth.* London: Putnam.

Alexander, F., French, T. M., et al. (1946). *Psychoanalytic therapy: Principles and applications.* New York: Ronald Press.

Bettelheim, B. (1983). Supervision of a borderline patient. University of Detroit Advanced Psychotherapy Workshop, Detroit.

Freud, S. (1909). Notes upon a case of obsessional neurosis. *Standard Edition, 10,* 153–318. London: Hogarth Press, 1955.

Freud, S. (1910). "Wild" psychoanalysis. *Standard Edition, 11,* 219–230. London: Hogarth Press, 1957.

Freud, S. (1912). Recommendations to physicians practising psychoanalysis. *Standard Edition, 12,* 109–120. London: Hogarth Press, 1958.

Freud, S. (1916–1917). Introductory lectures. *Standard Edition, 15–16.* London: Hogarth Press, 1961–1963.

Freud, S. (1933). New introductory lectures on psychoanalysis. *Standard Edition, 22.* London: Hogarth Press, 1964.

Freud, S. (1963). *Therapy and technique.* New York: Collier Books.

Fromm-Reichmann, F. (1960). *Principles of intensive psychotherapy.* Chicago: University of Chicago Press.

Karon, B. P., & VandenBos, G. R. (1981). *Psychotherapy of schizophrenia: The treatment of choice.* New York: Aronson.

Knight, R. P. (1954). The present status of organized psychoanalysis in the United States. In R. P. Knight & C. R. Friedman (Eds.), *Psychoanalytic psychiatry and psychology* (pp. 7–26). New York: International Universities Press.

Malan, D. (1979). *Individual psychotherapy and the science of psychodynamics.* London: Butterworth.

Sterba, R. (1935). Psychoanalytic therapy. In *The collected papers* (H. Daldin, Ed.), pp. 71–86. Croton-on-Hudson, NY: North River Press, 1987.

Thoma, H., & Kachele, H. (1987). *Psychoanalytic practice.* Berlin: Springer-Verlag.

The Mastery of Countertransferential Anxiety: An Object Relations View of the Supervisory Process

Joseph W. Newirth, Ph.D.

Psychoanalysis has maintained a traditional apprenticeship model of education. This apprenticeship model, the intensive psychoanalytic supervisory experience, has developed around a didactic and personal relationship with a senior practitioner or mentor. As in other fields, this educational model has great advantages in allowing the student to learn about and to integrate complex tasks through the processes of instruction and identification. The purpose of this paper is to distinguish critical issues in the personal and technical development of psychoanalytic psychotherapists from the perspective of object relations theory. This paper focuses on those critical developmental issues in the supervisory process that occur in a regular sequence for most supervisees and lead to the development of clinical competence in psychoanalysis and psychodynamic psychotherapy. In focusing on the development of clinical competence through the critical stages of the personal development of a psychodynamic psychotherapist, several important aspects of education and training will be ignored in this discussion. It is assumed: that the student therapist or analyst has begun personal therapy or analysis and has developed a comfortable mode of personal self-observation and understanding; that the relationship with the

An earlier version of this paper was presented at the annual meeting of the American Psychological Association. August 31, 1987, New York.

157

supervisor provides a safe and supportive atmosphere for growth and understanding; and that the student therapist has acquired sufficient technical competence to develop a working relationship with the patients.

The supervisory process includes many different educational and emotional experiences; the most important involves the development of the therapist's ability to use his or her self as the major emotional force or fulcrum in the treatment situation. As with many developmental models, the stages that will be presented are a simplified schemata, which organizes the developmental tasks of becoming a psychoanalyst around the difficult, albeit critical counter-transferential anxiety situations, while allowing other experiences, those involving the development of nurturance and understanding, to remain in the background. Each stage in development represents an important capacity in the psychoanalytic clinician's ability to use the relationship in a dynamic and constructive fashion. After these stages are confronted and initially mastered, clinicians will return to these critical emotional focal points over and over again within their training and afterward.

Object relations theories, as compared to classical psychoanalytic drive theory and ego psychology, present a different metapsychology, a different view of etiology and different techniques and goals for the practice of psychoanalysis and psychotherapy. These theories emphasize the importance of continued growth rather than the resolution of conflict. Unlike psychoanalytic theories, which are oriented around drive and conflict models and emphasize repression as the core defensive process, object relations theories emphasize the processes of projection, dissociation, and introjection in the development of internal structure. Object relations theories represent a hermeneutic as opposed to a positivistic approach to treatment, one in which the important psychological processes involve the development of meaning, the capacity to use symbolic thought, and the development of the self. There is an emphasis on psychological disorders as adaptations to pathological family systems and failures or arrests in the development of a core, true or subjective self. The subjective self is conceptualized as the center of experience, pleasure, and initiative.

The analyst's or therapist's task, from the object relations perspective, is to create a holding environment, that is, an intense affective relationship that facilitates the development of a therapeutic symbiosis in which the patient can both begin to live through past transference fantasies and develop and integrate those aspects of the self that have been dissociated and externalized. The expectation for the therapist from this theoretical perspective involves the ability to symbolically enact the transference and countertransference fantasies, which have been dissociated, and to utilize the relationship within the therapeutic dyad as a significant symbolic reparative experience. Two primary concerns of the supervisory experience are to assist the developing therapist in his or her ability to be available to the patient and to overcome the anxiety that develops in the psychotherapeutic or psychoanalytic situation.

Schizoid Anxiety: Being Abandoned in the Analytic Situation

One frequent early experience of countertransferential anxiety concerns the therapist's growing awareness of being alone in a room with a patient and feeling abandoned by the supervisor. This anxiety is expressed by the student therapist in one of two ways: as an intense need to know what to do to help the patient with his or her problems, or as panic over not knowing what to do to effect change in the patient. The anxiety over being abandoned marks an important transition between experiencing psychotherapy as an academic-technical pursuit and as an extraordinarily personal and subjective meeting of two individuals and their efforts to create meaning for each in the world. The supervisee's terror of being abandoned with a patient echoes Freud's early warning of the potential dangers of "wrestling with the demons of the unconscious."

There are several issues that must be confronted with the student therapist at this point. Rather than discussing them discursively, the supervisory relationship can be used as a stage upon which to begin to enact them in the here-and-now with the intention of creating in the supervisory relationship a parallel affective situation to the therapeutic dyad. For example, I try to communicate the idea that I am not interested in what happens to the patient, that my interest is exclusively with the therapist's development. I often appear to be disinterested in the patient's well-being, and I like to emphasize the potential playful and game-like aspects of the student's relationship with the patient. In disregarding the student therapist's anxiety, the supervision emphasizes the experiential reality that at any moment one is ultimately alone with the patient and that, therefore, within this psychological field, one becomes vulnerable to all the manifestations of being attacked and loved by the patient and of attacking and loving the patient. As a result of feeling alone and abandoned in this unique and intense affective relationship of psychotherapy, all of the hidden paranoid and depressive anxieties and possibilities are brought to the foreground for both patient and supervisee.

The second issue arising out of the confrontation with this abandonment or separation anxiety is the recognition that the supervisory situation is one of mixed purposes and loyalties. The therapist is primarily committed to the patient's development and to his or her own future development and professional identity. The supervisor, on the other hand, is primarily committed to the therapist's development and to the ideals of the field of psychoanalysis and psychotherapy through which his or her own professional identity is affirmed. Recognition of the mixed loyalties in the supervisory situation facilitates the analysis of the various relationship configurations: the relationship between the therapist and patient, between the therapist and supervisor, and those based on the projections of each of the three individuals. As a result of the student therapist's ability to work with this countertransference anxiety, he or she is able to segregate the analytic or therapeutic space and relationship from that of the external, objective world of non-analytic or therapeutic relationships, and is able to move the treatment forward from a focus on problem solving to a focus on structural change and issues of the development of the patient's self. The achievement of this crisis in the development of a psychoanalytic psychotherapist is the capacity to be deeply involved in a therapeutic and analytic relationship and to recognize that one can create and also let go of this intense affective relationship. That is, it allows the new therapist to struggle with and become comfortable with his or her ability to regulate and control the intense transference-countertransference relationship, in spite of the potential guilt of hurting and abandoning the patient.

Paranoid Anxieties: The Loss of Boundaries

In the development of a psychoanalytic psychotherapist, the next stage of countertransference anxiety is engendered by the inevitable confusion arising from a loss of boundaries between the therapist and the patient or, more accurately, between the patient's unconscious fantasies and the therapist's unconscious fantasies. Through empathic relatedness and processes of projective and introjective identification, there has been a dedifferentiation of the transference and countertransference. This dedifferentiation of the transference and countertransference is part of the development of a constructive symbiotic relationship between the therapist and the patient. The countertransference anxiety mounts as the therapist experiences an absolute similarity, an unconscious identification, between the patient and him- or herself. During this critical phase, the student therapist will be filled with feelings of despair, inadequacy, and stupidity. As a result of experiences of merger and projective identification, the therapist will believe that the supervisor should not allow him or her to be functioning as a psychotherapist to this patient. The therapist will feel at least as "sick" or "crazy" as the designated patient and that he or she should be hospitalized or simply be told to find another occupation.

The anxiety that develops as the therapist merges with the patient and the boundaries dissolve between therapist and patient involves loss of the therapist's sense of omnipotence, superiority, and grandiosity, which are the defenses against helplessness and the recognition of a shared primitive core of experience. At this point, some therapists attack the patient, that is, "objectify" the patient, in order to externalize this anxiety in an attempt to overcome this situation via the use of paranoid defenses. Implicit in the therapist's perception of the supervisory relationship is a view of the supervisor as possessing the omnipotence and omniscience that the therapist feels that he or she has lost, but has in fact projected into the supervisor as a means of maintaining this grandiose fantasy. The supervisor's capacity to empathize with the therapist's experience of despair and inadequacy, and thus accept the possibility that the therapist should leave this field, seems to be critical for the development of the therapist-in-training's ability to progress past this point of hopelessness and helplessness. It is only by accepting the supervisory failure in the possibility of rescuing the therapist that a future identification with the necessary work of analysis can be forged.

Under the press of the intense affective experiences that grow out of the loss of boundaries between the patient and therapist, the therapist loses his or her ability to distinguish between fantasy as internal and symbolic experiences and fantasy as real and frightening events in the external, objective world. The work of supervision becomes the process of demonstrating to the therapist the relationship between the therapist's experiences and the empathically perceived and projected aspects of the patient within him- or herself. It is through this process of symbolic elaboration of patient's and therapist's fantasies that the therapist is able to experience the transformative effects of the development of symbolic discourse in psychoanalytic psychotherapy. As the therapist becomes able to differentiate fantasy and objective reality, then, through the elaboration and playful enactment of the patient's dissociated fantasies, the patient can begin to develop a sense of the inner world and of him- or herself as an independent "center of initiative" and action and to develop and internalize a subjective or true self.

Depressive Anxiety: Tolerating Hatred and Guilt

In the final stages of the development of a psychoanalytic psychotherapist, the main source of anxiety lies in the therapist's capacity for and recognition of hateful feelings toward the patient. This anxiety frequently manifests itself as feelings of boredom, having hateful and sadistic feelings toward the patient, or finding oneself distracted and preoccupied with money or other private pleasures. The therapist must recognize, through self observation, that he or she has been bad and hateful toward the patient. This recognition causes the therapist to experience feelings of guilt, shame, and depressive anxiety. The capacity to experience hateful, sadistic, and aggressive feelings toward the patient involves relinquishing the nineteenth century, classical psychoanalytic posture of helping patients to give up their maladaptive, infantile, neurotic, or unhealthy behaviors, while remaining, oneself, well-intentioned, pure, and sincere. An interesting and paradoxical expression of this countertransference anxiety involves the premature interpretation of an idealizing transference, which attacks and devalues the patient's positive feelings about the therapist and negates the idealization and development of gratitude in the therapy situation. This countertransferential anxiety of the depressive experience is usually not presented directly in supervision, rather it is often expressed in the form of parallel processes.

Object relations theory encourages the development of the therapist's capacity to accept and enjoy his or her aggressive feelings and fantasies toward the patient, and encourages the articulation of those elements in the transference and countertransference. These countertransferential experiences of hatred are indicative of the development of the capacity for concern, thus the depressive position, because of the recognition that one may have hurt the patient or simply not been able to do enough for the patient. However, as painful as the acknowledgment of failure in one's therapeutic ambition may be, the therapist must also become able to do a far more difficult task in acknowledging what he or she has been able to do for the patient and the ways in which he or she has contributed to the patient's growth.

In a discussion of the process of identity formation in early development and in psychoanalytic treatment, Searles (1979) has discussed the painful necessity of the parent's and therapist's recognition of the pleasure that is centered in their own individuality and the importance for the developing person to both see and identify with the part of the caretaking other that is separate and cannot be destroyed by hostile attacks. Winnicott (1975) similarly talks about the importance of the therapist and parent being able to tell the developing person what they have gone through for the other and how they have been able to survive in spite of the presence of hostility from both members of the dyad. For both Winnicott and Searles, a critical importance is placed on the therapist's ability to acknowledge separateness, limits, and the unwillingness to sacrifice everything for the patient. In supervision, it is necessary for the supervisor to allow for and enjoy the expression of his or her and the student therapist's hatred, as well as to recognize the processes of idealization as a part of reparation and the development of concern for a separate individual.

Conclusion

In the course of supervising both graduate students and psycho-analytic candidates, it has been my experience that it is necessary for the student to master these three countertransference organizations in order to be able to work psychoanalytically and confront the patient's internal world. Oftentimes, it is not until late in a student's career that he or she has been able comfortably to integrate these three stages. Invariably, these stages have emerged as a function of the level of the student's experience with the early levels of development, marked first by schizoid anxiety over abandonment, followed by paranoid anxiety over loss of boundaries with the patient, and finally by coming to terms with the depressive anxieties of one's own hatred and cruelty. The supervisor's task must be to maintain the focus on these critical issues and to support the exploration of these experiences.

This approach to supervision leads to an intense relationship between supervisor and supervisee, which differs from personal psychoanalysis in that it is focused exclusively on the anxiety that arises out of one's relationship with the patient and on the anxiety that surrounds the ability to function constructively within the analytic situation. As in all psychoanalytic supervision, there is the expectation that the student has available an analyst with whom issues arising out of the supervision can be addressed. I want to emphasize that these experiences of intense countertransference anxiety are a necessary part of the work of psychoanalysis and psychoanalytic psychotherapy. Experience and training progressively allow the analyst to be able to use these experiences in the service of growth for both the patient and him- or herself. It is important to emphasize that we all remain permanent students of psychoanalysis as we continue to confront the inner demons that are called forth both through our work with patients and in our own personal and self-analysis. The ability to master these countertransference anxieties leads to the development of individuality, power, and joy in one's therapeutic actions, and to the development of a psychoanalytic identity and the capacity to function within the subjective realms of the psychoanalytic situation.

References

Searles, H. F. (1979). Concerning the development of an identity. In *Countertransference and related subjects*. New York: International Universities Press.

Winnicott, D. W. (1975). The depressive position in normal emotional development. *Through pediatrics to psychoanalysis*. New York: Basic Books.

The Supervision of Graduate Students Who Are Conducting Psychodynamic Psychotherapy

Jerome L. Singer, Ph.D.

The question of how to train psychodynamic therapists in graduate school, relying heavily on the supervision of their treatment of patients as the modality of teaching, is a central issue in clinical psychology education. As someone who experienced extensive psychodynamic therapy supervision (including exposure to supervision by six different psychoanalysts, such as Clara Thompson and Erich Fromm in my own institute training) and who has conducted supervision of graduate students and some analytic candidates for 35 years, I looked forward to this symposium. After reading the papers, I found myself in somewhat of a dilemma. It seemed as if I was adrift in a sea of jargon and theory and that somehow I had lost touch with the real students I have worked with and their very real patients who were coming to these young incipient therapists desperate for help with urgent problems in living. I had to confront the question: What are these papers about? Are they confronting the charge posed by the Symposium Chair, Dr. Ochroch, which I read as describing the training of graduate students and addressing differences between psychoanalysis and psychodynamic psychotherapy in the training process? What was presented, however, in at least two of the papers, was heavy doses of theory and a kind of abstraction that failed to confront some of the basic realities of the supervisory situation in a graduate school. What are the formal relationships that actually exist between supervisees and supervisors? What is the ultimate target of the supervisory process—the expansion of the trainee's psyche or the welfare of the patient? Is supervision designed to teach the psychoanalytic process or at least some modified form and, if so, what brand-name version of analysis? Since these are graduate students in psychology, not yet psychoanalytic candidates, ought we not train them more generally for effective intervention rather than focus on a very specific procedure or narrow theory-driven approach? How much ought we to be delving into their fantasies and private experiences, especially since, in contrast to a psychoanalytic institute, 1) we never warned them of this possibility in our graduate school brochures, and 2) our roles as mentors and evaluators are different from those we assume as therapists?

Let us face the issue squarely as psychologists who ought to know something about the social psychology of contextual demands and multiple role relationships. We have several not necessarily overlapping motives for engaging in supervision of therapy with graduate students. First of all, we bear an obligation to the patients who come for help to our department clinics or practicum settings. Supervision affords those patients some protection against the limitation of neophyte therapists and some benefit of having experienced and well-trained professionals monitoring their cases for maximum benefit. Second, we are providing students with the personal support they need and with a teaching relationship constructed around an ongoing therapeutic process. Finally, let's be honest about it. We are evaluating the student. The therapy experience is a course which yields at least a pass-fail grade in most institutions. While few fail, we have a responsibility to those students who lack talent or who are too disturbed, to provide them with appropriate feedback and counseling about seeking help or changing their career goals. And we have a responsibility to our profession to screen out students who may represent potential hazards to their patients.

Review of the Models Presented

In turning to the specific presentations I would like first to call attention to one of the few formal research studies of supervisory styles in psychodynamic therapy I know about. Vivian Nash (1975), after interviewing student therapists and obtaining questionnaire responses describing their experiences with a variety of current and recent supervisors, found that supervisors' styles could be quantitatively ordered along three dimensions. The first model of supervision might be termed Authoritarian-Didactic and was characteristic of some senior psychoanalysts who, in effect, sought to teach students about psychoanalytic concepts in a rather formal, dogmatic fashion. They paid little attention to the ongoing therapist-patient interaction except as a launching ground for discussion of theory. In general, student therapists, while in awe of these supervisors, did not feel they were very helpful.

The second pattern might be described as a Quasi-Therapeutic supervisory style. Here the supervisor focused on student-therapist feelings, fantasies, fears, countertransferences. The patients were considered only insofar as they were the catalysts for supervisees' reactions. This style was more popular with student-therapists, especially the more junior ones.

The third pattern might be termed Case-focused. Here the supervisor sought to establish a kind of working alliance with the student therapist to try to provide the optimal treatment for the patient. It was a stance suggesting, "We're both in this together to treat this person." This approach was more appealing to the more experienced student therapists.

Where do the orientations presented in this symposium fall on the dimensions of supervisory style I have just mentioned? Karon seems most clearly to be case focused, but with a special effort to create a mutually respectful style. Although details of actual supervisor-therapist interaction are vague, the approach has a didactic thrust, chiefly by the requirement of more frequent sessions and the clear identification of the supervisor as psychoanalytically oriented. But what brand is Karon purveying and how does his particular theoretical orientation express itself in the actual case discussions? It is a far cry, I submit, from the readings he requires in Freud's *Introductory Lectures* to the more interpersonal Sullivanian approach of Fromm-Reichmann or to Malan's shorter-term, more interpersonally oriented approach. On the whole, what does come through in his presentation is a profound sense of respect for the student and a strong communication that "I'm here to help you with this patient anyway I can!" But what differentiates such an approach from the stance a responsible Rogerian or cognitive-behaviorally oriented supervisor might assume?

Gassner's approach is strongly focused on a specialized revision of classical psychoanalysis, which is not yet widely accepted, that of Joseph Weiss (Weiss & Sampson, 1986). Gassner's orientation is, however, strongly case focused. Gassner's emphasis is on concrete issues: the early formulation of a problem, goals, and subgoals; the identification of "pathogenic beliefs"; the identification of the ways in which the patient's stance or communications to the therapist reflects attempts to reverse roles from a passive victim to active pursuer—all of these reflect an embedding of a teaching method in a patient-oriented supervisory role. My own hesitations reflect more concerns that Gassner may be indoctrinating students into a psychoanalytic position that may be much more specific and novel than the students realize.

While Weiss and Sampson and their group are to be commended for the effort to conduct serious research on the method and theory, I find myself somewhat unconvinced of the genuine novelty of the orientation. The critical role played by unconscious beliefs seems very close to more general, nonpsychoanalytic theories about the role of self-schemas, scripts, or personal constructs in the work of cognitive-behavioral therapists or the followers of George Kelly's psychology of personal constructs (Beck, 1976; Ellis, 1973; Kelly, 1955; Meichenbaum, 1977). Indeed Weiss's position is that "psychopathology may arise from any of a number of pathogenic beliefs, including beliefs about dangers stemming from a variety of motives not just Oedipal motives. . . . The views proposed here extend Freud's views by assuming that a patient may need to change a variety of pathogenic beliefs, not just those opposing Oedipal impulses" (Weiss & Sampson, 1986, pp. 324–325). Except for Weiss's emphasis on the unconscious nature of these beliefs—something not easily demonstrable—this view doesn't appear especially psychoanalytic, and the description of treatment, except for emphasis on the transference, seems quite compatible with cognitive orientations. Indeed the notion of "pathogenic belief" links this model squarely to current research in social cognition, where great progress has been made in operationalizing beliefs into schemas about self and others, prototypes, and scripts (Markus & Wurf, 1987; Singer, 1985; Singer & Kolligian, 1987).

I don't fault Gassner for adopting the Weiss position, which seems such a reasonable one, or for training students in the approach. But as a psychologist I would urge that students be helped to see that they are not *really* being inculcated into the *mystique* of a psychoanalytic method. Instead, the supervision is built around a widely held position, supported by considerable nonpsychoanalytic research, that the key areas for exploration in psychotherapy involve overlearned (automatic or "unconscious") schemas and scripts and that our goal as therapists is to use a variety of approaches (including identification of transferences) to help patients perceive their self-defeating expectations about relationships and to encourage them to try to reshape their belief systems.

Finally, we come to Newirth's orientation. This is clearly built along the lines of an object-relations model with its focus on achieving growth in the student therapist. There is an explicit expression that emphasis is on the supervisee not the patient and so it falls into Nash's Quasi-therapeutic category. In all candor I must assert that I was most troubled by this paper. Newirth's explication of the essential position of a Kleinian-derived object-relations theory superimposed on the graduate student therapist is a tour-de-force. The effective use of terms like "countertransferential anxiety" and "feeling abandoned by the supervisor" set an awesome and momentous tone around a relationship that becomes increasingly like psychotherapy rather than training. I think back over my years as supervisee or supervisor and I cannot connect with this representation of the relationship. It was a rare student indeed (and, remember, Newirth works with *advanced* graduate students) who seemed to feel abandoned, terrorized or deeply in despair during work with patients. Maybe more of them should have felt such powerful emotions but I believe the combination of a good psychology background and the special (if somewhat illusory) power associated with the role of therapist fended off such existential anxiety.

I believe Newirth's strict application of object-relations theory has led him (and his supervisees along the way) into what Mitchell (1984) has called the "developmental tilt." In order to preserve some vestige of the classical drive model and the psychosexual stages while strongly advocating a more cognitive, interpersonal relations perspective, many object relations theorists, as Mitchell has documented, push the relational model earlier and earlier in childhood into the presumed but unverifiable fantasy world of the infant. That explains to me why I'm so uncomfortable with Newirth's account of his quasi-therapeutic supervisory approach. He's treating his students like babies and, alas, he may be encouraging them to treat their baffled patients accordingly.

I just don't recognize my own generations of supervisees in his highly abstract depiction. While a few were certainly somewhat immature socially or inept interpersonally, the vast majority of trainees I worked with in five different settings were not only intelligent and autonomous but also socially relatively effective. They were more like colleagues than terrorized children. They were generally curious and eager to understand and help their patients, but they only rarely lost their sense of boundaries. Contrast Karon's approach with Newirth's and you can see a vast gap between the former's respectful mutual alliance stance and Newirth's abstract, theory-driven account, which seems to me to demean the student. I wish I knew what *actually* goes on in the supervisory sessions Newirth describes—what the two participants actually talk about. I've had many students confront their flashes of anger or impatience with patients or supervisors, but when Newirth talks of "hatred" in both therapist and supervisor, I'm at a loss to know what he means. In summary, my concerns about Newirth's paper are oriented around its high level of abstraction and the *appearance* (in the way object relations theory is employed) of a somewhat demeaning or condescending tone. The object relations perspective itself, if it emphasizes interpersonal cognitions, differentiation of self-other schemas and expectancies about the attachment-individuation dilemma in human development, seems a valuable framework. It is the tilt toward treating adult attitudes as if they were babies' schemas that is problematic.

Reexamining the Uses of Supervision in Psychotherapy Training

Why Do We Need Supervision?

I would like to close by presenting a personal perspective on the supervisory process, specifically as it bears on the training of graduate students in clinical psychology. We may first ask why we need supervision at all. Clearly, if we offer the therapeutic services of students to clients, we are obligated to strengthen the students' effectiveness by experienced oversight and assistance. This is an ethical protection for the client. As I've already stated, we must also monitor the quality of the students' work to insure that they are progressing in skill and will not eventually prove to be inept or hazardous therapists. Finally, we provide expert supervision as a major form of hands-on teaching. The supervisor, whether or not a member of the full-time faculty, is essentially a teacher. There is a caveat here—unlike the situation in a psychoanalytic institute—the supervisor in a graduate school is stepping outside an appropriate role if he or she plays a psychotherapeutic role and offers interpretations of presumably unconscious fantasies of the supervisee. Tactful counseling is a different matter and is a valuable part of providing feedback as part of the mentoring role.

Let us take a closer look at the teaching role of the supervisor.

There is an inevitable tension between the supervisor's responsibility to the patient and to the student therapist. It requires continual tact and sensitivity, perhaps the supervisor's hardest task, to identify and point out therapist errors without paralyzing the therapist. Coming on too forcefully when a student may be too pushy or too silent or is simply missing obtaining important information can lead students to be so self-conscious that they can't listen to the patient because the forbidding face of the supervisor intrudes in their thoughts.

With supervision we seek to identify the neophyte therapists' styles, language usage, skills, and to some extent their personal distortions or limitations of life experience. While videotapes might be ideal, they're not readily available and often more anxiety provoking for the therapist than for the patient. Audiotapes should be routinely used; most patients accept them from the start, with the explanation that they will be of help to therapists in note-taking and in studying the process for the patients' benefit. Therapists should use the tapes for preparing process notes, which can be used in supervision. The supervisor can also listen to occasional tapes to get a sense of the stylistic patterns of the therapist and the flow of interaction.

Identification of styles, skills, distortions, or fears can be accomplished if an atmosphere of a mutual alliance, so well described by Karon, is established. One can never eliminate the subtle evaluative features; still, a task-oriented cooperative approach of "we're both trying to help the patient" can go a long way toward permitting the student therapist to identify areas in which identifying personal style or other self-awarenesses can improve the effectiveness of treatment. Keeping the focus on helping the patient can permit the student to deal with countertransference issues, such as the male therapist who may be too welcoming of the female patient's seeming positive transference, or the female therapist who recognizes her fear when hearing a male patient's fantasies of rape or actual accounts of seeming date-rape behavior (Gornick, 1986).

Supervision certainly affords an opportunity to link theory to practice. But it also must help the student to recognize the limitation of our theories, or at least of any specific theory. By focusing as much as possible on what the student needs to do to understand the patient more fully or to be of some assistance to the patient, one soon sees how recognizing one's own personal patterns or trying approaches from *other* systems of treatment may actually prove useful.

I believe supervision can be of great help to the student

therapist's personal growth without creating a quasi-therapeutic atmosphere with its attendant risks. It can broaden students' intellectual scope, as supervisors not only point out theoretical issues but also help the students recognize the range of cultural variations reflected in their clients, and the impact of religious or socioeconomic factors on patients' belief-systems. It can be ego-boosting by helping students recognize their genuine competencies, personal and intellectual. However alone students may feel out there with the patients, the fact is, any reasonably well-prepared student therapist should have a considerable edge on the patient in psychological and sociological knowledge and in some degree of communication or interviewing skill. Helping the student to recognize how the therapeutic role itself affords one some initial respect and one-upmanship in the early encounters with any but the most psychopathic clients eases the way for greater personal confidence.

The supervisor can help the student use these positive skills but must also be alert to helping the student confront certain fundamental realities. These include: 1) the limits of a particular patient's ability to use therapy; 2) the limitations of therapy in the face of a complex life situation, which client-insight or personality change cannot restructure; 3) the limitations of therapy in *any* case. Confronting the fact that life is not fair, or helping the student to see what Freud meant by reducing neurotic misery to everyday misfortune, can help the students avoid either the grandiosity of "I can cure anyone" or the self-doubt of failure when, inevitably, clients drop out prematurely because of external pressures.

Newirth has pointed out the problem of the therapists' being out there "alone" on the front lines. The supervisor can never overcome this feeling (except in those rare instances where supervisors watch through one-way vision screens and communicate to the therapist via "bug-in-the-ear," a technique that would drive me mad if I were the therapist, but which some students welcome). Tactful use of audiotape and process notes and a respectful attitude of "we're in this together" can alleviate some of that feeling. I believe the communication to the student of a sense of respect for the effort and some positive reinforcement for listening carefully and for empathic responses can go a long way to building confidence.

Perhaps the best thing we can offer students as supervisors is to model for them an attitude of deep curiosity, empathy for the patients' dilemmas and excitement about the *process* of trying to understand and to help troubled clients. Clearly we can't fake such an attitude, especially with the bright students we're working with.

But we have to be willing to show them our persisting curiosity about the puzzles of the human psyche, our continuous surprise at what people come up with, and our eagerness to find better ways of communicating with clients. Such enthusiasm is catching and I believe can do more for the students than delving into their presumed infantile fantasies.

The Special Role of Psychoanalysis

I come, finally, to the issue of psychoanalytic treatment versus psychodynamic therapy. Personally, I believe it is not realistic to talk of psychoanalysis in the training of graduate students. We are training clinical psychologists, individuals who will have long and varied careers in a variety of settings once they graduate. A few may go on to psychoanalytic or other specialized therapy training. But things change over a long lifetime. Students are being increasingly attracted to opportunities for work in the health psychology field where cognitive-behavioral or psychophysiological interventions may be more appropriate than psychoanalysis. As our population grows older, there will be more work with the aged, and treatment approaches, while psychodynamically informed, may scarcely approximate a long-term analysis. We have an obligation to our students to provide them with the basic tools in general psychology and with at least some skills in behavioral or cognitive as well as dynamic approaches for the many different tasks they will confront.

What features of psychoanalysis should we emphasize with students? Besides reading from some classics, they should be brought up to date on the current state of the personality theory and the clinical approach of psychoanalysis as it is currently practiced. That means attention primarily to ego psychology, object relations, and self-psychology in the theory, and to the psychodynamic, interpersonal approach in practice. The manuals of Strupp and Blinder (1985), Luborsky (1984), Horowitz (1984), and Klerman et al. (1984) are especially useful, as is the book by Malan (1979) already cited by Karon.

In supervision, we can help students grasp, through their direct work with patients, the great conceptions that psychoanalysis has added to psychotherapy. These include, first of all, the identification of transference phenomena expressed by the patient toward significant others as well as toward the therapist, and the recognition that we all bring into any interaction a series of hidden agendas, some not only hidden from others but from ourselves. The identification and modification of these hidden agendas in relation to the current realities of the patient is the heart of a psychodynamic orientation. We can help the student to use free associative techniques, exploration of daydreams or night dreams, the identification of resistances and defenses, and, when appropriate, interpretation of transference to help the patient. But these procedures are applicable to the relatively shorter term, once- or twice-a-week treatments that are likely to be most available to student-therapists.

The art of supervision is delicate, but it is a key feature of graduate training. Indeed, it is a luxury of professional training available to only very few in our society. We can use it to offer our students a first-rate introduction to psychodynamic therapy. But we must be honest and recognize that the graduate school is not a psychoanalytic institute. We must keep the psychodynamic approach in reasonable balance with other forms of intervention. We should not cripple our students by limiting them to a special brand of psychoanalysis without exposing them to other approaches. Varying supervisors can be a help in this respect.

In conclusion I would like to suggest that, as psychologists, we conduct more research on the effectiveness of different supervisory styles. We need to go beyond dogmatic assertions to find out the best ways of conducting the delicate art of teaching psychodynamics through supervision.

References

Beck, A. (1976). *Cognitive therapy and the emotional disorders.* New York: International Universities Press.

Ellis, A. (1973). *Humanistic psychotherapy: The rational-emotive approach.* New York: McGraw-Hill.

Gornick, L. (1986). Developing a new narrative: The woman therapist and the male patient. *Psychoanalytic Psychology, 3,* 299–326.

Horowitz, M. (1984). *Personality styles and brief psychotherapy.* New York: Basic Books.

Kelly, G. (1955). *The psychology of personal constructs* (2 vols.). New York: Norton.

Klerman, G., & Weissman, A.; Rounsaville, B., & Chevron, B. (1984). *Interpersonal psychotherapy of depression.* New York: Basic Books.

Luborsky, L. (1984). *Principles of psychoanalytic psychotherapy.* New York: Basic Books.

Malan, D. (1979). *Individual psychotherapy and the science of psychodynamics.* London: Butterworth.

Markus, H., & Wurf, E. (1987). The dynamic self-concept: A social psychological perspective. *Annual Review of Psychology, 38,* 299–337.

Meichenbaum, D. (1977). *Cognitive behavior-modification.* New York: Plenum.

Mitchell, S. (1984). Object relations theories and the developmental tilt. *Contemporary Psychoanalysis, 20,* 473–499.

Nash, V. (1975). *The clinical supervision of psychotherapy.* Unpublished doctoral dissertation, Yale University.

Singer, J. L. (1985). Transference and the human condition: A cognitive-affective perspective. *Psychoanalytic Psychology, 2,* 189–219.

Singer, J. L., & Kolligian, J. (1987). Personality: Developments in the study of private experience. *Annual Review of Psychology, 38,* 533–574.

Strupp, H., & Blinder, J. L. (1985). *Psychotherapy in a new key. A guide to time-limited dynamic psychotherapy.* New York: Basic Books.

Weiss, J., & Sampson, H., & the Mount Zion Psychotherapy Research Group (1986). *The psychoanalytic process: Theory, clinical observation and empirical research.* New York: Guilford.

Symposium

*The Psychoanalytic
Supervisory Process*

Introduction

Gayle Wheeler, Ph.D.

The papers presented here by Drs. Caruth and Oberman and the discussion by Dr. Mayman emphasize some aspects of the supervisory situation not commonly focused upon. The expansion of the analyst's working self to include a professional commitment to supervision is more than simply the addition of an important role. Isakower's unpublished references to the unconscious as the "instrument" of analysis paved the way for further elaboration of the functions and traits of the analyst in the process of analyzing—an elaboration that may also be fruitfully applied to the analyst in the process of supervising. The state of mind of the analyst at work— whether analyzing or supervising—may be referred to as "a subsystem in the ego" (Gill & Brenman, 1959), "a categorical person . . . the temporarily built-up person who [functions] under the circumstances and for the period of his work" (Fliess, 1942), or perhaps somewhat less precisely as "work ego" (Olinick et al., 1973). The differences between these analytic and supervisory functions have previously been discussed at length, and that discussion is carried forward and refined by our panelists.

Supervision, this most critical vehicle of psychoanalytic training appears rarely to be formally taught as a course, nor is supervision of the beginning supervisor often considered mandatory. Status as a master clinician with proven abilities in the areas of pedagogic skill, tact, and patience are considered the qualifying credentials. Supervi-

Symposium presented at the mid-winter meeting of the Division of Psychoanalysis (39) of the American Psychological Association, February 26, 1988, San Francisco.

sion itself, similar to a tutorial, is at times frankly didactic, at times illustrated with case vignettes and personal reactions from the supervisor's practice. In this intimate learning situation, the complexities of the supervisor's cognitive and affective teaching task are grounded not simply in knowledge of theory and practice but also in the supervisor's own multiple identifications. The supervisor at times identifies with the therapist, with the patient, and with his or her own previous supervisors. These identifications—insofar as they remain transient, partial, and can be made conscious—will inform supervisory empathy. Empathy—often called the sine qua non of psychoanalysis—can likewise be the bedrock upon which the supervisor constructs a model for understanding the therapist's working self and learning difficulties. Multiple identifications by the supervisor can provide many avenues toward empathically informed teaching. Nevertheless, if these identifications remain prolonged or unconscious, they may fuel unproductive parallel processes which reverberate throughout the supervisor-therapist-patient system.

Empathy's application in supervision may take quite different forms than in treatment, but its importance in this aspect of the analyst's functioning ought not be minimized. In the papers by Oberman, Caruth, and Mayman, in which each raises unique and important questions about the nature of supervisory interactions, one hears repeatedly the echoes of supervisory empathy at work.

References

Fliess, R. (1942). The metapsychology of the analyst. *Psychoanalytic Quarterly, 11,* 211–227.

Gill, M. M., & Brenman, M. (1959). *Hypnosis and related states. Psychoanalytic studies in regression.* New York: International Universities Press.

Olinick, S. L., Poland, W. S., Grigg, K. A., & Granatir, W. L. (1973). The psychoanalytic work ego: Process and interpretation. *International Journal of Psycho-Analysis, 54,* 143–151.

Interpersonal and Intrapsychic Complexities and Vulnerabilities in the Psychoanalytic Supervisory Process

Elaine G. Caruth, Ph.D.

This paper will review briefly certain pressures put upon the supervisor and supervisee during formal psychoanalytic supervision and contrast them with those put upon the training analyst and analysand. Emphasized particularly will be the dyadic, preoedipal areas of narcissistic vulnerability and self-esteem that are so prevalent for both participants in the supervisory process. Oedipal issues in relation to the triadic aspects of this teaching and learning relationship will also be discussed.

Analytic supervision comes at a relatively advanced stage of a candidate's training, and it almost inevitably arouses a feeling or experience of regression in the supervisee. Whatever status of maturity and competence candidates may have achieved in other areas of their professional and personal life, including that of being a psychotherapy supervisor or teacher in other settings, they are again placed in the metaphoric position of the dependent child needing and receiving help from the adult who is in a position of authority and responsibility. Furthermore, this helping person is designated as a *super*-man, so to speak, a super-visor with super-vision, who may additionally be endowed, by virtue of the learning transference, with all kinds of super-powers, which are sometimes unhappily interpreted or experienced by the supervisee as omniscience. This is in addition to the actual powers that are bestowed upon supervisors by virtue of their position of authority over the candidate in relation to advancement in the particular training institute, as well as those powers with which they might be intrinsically endowed as a result of their training, experience, personality, and particular abilities. Similarly, supervisees must attend to their patients' needs and, therefore, often try to make immediate application of what they are learning from their supervisor, not having the luxury of an "interminable" exploration of their own needs and learning processes.

Although supervision, like psychotherapy and psychoanalysis, places the adult in the regressive position of having to ask for and receive help from a helping person, it is unlike the situation in therapy or analysis, where the perceived power is optimally bestowed upon the therapist *only* through the experience of the analysis and of the transference. Practically speaking, such optimal situations are rare since the candidates frequently have considerable information or misinformation about the training analysts available to them. In supervision there is, as mentioned above, a "real" power relationship when such supervision takes place within an institute requiring candidate evaluations and graduations. For the candidate, this involves comparisons and competitions with other candidates, often in relation to the speed with which they pass the requisite supervisory hours. Furthermore, unlike the usual situation in choosing an analyst, in some institutes the student may be assigned to a supervisor or the choice may be limited. (This, of course, is not an issue in private supervision, unless there is a paucity of analysts in the community.)

In like manner, there are both similarities and differences between the tasks and stresses experienced and placed upon the training analyst and those experienced and placed upon the analytic supervisor, analogous to those similarities and differences between those tasks placed upon the analysand and the supervisee. The supervisor is in the position of ultimately having to make decisions affecting the student's real-life situation. Unlike analysis, which is guided by principles of delay, reflection, understanding, and interpretation, supervision, particularly with the beginning candidate, may frequently involve making suggestions, giving some specific advice, and making decisions, if only, for example, in approving the choice of a patient as a training case. Furthermore, unlike the analyst, the supervisor must have concern and empathy for the patient in the supervisee's office as well as for the supervisee in the supervisor's own office, a responsibility that has both ethical and legal implications.

Another significant difference between the two processes lies in the difference between the intrinsic nature and goals of pedagogy and those of psychoanalysis. In analysis, the therapist is optimally not a conscious model for the patient except, in the ideal situation, as a model of a way of understanding oneself. (Unfortunately, we know that in actual practice this is not always the situation, particularly concerning the objective aspects of the treatment situation which are often copied by the candidate from the structure experienced in his or her own analysis.) In supervision, on the other hand, the supervisor may present his or her way of working as a model of technique and offer vignettes from his or her own practice as well as technical and theoretical advice and information. This is particularly true of the supervision of beginning candidates, where it may be necessary to help with the acquisition of certain technical skills in addition to facilitating the development of the intrapsychic, em-pathic, intuitive, and introspective processes that form the core of the practice of analysis. Some supervisors limit themselves to helping the supervisee to understand the process taking place between candidate and patient, while others utilize the parallel process between candidate and supervisor to enrich the candidate's understanding of the patient's struggles (Ekstein and Wallerstein, 1958). By parallel process they suggest that, in fact, supervisees repeat with their supervisor those problems with which they and their patient are dealing. This powerful approach tends to blur the boundaries between supervision and psychotherapy. Furthermore, the supervisory learning transferences may be revealed, before the candidate ever sees the patient, in the very way the candidate approaches supervision. For example, the resistance to being in what is experienced as a passive position was expressed by one super-visee who came in and put on the light, thereby subtly taking charge and reversing the situation of the light that was to be shed upon his own work, as it were. Some supervisees query their supervisor upon his or her own background or orientation or suggest that the two of them work together for a while to "see how it works out" for them. I believe that supervisor's understanding of such feelings and resis-tances is important, but I am not sure that conveying this to supervisees will be necessarily experienced as helpful, unless such resistance has been actively interfering with the work with their own patients. Similarly, placing the entire responsibility for the areas of discussion about the work upon the supervisee will certainly reveal conflict spots quickly, if only by omission, but I suspect this may be less safe for the supervisee than taking the initiative and raising one's own concerns when it is clear that there are problems.

Techniques of supervision will obviously vary depending on the underlying philosophy, particularly so with respect to note taking and/or note reading during supervision. Those persuaded that the only important material is that of the countertransference and inner processes will frown on either note taking or note reading, but in actively insisting upon this position, they may be acting out an authoritarian role with which the candidate eventually identifies and repeats with his or her own patients. Supervisors who are convinced that the parallel process is the only significant source of information may encourage notes being submitted ahead of time (Ekstein and Wallerstein, 1958) and deal in the session with whatever the supervisee chooses to focus upon, but see it as a relating to both supervisory and therapeutic issues. Technique and content-oriented supervisors will obviously find note taking and note reading more acceptable, but need to be attuned to whether the notes are being used adaptively or defensively, that is, whether the supervisee is hiding behind or merely being supported by the note taking process, whether the supervisee is using the notes to assess his or her inner life or to avoid it.

It is apparent I am suggesting that all of the above approaches have something to offer and that perhaps, unlike the situation in treatment, an eclectic approach to supervision may be more valuable, one that gives information and thus structure when such is needed, either cognitively or affectively, one that can help the supervisee understand his or her resistance to supervision as a means of understanding the patients' resistances when they are interfering and, finally, one that can help the supervisee understand his or her own inner processes as a countertransference response to the transferences of the patient. In the latter instance, it becomes essential that we work with a candidate who has demonstrated sufficient health and maturity to be able to distinguish between his or her own projections and projective identifications from those of the patient, between his or her transference, so to speak, to the patient emanating from personal infantile conflicts and the countertransference responses elicited in response to that particular patient. As supervisors, it is important to recognize that structure and knowledge can provide safety and guidelines for enabling experimentation with freedom and structure without being restrictive or authoritarian.

While it is true that analysts often and, perhaps, inevitably become models for their analysands, this may serve as a defense against candidates becoming deeply and experientially involved in their own analytic process. The analysand who is lying on the couch primarily to learn how to do analysis is unlikely to become fully involved as a patient, experiencing, and participating in his or her own analysis. Such conscious imitation is not a true identification and interferes both with the therapeutic and the learning processes. I believe it is important that we begin to explore, compare, and understand the kinds of imitations, identifications, and learning on all levels of consciousness that take place in supervision with those that take place in the training analysis if we are to achieve our goal of helping candidates to achieve and fulfill themselves as truly autonomous and skilled professionals.

Our understanding of how supervision educates, as opposed to trains, as in training to do behavior modification, for example, is probably about as limited as is our understanding of how treatment cures. Blatt and Behrends' (1985) model of the processes of change in development and in therapy may well be applicable here. They suggest that growth occurs and internalizations take place when an affectively gratifying object involvement is followed by an experienced incompatibility. Applying this to the supervisory situation, one might suggest that the gratifying involvement with the supervisor during the supervisory session in which supervisees feel safe, secure, understood, and protected is followed by the inevitable separation and separate experiences with the patient. Initially supervisees metaphorically bring the supervisor along with them, the owl perched on the shoulder, so to speak, but gradually begin to internalize and identify with those aspects of the supervisor's way of working that they chose to make their own. The supervisor is no longer in the room with them consciously, and they eventually begin to feel that they indeed are no longer in need of supervision, either for a particular case or, ultimately, for all their cases. One might compare such a process with a successful piece of mourning during which a gratifying relationship is gradually replaced by stable internalizations, conscious and unconscious, of pieces of the person and memories of their experiences together so that the individual is finally able to resume a life gratifying to both self and object needs.

In comparing the experience of being supervised with that of being analyzed, it is interesting to note that supervision may at times present a more threatening experience than does the analysis for certain kinds of candidates. First and perhaps foremost, supervisees have to reveal much about their inner processes in a situation where they are simultaneously being evaluated and expected to change. It has been suggested (Hedda Bolgar, personal communication) that this may, in fact, be an impossible situation, paralleling the one of earlier years when the training analyst was expected to report back to the Education Committee concerning the analysand. In addition, the kind of exposure in supervision may be experienced as a more drastic, unremitting, and shameful one. Perhaps this is so primarily for the conscientious supervisees who attempt to present a complete and verbatim picture of their interpersonal interactions with the patient as well as a painstaking account of their internal responses, knowing at the same time that their responses to the supervisor are being observed and evaluated. Candidates reveal much about themselves in a way that may make them feel less under control than in the analysis, where more censorship may be tolerated, since as analysts we are more accepting of "keeping secrets" and are concerned more with analyzing the need for them rather than ascertaining their contents (Ekstein & Caruth, 1972).

As supervisors, however, we may feel more concern about the contents of what the candidate may be omitting or concealing, particularly if we believe that such material might be detrimental to the patient.

Furthermore, in reporting to the supervisor about what transpires in the work with the patient, the supervisee has to reveal both cognitive difficulties and ignorance (dumb spots) as well as difficulties in the work with the patient that arise out of personal conflicts and inner dynamics (deaf and blind spots) (Ekstein, 1969), which lead to transference and countertransference phenomena, both with the patient and with the supervisor.

Dumb spots yield to further learning. Deaf and blind spots—the inability to hear certain aspects of what is being said or to see certain aspects of the self—may contribute to current difficulties the student is experiencing in the supervisory process, which need to be explored with the supervisor, or they may reflect more deep-seated intrapsychic conflicts interfering with the therapeutic practice, which need to be explored more deeply or possibly referred "back to the couch," so to speak.

This is, of course, a particularly difficult recommendation if the student is not currently in analysis and one of the compelling reasons for requiring simultaneous treatment and supervision during analytic training. Parenthetically, there are differing opinions about referrals "back to the couch"; some analysts feel this is inappropriate and even an intrusion (Ernest Lawrence, personal communication). Such a reaction is analogous to the concern of the child analyst with parents who instruct their children what to report to the therapist, particularly as it is generally "bad" behavior in the eyes of the parent.

Deaf and blind spots creating conflict in the supervisory process may be repeated in an analogous difficulty that the student experiences in the treatment process. Similarly, deaf and blind spots emerging in the work with the patient may be repeated in the work with the supervisor. The supervisor must attend to this parallel process between the supervisory and the treatment processes. The dominant anxiety for the student may lie either in the supervisory or in the treatment process. Which of these is the primary source of the difficulties may distinguish between different kinds of underlying dynamics in the candidate (which will be discussed further below).

It is in dealing with the deaf and blind spots that the supervisor has to exercise the greatest skill to maneuver, as it were, between the Scylla of becoming too intrusive and interpretative and the Charybdis of remaining too didactic and content oriented.

The impact of the supervisory process upon the supervisee and his or her therapeutic work must not be underestimated and has been generally recognized. However, the impact of a particular patient's treatment process upon the student must also not be underestimated in understanding the supervisory process. For example, work with very disturbed patients may lead to an appearance of greater disturbance in the candidate during the supervision process than actually exists intrinsically in the supervisee. This may arise from the student's transitory identifications in the service of empathy with a very sick patient, rather than from a pervasive on-going pathology in the student.

The impact of supervision upon the nature of the supervised treatment requires careful consideration. Even under the most optimal and benign circumstances, supervision turns the dyad of student-patient into a triad—into a crowded room, so to speak. This creates a situation akin to gossiping, in that the intimacy between patient and supervisee is intruded upon by the supervisory relationship and requirements (Caruth, 1985). In addition, students *may* experience a feeling of guilt and weakening of their sense of professionalism over what they may perceive as a betrayal of the patient's confidences necessitated by the supervision. This may be particularly true if they have not informed the patient of the supervision. Furthermore, students often speak of the feeling that the supervisor is in the room with them—an owl perched on their shoulders, or, in less benign circumstances, a raven quoting, "Nevermore!"

Another consequence of the supervision may be its direct impact upon the patients themselves, who often reveal, implicitly or explicitly, their awareness of and/or preoccupation with their therapist's supervisor, about whom they may or may not have been openly informed. This may occur in their dreams, their associations, or in direct questions concerning the supervision. It would be interesting to systematically study the range of reactions to knowing that the therapist is being supervised. I suspect the responses vary from feeling more secure, as is the case with patients who prefer a clinic to a private practice, to feeling threatened either by the learning status of their therapist or by the exposure to a third person of their personal confidences. In addition, and of course of focal significance, are the candidates' own feelings about being in supervision and "a student" either in their own eyes or the eyes of their patients. Some candidates have found it comfortable to justify a low fee because of the fact that the patient is a "control case," while others who are seeing a full-fee private patient find it almost impossible to present this information.

This triangle does not exist in isolation however. In an institute setting, there are parallel processes impacting upon the supervisor as well as supervisee. Both are accountable to the administration, which becomes a kind of meta-supervisor to each of them, observing the supervisor as a teacher, the candidate as a learner, and thereby complicating the existing learning and teaching transferences and countertransferences for both. Furthermore, both supervisor and supervisee have their own respective peer group relationships. The peers of the student generally form a support group, particularly if he or she is experiencing difficulties in the supervision. This then may, to some extent, be experienced as a threat to the supervisor, who is now the "gossiped of" about whom the student-gossiper may be complaining to the other students, the "gossiped to." The student's peers, however, are also potential competitors and thus can be for certain students a source of threat rather than support.

The supervisor may also be ambivalently involved in supportive or competitive relationships vis-à-vis peers and the administration. In addition, ethics require that the supervisor not discuss the supervisees indiscriminately, outside of evaluations to the administration. The supervisor, therefore, may not defend him- or herself against the complaints of the supervisee to the other candidates, among whom may be numbered his or her own patients. One supervisor's student challenged him by reporting his reputation for toughness, even as the administration was condemning him for being too softhearted in his evaluations! In general, candidates share conflicts about supervisors with their peers, while supervisors bring their doubts to the administrative powers. However, additional complications can exist at analytic institutes where the student may simultaneously be in analysis and relating difficulties in supervision to the analyst—the supervisor's peer or possibly even administrator. The student may do this with the luxury of total analytic confidentiality, that is, unless the analyst also happens to be in treatment with his or her own training analyst in the institute, who may also be the student's supervisor, which does occasionally occur! Overlapping triangles clearly exist, with all kinds of communications going on at different levels and in different directions.

At this point it is important to note that although I have been discussing "the student" and "the supervisor," there is, of course, no such thing as a homogeneous class of either candidates or supervisors. Candidates vary with respect to level of training, information, and expertise, and even more importantly, with respect to their personalities and accompanying learning styles and transferences.

I shall describe here only two of the many possible kinds of personalities presented by the candidates, with their corresponding impact upon the supervisory process potentially leading to what Lane (1986) has designated as a Negative Supervisory Reaction. The first type of candidates might be described as psychologically immature, vulnerable, dependent, outer-directed, and needy of affirmation and approval from authority figures. For this kind of a student, narcissistic issues predominate over more mature learning needs. Such students tend to assume a passive, often idealizing relationship to the supervisor, and they may become more involved in issues in the supervisory process than in the therapy process with their patients. In such instances, the parallel process may bring issues into the therapy more than the therapy process brings issues into the supervision. For example, there may be a "passive," or uncritical, imitation of the supervisor or of what they think the supervisor is saying in order to emulate and please the supervisor. In other instances, where the supervisor may express empathy or concern for the patient, they may experience a kind of angry sibling rivalry, as it were, with the patient, feeling themselves in competition for the supervisor's approval and love. Parenthetically, this may occur most noticeably around setting or changing fees or schedule arrangements. A supervisor's attempt at understanding how the patient may be experiencing the therapist's interventions may lead to the therapist feeling misunderstood, criticized, and defensive about his or her own needs.

A second type of student might be characterized as seemingly independent, and may actually be engaged in a competitive struggle with the supervisor. These students tend to be more aggressive, assertive, and preoccupied with autonomy and control. In these instances, the underlying oedipal goal is to impress the supervisor by doing better than he or she could do. In this case, rather than idealizing the supervisor, the secret wish may be for the supervisor to idealize the candidate. This can lead to competitive attempts to be a better therapist—symbolically an oedipal victory from which the patient may or may not benefit.

It is clear that these two kinds of supervisees may be matched or more likely mismatched with supervisors with similar or conflicting kinds of problems. Some supervisors seem driven by the need to demonstrate their brilliance or omniscience, with the hidden, or not so hidden, agenda of impressing more than teaching. Others feel the need to appease their students in order not to arouse any negative feelings and to become "pals," so to speak, thereby wiping out the generation gap between supervisor and supervisee in a kind of quasi-democratic effort to demonstrate that "we are all struggling together with similar problems," a message that the more competitive supervisee is most eager to hear. While this message may be true in one sense, it is not true to the degree that it wipes out differences between the learner and the learned and, I believe, subtly minimizes the value of training and experience.

I suspect that in many ways the task of the supervisor is the most complicated of all the tasks involved in training the young analyst. The supervisor does, at varying times, need to convey certain kinds of information of both a clinical and theoretical nature, for we expect our analysands to be more than intuitive, empathic, and gifted artists, even as we value those qualities. The supervisor is faced constantly with the interaction of the candidate's personal problems with those of the patient, and must help him or her to utilize personal reactions for understanding the patient and differentiate those that arise strictly out of personal problems. In differentiating between the student-therapists' countertransference and transference reactions, the latter have more to do with on-going repressed infantile conflicts from the past that arise in all the work, whereas the former have more to do with responses to a particular patient in the present. I believe this is an important distinction, although perhaps a difficult one to make in practice. It is of particular importance, however, when one works with the internal responses of the therapist as the primary material of supervision. Supervisors working in this way frequently discuss with their supervisees issues of projective identification, and it becomes essential to help the candidate differentiate who does what to whom.

This in itself may be an impossible task for, as Ogden (1986) points out, both the container and the contained are changed in the process of projective identification. So far I have been referring to the projective identifications occurring in the therapeutic process, but they occur as well in the supervisory process and must also be attended to by the supervisor.

Analytic supervision, which generally coincides with the didactic analysis, is confronted frequently with complications arising from differences between the supervisor and the analyst as well as other supervisors and instructors. As a supervisor, it is most difficult to deal with a candidate whose reason for doing something is, and I quote, "That's what my analyst does." I have run into this explanation when trying to explore with a supervisee his/her use of a secretary to handle fee and insurance matters. When I tried to explore with a supervisee the complexities of responding to a patient who wanted to borrow material from the waiting room, I was told, with some perplexity as to why this was an issue, that his own analyst had just borrowed a book from him! As a supervisor one is frequently faced with parameters that may have been introduced by the supervisee's analyst, and such problems verge on the insoluble.

These kinds of problems may often be behind those supervisory impasses that may necessitate a termination of the supervisory process with a change to a different supervisor. Here again it would be valuable to have more information about such "failures" in supervision, from whence they arise and how they can be resolved so as to enable the resolution to become part of the learning process itself. This might also model for the candidate the fact that there may be times when therapeutic impasses may similarly be unresolvable with a particular therapist and require termination and transfer. It is a valuable lesson for any candidate to learn that both supervision and treatment are impossible tasks and that to err is human and to acknowledge is divine.

These are examples of but two kinds of situations where the particular needs of the student and/or supervisor may complicate the difficult task of the supervisor, who optimally needs to remain equidistant in the three-pronged task of understanding the inner life of the patient, of enhancing the learning processes of the student therapist, and of evaluating and communicating recommendations back to the administration. The supervisee also has the equally monumental task of simultaneously trying to understand the inner experience of the patient and relate it back to the supervisor, even while engaged in a learning transference with the supervisor, a therapeutic transference with his or her own analyst, a countertransference with the patient, and a somewhat overdetermined, albeit ambiguous relationship to the administration in whose control some of his or her future professional life has been placed!

When one tries to conceptualize the immensely complex nature of the teaching and learning task, one is tempted to turn to what I have labelled the "earthworm theory" (see Appendix) of learning, which I suspect may be the occasional secret fantasy of every supervisor and every supervisee. I refer here to the experiment in which untrained earthworms were fed trained ones and thereby acquired all their knowledge (McConnel, 1962). In the long run, after all is said and done, this may be what "really" goes on in the supervisory process, and incorporation, like imitation, may be not only the sincerest form of flattery but also the basis for all clinical learning!

References

Blatt, S., & Behrends, S. R. (1985). Internalization and psychological develop- ment throughout the life cycle. *The Psychoanalytic Study of the Child, 40,* 11–39.

Caruth, E. (1985). Secret bearer or secret barer? Countertransference and the gossiping therapist. *Contemporary Psychoanalysis, 21,* 4, 39–49.

Ekstein, R. (1969). Concerning the teaching and learning of psychoanalysis. *Journal of the American Psychiatric Association, 17,* 2, 419–438.

Ekstein, R., & Caruth, E. (1972). Keeping secrets. In P. L. Giovacchini (Ed.), *Tactics and techniques in psychoanalytic therapy* (pp. 200–218). New York: Science House.

Ekstein, R., & Wallerstein, R. S. (1985). *The teaching and learning of psychotherapy.* New York: Basic Books.

Lane, R. C. (1985). The recalcitrant supervisee: The negative supervisory reaction. *Current Issues in Psychoanalytic Practice, 2,* 2, 65–81.

McConnel, J. V. (1962). Memory transfer through cannibalism in plenariums. *Journal of Neuropsychiatry,* Supplement 1, 3, 42–48.

Ogden, T. H. (1986). *The natrix of the mind: Object relations and the psychoanalytic dialogue.* New York: Jason Aronson.

Appendix

ODE TO THE EARTHWORM

Pity the poor earthworm—
His life was so drab
Until he hooked up with
A psychology lab.

He trained and he trained
With a researcher so firm
That very soon he became
The most learn-ed earthworm.

Then alas for this worm,
Who held sway for a term,
They fed him (don't squirm!)
To an untrained earthworm.

And, lo and behold,
A miracle came to pass;
The ingesting earthworm
Was soon head of class!

For now it turned out
That he reigned supreme;
He had acquired the clout
Of the trained earthworm's gene!

But, alas and alack,
His fame was quite short;
New researchers brought back
No similar report!

So pity the poor earthworm—
For as you can see
He neither has fame
Nor longevity!

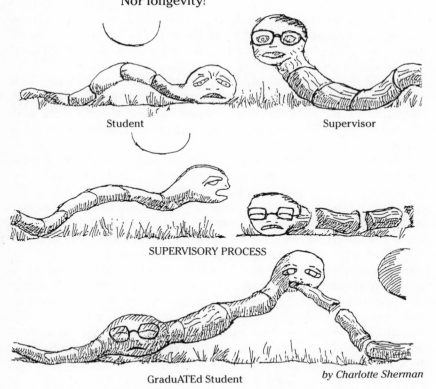

Student   Supervisor

SUPERVISORY PROCESS

GraduATEd Student   *by Charlotte Sherman*

IDENTIFICATION IN SUPERVISION: THE EARTHWORM MODEL

Supervision and the Achievement of an Analytic Identity

Norman C. Oberman, Ph.D.

Two studies of psychoanalytic supervision in recent years have, indirectly, cast serious doubt on the efficacy of the traditional supervisory process: Wallerstein's *Becoming a Psychoanalyst* (1981) and Dewald's *Learning Process in Psychoanalytic Supervision* (1987). In both studies, well-trained and respected clinicians illustrate how they conduct supervisory sessions with gifted candidates. In Wallerstein's book, Herbert Schlesinger summarizes his work with Howard Shevrin; Dewald's study presents verbatim transcripts of his supervision of Mary Dick.

Both studies break new ground in the richness of the material they provide. Not only do they offer detailed records of the supervisory hours, they also include the candidate's candid views of the experience, considered as an aspect of their development as analysts. What they say about the experience is disquieting. We learn from Shevrin that he felt consistently misunderstood, that he struggled with the patient until the supervision was completed, and that it was only after a change of supervisors that the patient began to make substantial progress. The success of the treatment, we are told, came as a surprise to Schlesinger. Dick describes her idealization, occasional hostile transference, and difficulties learning with Dewald. She writes, "In the second year of the supervised analysis, I presented the case in a continuous case conference. I began to listen to and hear my patient more independently of the vision of her I had developed with my supervisor, which I now realize was restricted by distortions in my transference" (p. 460). Reformulating her concept

194

of the patient, she presented her views to Dewald and was relieved to have him take it in stride. She adds, "I am aware that after working through . . . [this particular] defense in my patient's analysis I gained a greater, more substantial feeling of confidence in my evolving clinical judgment, and in my growing ability to use myself, my knowledge, my senses, to understand my patients" (p. 462).

If these had been inexperienced supervisors or less talented candidates, there would be less cause for concern. After all, the candidates did get through the experience, even though, to the candidates, the supervisors often appeared as more an obstacle than a help. Can we then say that the system works well enough, that the learning difficulties of the candidates reflect no more than their self-serving narcissism, which makes them reluctant to credit their supervisors' accomplishments? The problem seems to go deeper than that. For the most part, the record of these supervisions is of mutual misunderstanding. Anxiety and confused self-doubting on the part of the candidates were both cause and consequence. While it is true that the candidates managed successfully to complete their work, it was despite the system as much as through it that they succeeded. Most importantly, given the recognized experience and skill of the supervisors and the self-evident potential of the candidates, we are left to wonder how numerous other candidates, less gifted, working with less sensitive supervisors, may struggle and fail for lack of adequate understanding and guidance.

The principles of psychoanalytic supervision, according to Schlesinger (1981), place "facilitating . . . [the] process of combined personal and professional growth in the candidate" (p. 30) central in the supervisor's concern. Yet, in actuality, the supervisor contends with conditions that often deprive these aims of meaning. Unlike the candidate's analyst, the supervisor does not have the candidate's associations to work with, except as the candidate chooses to reveal them. Thus, the assumptions the supervisor makes about the candidate's states of mind are likely to remain untestable and may be seriously in error. For example, Dewald (1987) tells us candidly that he was unaware of Dick's transference, despite its pervasiveness and covertly disruptive consequences for their work. Lacking insight into candidates' conflicts and transference, supervisors can do little more than create settings in which candidates have the opportunity to learn, if they want to. However, supervisors have no reason to believe their efforts will be seen as helpful or even as benign by candidates. Inevitably, inescapably, candidates experience supervisors in a private way, known only to themselves. While it may be an understatement to say candidates are limited by "blind spots," it is self-evident that supervisors, like blind Oedipus, must make their way alone in the dark.

It is possible to posit, as does Schlesinger (1981), that the capacity to form a "learning alliance" (p. 35) with the supervisor is a prerequisite for supervision, and that the problems described, where they do arise, are a function of failed selection criteria. Consequently, the conclusion can be drawn that it is not supervision that must be reconsidered but rather the methods of selecting and promoting candidates. Selection procedures are obviously important; but it is also true that, after selection is completed, the training situation itself promotes regression in the candidate, reawakening oedipal conflicts that are likely to be silently disruptive of the supervisory relationship.

Among the factors that contribute to regression is the structure of training itself, which returns the candidate to the child-like dependency of the family. In addition, extraanalytic contacts between candidate and analyst, both during and after the analysis tend to perpetuate an infantile relationship with the analyst. The consideration has led Greenacre (1971) to describe the ending of the training analysis as the "final phase" rather than as "termination," in recognition of its incompleteness. Furthermore, as Atkins (1970) points out, both the candidate and the analyst know that someday the candidate will, in actuality, displace his own analyst. Eventually, the training analyst will retire and the candidate will be eligible to take his place. Thus, the training program in general, and the training analysis, specifically, recapitulate the parent-child relationship and, in doing so, limit the possible resolution of the Oedipus complex.

One of the ironies of analytic training is that it is these selfsame oedipal issues, which remain unresolved in the training analysis, that critically influence the outcome of the candidate's training. Within an institute, oedipal conflicts constellate around the persons who pass or fail the candidate. The severity of the oedipal conflict determines whether the candidate dares achieve an analytic identity. Schlesinger (1986) has suggested that the function of supervision is to counteract some of the side effects of the training analysis. He observes that, rather than achieving a true termination, candidates are likely to identify with their analysts, and that supervision can help correct that by providing other models for comparison. We have noted, though, that regressed candidates' conflicts impair their ability to learn, including the ability to learn from the supervisor's example. It would seem that if the supervision is to be effective, it must somehow work within the interests of the candidate. Which is to say, it must offer hope of a meaningful resolution of the oedipal conflict. If that can be achieved, it offers the opportunity to engage directly the active cooperation of candidates in their own training. Failing to accomplish that, attempts by the supervisors to teach are likely to be construed by candidates as hostile to their ambitions and to increase the candidates' oedipal conflict, whatever the good intentions of the supervisors.

What are the interests of the candidate? On this issue, Masud Khan (1974) notes, "Today, there are few who would say that anyone comes to analytic training merely to acquire a skill to help to cure others without a primary need for a cure for himself . . . I would go so far as to say that those that are content to be helped to live with their problems seek treatment; those who seek a cure demand training. Hence in the analysis of students, one has to anticipate what is the other's expectancy of cure" (p. 117). The implication seems to be that something fundamental is demanded by students, something that other analysts have said cannot be obtained from the training analysis alone. Erikson (1954) appears to think along similar lines when he interprets the dream of a graduating professional. The analysand dreams he is lying on the couch while his analyst saws a round hole in the top of his head. After acknowledging the dreamer's castration anxieties, Erikson compares the dream's manifest content to the tonsure administered by bishops to young Catholic priests. In making that comparison, Erikson suggests that the graduate wants not only to understand his infantile roots; he also wants a sense of his appointed place, a sense of belonging and responsibility consistent with his roots. That is his "cure." By extension, I would add that the achievement of an analytic identity is the "cure" sought by most candidates. In order to appreciate the implications of this "cure" for supervisory practice, it will be necessary to consider first what is meant by an analytic identity.

The import of achieving an analytic identity has not escaped notice of those involved in training. Ekstein and Wallerstein (1958), referring to the education of psychoanalytical psychotherapists say, "If a psychotherapy training program were to succeed completely in helping its students acquire all the basic psychotherapeutic skills known today, and if this program would do no more than that, it would have failed to fully accomplish its chosen task; the training of psychotherapists. For in professional training, the acquisition of skill by itself would not be enough. What would still be missing is a specific quality in the psychotherapist that makes him into a truly professional person, a quality we wish to refer to as his professional identity" (p. 65). Dewald, writing almost 30 years later, affirms that attitude, placing the achievement of an increased sense of identity as an analyst first among the broader goals of psychoanalytic supervision. By addressing it as a broader goal, he implies that, unlike technique and theory, it cannot be addressed directly in supervision.

This apparent agreement on the centrality of an analytic identity appears on closer investigation to rest on the very ambiguity of the term. Certainly, there is much less agreement as to what constitutes an analytic identity or how it is best achieved.

The polar positions on this concept have been voiced by Edward Joseph and Daniel Widlocher (1983). Joseph suggests that analytic identity is achieved through identification with one's analyst, teachers, supervisors, and historical figures, assimilated into existing earlier identifications. These are brought together in the candidate's personal analysis; but the process is not fully completed until after the candidate graduates. The outcome, in Joseph's words, is that "his psychoanalytic identity will be that of the objective scientist constantly studying, seeking to understand further (p. 20). It includes a high degree of integrity in the search for truth as well as a moral commitment to the acceptance of truth" (p. 21).

Widlocher, unlike Joseph, seeks the analyst's identity in the analytic encounter itself. He writes, "Our identity rests on the specificity of our action, on what we 'do' with our patients. The psychoanalyst 'at work' is, without doubt, what defines us best and yet what is so difficult to transmit. To arrange for a certain interhuman encounter, to encourage and to spot in this situation quite specific processes, to communicate certain of its elements so that the patient feels free and secure when facing the instincts and the internalization process, seem to be the three aspects of this task" (p. 27).

We can say of these approaches, that each separately is intriguing, yet incomplete. Each is too general to enhance either clinical understanding or pedagogical process. Widlocher appreciates this deficiency and suggests the need for more detailed description. He writes, "A peculiar silence surrounds the difficulties we meet in the exercise of our practice. (p. 30) Would it not help an overall study of the resistances met in our work as analysts, and promote both freer communication regarding these difficulties and a revision of the defense mechanisms of the psychoanalyst at work, to specify better what constitutes the foundation of our identity?" (p. 33).

There have been thoughtful papers, if not on the analyst's identity, at least on the analyst at work. Fliess (1942) proposed that the analyst, through modifications in his ego and superego, could understand the patient by "trial identification." Under these defined conditions, the analyst can tolerate fantasies, impulses, and affects which in other circumstances would evoke anxiety and defense. Schafer (1983) proposes that it is commitment to the analytic tradition that allows the analyst circumscribed areas of relative professional freedom. Unlike Fliess, Schafer regards understanding as based not so much on trial identification as on the analyst's construction and reconstruction of the patient's character and history. Malcove (1975) as well as Baltar, Lothane, and Spencer (1980) describe and discuss unpublished proposals by Isakower regarding what he called the "analyzing instrument" and the process of regression shared by analyst and patient that promoted and sustained the analysis. Isakower considered teaching the "analysing instrument" as the prime task of supervision. Beres and Arlow (1974) consider the means by which analysts are able to recognize patients' unconscious fantasies. They propose that such recognition takes place when analysts experience an affect that alerts them to patients' motivation and fantasy. They suggest that analysts are stimulated by patients to have fantasies with meaning similar to the patients'. By acknowledging patients as instigators of the fantasies, analysts orient themselves to understand patients' experience.

While such studies have helped clarify the tools with which the analyst works, they have not added to our understanding of the analyst's processes in the encounter. They tell us little about the shifting motivational and defensive states of the analyst as the analytic work is done. Probably what has delayed investigation of the analyst's dynamics is the paucity of examples of the analyst at work. Thus, while there are endless case histories in the literature, they rarely include the experiences of the analyst. Theodore Reik is somewhat of an exception, but his associations emphasize his personal concerns rather than the more general characteristics of the analytic experience. Searles also presents his reactions, but they reveal more of what must be endured in order to treat severely disturbed patients than what is experienced while treatment takes place. Both analysts, in their writings, affirm the analyst's humanity, but they add little to our understanding of analysts' efforts to maintain themselves while comprehending their patients. Most case presentations are summaries of the work done, to be taken largely on faith. At best they include process notes. Almost never are they accounts with which we can compare our own experience, from which we can draw general conclusions.

A rare exception to this reticence is Schafer (1986), who presents a clinical example remarkable for its description of the analyst's silent struggle to maintain himself as he attempts to understand his patient. In citing Schafer's report of his experience as an example of the analyst's identity struggle, I will use the author's words wherever possible. The patient's background and associations, while summarized, are also in the analyst's words. Schafer's reflections during the hour are presented in their entirety .

The case involved the analysis of a young married woman. The analyst had just returned from a week's vacation. During his absence, his patient had begun a new job. She also took an examination to qualify for advanced specialty training. Much analytic time had been spent attempting to understand the intensely anxious way in which she was anticipating these events. In the first session after his return, the analyst notes she does not refer to his absence, and she alludes only vaguely and in passing to some uneasiness about having enjoyed the past week. She refers neither to her experience in her new job nor to how she had performed on the qualifying examination. She goes on to dwell on the ups and downs, mainly the downs, of her personal relationships. She lets drop again a hint that she had some "great" times, but develops the negative with considerable and mounting bitterness. In great detail she rails against her husband, but presents no specific or persuasive evidence. She comes across as demanding, intolerant, and "nagging," particularly in relation to her husband.

Schafer then describes his own internal processes: "On my part, I begin to respond silently with some countertransference, starting to wonder glumly whether the analysis of her presenting problem of depressiveness and inhibitedness will only eventuate in her becoming remorselessly vindictive. At this point, however, I realize that she is, so to speak, once again beginning to cast a spell over me. Under this spell, with which I am familiar in this analysis, I can no longer listen empathically or remember adequately; instead, I am moved increasingly to say something critical and thereby enter into a complex sadomasochistic interaction with her. By 'something critical' I refer not to criticizing her in the conventional sense but to pointing out some problematic aspects of her account that I could know in advance she would take only as criticism.

"Realizing all this, I begin to remember better. I recall once again that this mode of self-presentation has always been typical of the way she begins her sessions and that it used to be typical of her sessions from beginning to end. I also remember that it has deep roots in preferred patterns of interaction within her family. I recall, too, that recently she has been attempting to shift within her sessions from this 'nagging' initial self-presentation to collaborative thoughtfulness . . . In short order and with some chagrin, I realize that in this session I have been observing an expectable regressive response to my week-long absence."

Schafer's attention to detail and respect for the clinical process makes this a remarkable record of the analyst's crisis, a window into the analyst's world. His experience can be summarized as follows: After listening to his patient for a while, the analyst becomes abruptly aware that something has happened to him. He feels his patient is beginning to "cast a spell" over him, which is to say, he feels seduced into a state other than his usual analytic one. Under this "spell" he "can no longer listen empathically or remember adequately." Instead, he is moved to enter into a sadomasochistic relationship with her. "Realizing all this," he writes, "I begin to remember better."

What is implicit in Schafer's comments is that the first memory recaptured is the memory of who he is—he is an analyst. Almost simultaneously, perhaps even implicit in the first memory, he remembers what an analyst remembers, namely the patient he has known: her typical manner, the history they have renarrated of her life, and the history of the analysis itself. Himself restored, and with his internal object also restored, he is once again able to be an analyst, able to understand and to empathize with his patient. Achieving that, he can now compare the current hour's sado-masochistic seduction with the long-term relationship they have established, and in making the comparison, recognize the patient's attacks as no more than an expectable regression, a reaction to the vacation break.

Grinberg (1983) writes, "We may say that the mother-analyst contains—and is the depository of—the seed of the patient's rudimentary identity, memory, and synthetic function; the analyst contains the seed and the material with which the patient's identity will be built" (p. 55). It is apparent in the case illustration that Grinberg is indeed correct; the analyst, by containing the memory of the patient, also preserves the patient's identity. We are now also in a position to extend Grinberg's statement, and we can add to it that the analyst also contains his or her *own* identity in the memory that he or she is an analyst. In other words, the identity of analysts rests both on desire and on the ability to remember. A crisis of identity occurs as the analyst is torn between the seduction of archaic object relations and remembering that he or she is an analyst.

Returning to the case illustration, Schafer relates how he made his interpretation: The patient "asks me what I make of all the material of the session . . . I decide to answer by taking up two factors: her defensive avoidance of manifest links to the transference and her unconsciously active stereotyped attempt to seduce me into a sadomasochistic countertransference response. I say that she feels distant to me today, as in her making no mention of my absence and no mention of the new job and the examination on which we spent so much time before I left. Not only distant from me, however, but acting as though she has been trying to get me to feel distant from her and dissatisfied with her as someone who won't even tell me about her great times during my absence."

What appears evident in his interpretation is that, once the analyst has restored himself and his patient, he then is able to employ the affect and fantasy evoked by the patient to understand her. This understanding is the raw material of the interpretation. The interpretation itself is a complex function of the relationship with the particular patient, in their shared appreciation of her personal history and the history of their relationship.

While the clinical hour presented represents a kind of encounter that is commonplace to us, it is probably not what comes first to mind as typifying analytic work. Rather, most often, we follow the patient's associations until, as Bernfeld (1941) has said, the patient's "confession" fits the facts. Yet even the mundane hours rarely are as uneventful as they seem, at least for the analyst. Usually there is some momentary anxiety that can be recalled afterwards, though it may not be sufficient to trigger defense. Which is to say that even when the work is relatively routine, analysts are involved personally, and their ability to manage the ordinary rests on their confidence that when extraordinary events take place, they can use their experience to further the analysis.

Let us consider an example of another analytic hour, this one conducted by a candidate. The candidate in question described working with a bitter, withholding, contemptuous, single woman in her mid-thirties. She seldom spoke, and despite years of work together, still treated him as if he were of no importance in her life. During the hour in question, the patient, when she would talk, complained about a niece who had been a terrible disappointment to her. At one point in the hour, they once again fell into a prolonged silence. Lost in his thoughts, the candidate gradually became aware, first of feeling apprehensive, then of a vision that emerged in his consciousness and gripped his imagination. Several people huddled together in a cave where they had sought escape from a predatory, dragon-like creature. There had been no sign of the creature for a while, and they wondered, had the dragon gone or was it waiting for them in silence? They had to know, so one man fearfully, cautiously, moved out. He was immediately seized and torn to pieces by the creature. The candidate thought about the fantasy and then suggested to the patient that she seemed angry with him (to which she replied with some ferocity).

What commands attention in this vignette is less the patient than the unmistakable evidence of unresolved conflicts in the candidate himself. Although he was able to use his fantasy to further the analysis, one wonders why the candidate was not more sensitive to the patient's show of anger at him. Even without hearing the candidate's associations to his own fantasy, we can recognize conflicts over wishes to bite and tear, and I would suspect that we could make intelligent guesses as to their origin in his infantile phantasies. However, for our purposes, it may be enough to note that, without engaging in self-analysis, and without being seduced by his own infantile wishes, the candidate was able to sort through his fantasy well enough to find his way back to the patient.

In general, we can say that realization by candidates that their personal experiences relate to the state of the transference consolidates their professional identities. Their reactions are no longer only neurotic residues but become potential tools of the trade. Gaining trust in themselves to find the patient amidst the tumult of their feelings and fantasies, they can afford to turn their attention to the more impersonal issues of clinical theory and patient dynamics. Operationally, I believe this is what we mean by an analytic identity. It employs selective attention. It is a way of processing personal experience. It does not require complete resolution of personal conflicts. It works well enough for us to do our job. It is clear enough for us to teach and for candidates to learn.

The last example also raises questions about how we are to conceive of analytic failure, of countertransference. We can say that the analyst in a state of countertransference relates to the patient as to a stimulus for internal release rather than as to a separate person. The patient has become a part object, a stand-in for the analyst's archaic object, at whatever level that happens to be. Thus, what is remembered by the analyst in such a state has less to do with the patient and more to do with the organization of thought intrinsic to that regressed object relationship. Which is to say, it is difficult for the analyst to remember the finer points of a relationship if what matters is only to eat or be eaten. So the countertransference reaction itself implies drive organization of thought. And the drive oriented, regressed analyst has no obvious use for memories that are other than drive directed—for memories other than of a part object adequate to need.

Why then do we not act-out more often with patients, rather than remain the analyst? The answer is almost self-evident. Because we are analysts. Schafer (1983) discusses this issue with reference to Kris's well-known paper on regression in the service of the ego. Schafer points out that we work within a tradition, and that analytic regression is limited by our commitment to that tradition. Another way of saying it is that analysts remember because, in remembering, they affirm their identity as analysts, and that affirmation is more important to them than the instinctual release available through action or than their commitment to their archaic identity.

Thus, we are not surprised to learn, in Schafer's case illustration, that the realization that he had been seduced, momentarily, into betraying that tradition is marked by "chagrin" for his internal betrayal, possibly also for the instinctual gratification that must now be renounced. Nor would we be surprised to learn that when the analyst's sense of separateness returns, he is strengthened by his ability to remain loyal to himself as well as to his internal objects, and is better able to remember the patient and to consider her with the eyes of an analyst.

Summary

The structure of institute training places candidates in a child-like relationship to the faculty, encouraging regressive reactivation of oedipal conflicts. Political considerations require that candidates mask their inner struggles, and intellectual defenses support classroom participation and learning. The supervised analysis presents a more personal challenge to the regressed candidates, in their dealings both with supervisors and with patients. Supervisors, unlike candidates' analysts, do not have access to candidates' conflicts, but must proceed in their work with only conjectures about the candidates, which cannot be tested directly. The consequences, as evident in the two recent studies cited, are often a serious misunderstanding of the candidate and a potentially chaotic learning situation.

It is suggested that learning in supervision requires the active collaboration of the candidate, and that it is possible to achieve that collaboration if the supervisor and the candidate share a common goal. The oedipal ambition of the institute candidate is to achieve the inner (and outer) identity of an analyst. It is suggested that supervisors, to be effective, must do more than offer themselves as a model, or teach patient dynamics and clinical theory. They must initially address themselves specifically to the problem by demonstrating to candidates that they already have the means within themselves to be an analyst, but now must learn how to apply it. That task involves differentiating affect and fantasy from impulse, as well as learning to think about experience even while it is occurring.

The approach described is not presented as a panacea. It certainly is no guarantee of conflict-free supervision. Oedipal conflicts may be too severe to allow candidates to affirm their analytic identity. However, if it is important to candidates to be analysts, such supervision will help them achieve a core identity upon which traditional supervisory guidance can build.

References

Atkins, N. B. (1970). The Oedipus myth, adolescence, and the succession of generations. *Journal of the American Psychoanalytic Association, 18,* 860–875.

Balter, L., Lothane, Z., & Spencer, J. H. (1980). On the analyzing instrument. *Psychoanalytic Quarterly, 49,* 474–504.

Beres, D., & Arlow, J. A. (1974). Fantasy and identification in empathy. *Psychoanalytic Quarterly, 28,* 26–50.

Bernfeld, S. (1941). The facts of observation in psychoanalysis. *Journal of Psychology, 12,* 289–305.

Dewald, P. (1987). *Learning process in psychoanalytic supervision.* Madison, CT: International Universities Press.

Ekstein, R., & Wallerstein, R. W. (1958). *The teaching and learning of psychotherapy.* New York: Basic Books.

Erikson, E. (1954). The dream specimen of psychoanalysis. *Journal of the American Psychoanalytic Association, 2,* 5–56.

Fliess, R. (1942). The metapsychology of the analyst. *Psychoanalytic Quarterly, 11,* 211–227.

Greenacre, P. (1971). *Emotional growth.* New York: International Universities Press.

Grinberg, L. (1983). Discussion of E. D. Joseph & D. Widlocher. In E. D. Joseph & D. Widlocher (Eds.), *The identity of the psychoanalyst.* New York: International Universities Press.

Joseph, E. D. (1983). Identity of a psychoanalyst. In E. D. Joseph & D. Widlocher (Eds.), *The identity of the psychoanalyst* (pp. 1–21). New York: International Universities Press.

Khan, M. (1974). *The privacy of the self.* New York: International Universities Press.

Malcove, L. (1975). The analytic situation: Toward a view of the supervisory

experience. *Journal of the Philadelphia Association of Psychoanalysis, 2,*
    1–19.
Schafer, R. (1983). *The analytic attitude.* New York: Basic Books.
Schafer, R. (1986). Narratives of defense. Paper presented to the Los Angeles
    Institute & Society for Psychoanalytic Studies.
Schlesinger, H. (1981). General principles of psychoanalytic supervision. In R.
    S. Wallerstein (Ed.), *Becoming a psychoanalyst.* New York: International
    Universities Press.
Schlesinger, H. (1986). Supervision and the training analysis: Repetition or
    collaboration? Paper presented at the Clark Conference on Psychoana-
    lytic Training.
Wallerstein, R. S. (1981). *Becoming a psychoanalyst.* New York: International
    Universities Press.
Widlocher, D. (1983). Psychoanalysis today: A problem of identity. In E. D.
    Joseph and D. Widlocher (Eds.), *The identity of the psychoanalyst* (pp.
    23–40). New York: International Universities Press.

Discussion

Martin Mayman, Ph.D.

Dr. Oberman refers to the book on psychoanalytic supervision edited by Wallerstein (1981), reporting in detail on one supervisory process in which a skillful, sensitive, insightful supervisor finds himself increasingly at odds with the candidate, one who subsequently became an outstanding member of our psychoanalytic community. The difficulties that developed in that supervisory process had little to do with the relative competencies of analyst and supervisor. I suspect that the problem lay elsewhere. I believe it was a direct consequence of the supervisor's sense that, as Dr. Caruth tells us, "Unlike the analyst, the supervisor must have concern and empathy for the patient in the supervisee's office as well as for the supervisee in the supervisor's own office, a [double] responsibility that has both ethical and legal implications." True, but supervisors must be careful to clarify for themselves how that responsibility should be exercised.

In my experience, supervisors go awry, and with them often the treatment process as well, when they allow themselves to be drawn into the dialogue between patient and therapist. When supervisors feel pulled to step in and correct what a supervisee is doing wrongly, they have fallen victim to the pull of the patient's transference, or to the pull of the therapist's transference, or perhaps even to some pressure from their own unresolved transferences. Even if they successfully avoid acting on this pull, their feeling at cross-purposes with the therapist indicates a serious derailment of the supervisory process. Supervisors must be careful not to allow their empathy with a patient to develop into an identification with the patient, a joining with the patient in his or her transference complaints about the therapist or the treatment. This can have several deleterious effects.

No analytic candidate can listen intuitively, empathically, open-mindedly, and effectively to the patient if one ear is cocked for the supervisor's criticisms, outspoken or tacit, which he must brace himself for, or if possible, try to avoid. The situation is not like that in driver's training where the instructor can, with a flick of the switch, take over the steering when he thinks the driver is beginning to lose control. The psychoanalytic supervisor may be responsible legally and ethically for the patient, but he or she must be able to tolerate delegating that responsibility to the therapist if the treatment is to proceed constructively for the therapist, the patient, and the supervisor.

When we were designing the Doehrman study (1976) of parallel processes in supervision, one segment of the study called for tape-recording a series of sessions. We were concerned that this would distort the treatment and brought into question our ethical obligation to the patients. We found that the presence of the tape recorder had a far more potent effect on the therapists than it did on the patients. It was as if the therapist's relationship to the patient had suddenly been invaded by a looming, ever-present, ever-threatening superego.

I cite this anecdote because I think it is analogous to the more subtle but equally powerful impact the tacit presence of a supervisor can have on the therapist's freedom to listen and respond appropriately to the patient. The introduction of a supervisor into the treatment process has much the same effect as that tape recorder had. Supervisors should remain cognizant of their superego-ish impact on the therapist; it is essential that they avoid letting themselves be pulled into acting like a superego as well.

A related, but not nearly so disruptive effect of supervision has to do with another form of intrusion of the supervisory hour into the treatment hour. I find, especially with therapists in the early years of their training, that something therapists are told by their supervisor or learn from their supervisor becomes material they feel impelled to bring to the treatment hour. Without quite being aware that this has happened, they start the next hour with an extraneous agenda item carried over from the previous supervision session. This, as one would expect, has a disastrous effect on the timing of the intervention. It also gets in the way of their receptiveness to any new theme in the hour. The therapists become significantly less effective under these conditions than they would be if they were free of the supervisor's input!

In view of this, I have taken to laying down at the outset with a new supervisee a paradoxical and only half-facetious rule: that the therapist must promise to put completely out of mind anything that he and I discuss about the patient in our supervisory sessions when he enters the treatment room. Only he and the patient come together in the treatment process. The supervisor neither belongs there nor should be tolerated there. It is the therapist who is conducting the treatment, not the supervisor. In effect, the supervisor needs to decide whether he assumes that the therapist being supervised needs to be told what to think, how to comport himself, how to intervene with patients, or that the trainee can be trusted to set up and maintain a forward-moving treatment process, but may need some help clarifying for himself what is happening emotionally and ideationally in himself and in his patient as the analysis progresses. The supervisor helps him think about the material the supervisee brings to their sessions, helps him include in the larger equation elements he may otherwise minimize or overlook. I submit that what is required of good supervision is the same kind of neutral, integrative, nondirective reflectiveness we try to make optimal use of in analytic sessions with patients.

Supervisors almost without exception will find themselves addressing a related problem concerning the proper timing of interpretations. Except for that handful of students who seem to take to the psychoanalytic process as if they were born to it, most analysts in training must brace themselves not to respond too quickly, not to step in too soon to rescue a patient from mounting tension. It doesn't come easily to most analysts to let a theme develop over an entire session or over several sessions, to allow it to build and to run its course, before coming in with some formulation that is likely to interrupt the patient's free flow of associations. It takes training, experience, and in-touch-ness with the patient to know when a theme has ripened to the point where it is ready to be plucked, the point beyond which, if put off any longer, it would lose some of its coherence and cogency. Stepping in too soon is the most common error made by analytic therapists early in their training. Even the most experienced of analysts lapse occasionally into this error. Freud's early "rule of abstinence" can perhaps be imposed on the analyst, whether or not it still applies to the patient. Psychoanalytic therapists must learn to live with the insights they arrive at without immediately and enthusiastically sharing that understanding with the patient. Frustrating as it may be to withhold this information, especially when novice therapists are impressed with their own insightfulness, it is best, most of the time, to abstain. One must, once again, impose on oneself the discipline of respecting the patient's agenda in a treatment hour, rather than the therapist's. Strachey (1934), in his classical paper on the change process in psychoanalysis, tells us that the therapist should have his fingers on the pulse of the treatment process, in order to pick up the "moment of urgency" in the material the patient is presenting. The therapist learns to recognize and respond to that which is psychodynamically alive at the moment, as contrasted with intellectualized husks of ideas which will not lead anywhere if one picks up on them when they are lacking in "urgency." We must remind beginning therapists to keep in mind whose urgency they should be responding to—their own or the patient's? The two don't always coincide.

Strachey, in that same paper, also cautions against an "overdose of interpretations"—another common beginner's error. It is often difficult for the beginning therapist to believe that he also serves who only sits and waits. The therapist understandably feels a need to contribute something to the treatment process. It is difficult to hold onto the conviction that perhaps the most precious thing the therapist contributes is attentive listening.

Beginning supervisees who are unsure of their skill and talents lean heavily on theory. The supervisor needs to disabuse them of the idea that it is their job to arrive at insights and lay them before the patient. Getting this message across is a slow and arduous task. Teaching trainees forbearance, helping them to overcome their enthusiastic display to the patient of what they've discovered, and to accept the far more frustrating role of serving as a catalyst to the patient, who must learn to think about himself by himself and for himself, not just *what* to think about himself. We see this more often among beginners, but the temptation is never fully overcome, even with experience, of letting oneself fall into explaining the patient to himself. A good interpretation is something more than a good cognitive rendering of the analyst's sense of the operative dynamics at the moment. I don't mean to say here that the analyst must never become didactic in the course of an analysis. One must, however, not to confuse interpretations with didactic instruction regarding the psychodynamic formulas that apply to the patient, a course which serves only to intellectualize the psychoanalytic process and consolidates defenses rather than dissolving them.

I've suggested above that the rule of abstinence is a good one for the therapist to follow. I think the same can be said for Freud's basic rule. I find it consistently more useful to conduct supervision in a way that parallels the way we expect patients to conduct themselves in the treatment, that is to come to the session without notes, without having organized their ideas beforehand. So, too, I ask therapists to present their material freshly, spontaneously, without verbatim notes, allowing the material to structure itself as they go along. I find I can much more quickly grasp the implicit theme of a session when the session is presented this way. More importantly, we can also more quickly identify trouble spots, difficulties the therapists seem to be having with their patients, or with their own responses to the patients. A patient's transferences or a therapist's countertransferences show through more clearly in such spontaneously rendered accounts of a treatment session, using only sketchy process notes, or no notes at all.

The ability of the supervisor to function as an auxiliary ego to the therapist rather than as an auxiliary superego becomes particularly important as one turns attention to a therapist's entanglements in a patient's transference. When therapists find themselves increasingly locked into a transference-countertransference bind, it is essential that their relationship to the supervisor be trusting enough so that they can dare to explore openly with the supervisor the array of feelings evoked in them by the patient. I have in mind here not a therapeutic exploration of these feelings, but rather a cathartic expression of the feelings, so that the therapists can have a clearer sense of what the patient has been "doing to them." I find that this often leads to sufficient clarification for the analysts to be able to step out of the transference bind and resume their more neutral stance.

I've spoken so far of a set of problems referable directly or indirectly to the supervisor's impact on the therapy process, all bearing in one way or another on the therapist's relationship to the patient and to the supervisor. None of these reduce easily to simple rules of thumb. They fall midway between practical advice on technique on the one hand and such broader issues as Oberman and Caruth address. These authors stress that no amount of teaching an analyst good technique or the nature of the change process in psychoanalysis will serve us well without the concurrent development in the analyst of a psychoanalytic professional identity, integrated around a particular value system, a sense of commitment to the patient and the process, an acceptance of one's mature responsibility for the well-being of another person, and an identification with the best in psychoanalysis and the psychoanalysts who have preceded us. We have all run into trainees who approach the conducting of an analysis as if what is required of them is the learning of a manual of techniques: techniques for listening, techniques for drawing inferences, techniques for intervening. Certainly we would all agree that it takes more than technical proficiency to achieve competence as an analyst if one falls short of those personal qualities that are essential to the psychoanalytic enterprise.

Nonetheless, some mundane advice on technique is not out of line in a properly conducted supervision. In the course of training one picks up such rules of thumb. Schlesinger (1981) cites a number of these in his excellent paper on empathy. For example, we advise our trainees to "respond empathically to their patients." "A common vulgarization," Schlesinger cautions, "is to speak of 'giving the patient empathy,' to speak of empathy as though it were an oozy substance that could be applied like butter to an otherwise unappetizing piece of dry toast." Schlesinger cites other such rules of thumb: "to look through the transference at what the patient is saying"; to examine not only the content, but the affect with which that content is conveyed, in fact, to "go with the affect." Another such familiar guideline is to "interpret defense before content." We could add the advice to listen always for the metaphors, in fact, to attend to the metaphors in the patient's figures of speech, but also to the metaphors in the patterns of his or her behavior. Brenner (1976, p. 48) speaks of "the importance of precision, of avoiding analytic terms and of using the patient's vocabulary." We could well add to these several rules of thumb the suggestion that a major element in good technique is tact.

One could go on and on, but I would like to dwell some on the intriguing question raised by Oberman concerning how one comes to know what goes on in one's own and in the patient's unconscious. He illustrates how one uses the intuitive approach rather than a logical or an empathic approach to the conclusion that the patient is "angry." Oberman then adds that one might well puzzle over why it required this roundabout way of identifying the fact that the patient was in fact struggling with her primitive oral-agressive rage. But such a roundabout way to an inference need not be the only channel one has to the unconscious. Brenner (1976) writes:

> Intuition, conscious reflection, unconsciously motivated affec-
> tive reactions or fantasies—all are potential methods of forming
> a correct and useful conjecture about a patient in analysis.
> There are analysts who are especially enthusiastic about one
> method or the other, but the fact is that it makes little difference
> which method an analyst uses if it leads him to the desired

result. Most analysts have probably used them all at one time or another. Special preferences are doubtless determined by an analyst's own psychic conflicts. They are of interest to him as part of his own analysis, perhaps, but unless they interfere with his analytic work they have no other practical significance. They constitute an element of what one might call an analyst's professional style.

How an analyst arrives at psychoanalytic truths about the patient is one of the most important and challenging things we can teach in the course of supervision. More needs to be said about the nature of psychoanalytic inferences and the relative strengths and weaknesses of one way of knowing over another. Brenner's suggestion that all avenues to understanding are equally good may have been intended more as a diplomatic statement than a scientific one.

It is not easy to be a proper discussant. I refer here not to the tone one adopts or the tact one displays in response to the presenters, but rather how successfully one can deal with the temptation to avoid becoming a third presenter rather than an honest-to-goodness discussant. I am afraid I have let myself be more the former than the latter. I think I felt daunted by the task of doing full justice by the richly textured paper of Dr. Caruth and the thoughtful and somewhat troubling paper of Dr. Oberman; if so, I opted for self-indulgence, rather than the more ambitious analysis these two papers rightly deserve.

References

Brenner, C. (1976). *Psychoanalytic technique and psychic conflict.* New York: International Universities Press.

Doehrman, M. (1976). Parallel processes in supervision and psychotherapy. *Bulletin of the Menninger Clinic, 40,* 9–110.

Schlesinger, H. J. (1981). The process of empathic response. *Psychoanalytic Inquiry, 1,* 393–416.

Strachey, J. (1934). The nature of the therapeutic action of psychoanalysis. *International Journal of Psychoanalysis, 15,* 127–159.

Wallerstein, R. S. (1981). *Becoming a psychoanalyst: A study of psychoanalytic supervision.* New York: International Universities Press.

Index

Levenson, E. A.
  on levels of abstraction in supervision, 35
  on metapsychology, 37
  on phases of supervision, 40
  on supervision in psychoanalysis versus in psychoanalytic psychotherapy systems, 138
  on supervisory styles, 19–20
  on therapists' participation in patients' psychological systems, 59
  on work with Clara Thompson, 39
Lewis, W. C., 1, 5
  on transference in cross-gender supervision, 124–127
Liebert, R., 115
Loewald, H. W., 106, 132
Los Angeles Institute for psychoanalytic Studies, 1
Lothane, Z., 199
Lower, R. B., 19, 20
Luborsky, L., 173

McDougall, J., 138
McLaughlin, J. T., 107
Mahler, M., 26, 39
Malan, D., 152, 167, 173
Malcove L., 199
Manhattan Institute for Psychoanalysis, 1
Masterson, J. F., 137
Mayer, J. E., 20
Mayman, M., 1, 2, 8, 179, 180, 207–213
Meltzer, J., 55
men
  expected behaviors of, 130
  as supervisors of female analysts, 117
  transference by men to, 115
Mendell, D., 1, 5, 129
  on cross-gender supervision of cross-gender therapy, 114–117
metaphors, 212
Michigan Psychoanalytic Institute, 1
Michigan Society for Psychoanalytic Training, 1–2
Mitchell, S., 137, 169
Modell, A. H., 59

Moldawsky, S., 115
Mount Zion Psychotherapy and Psychoanalytic Group, 1, 5, 140, 145
Munson, C. E., 21
Murphy, T. C., 15

Nash, V., 166, 169
negative supervisory reactions, 189
neurosis, 84
neutrality, 31
Newirth, J. W., 1, 2, 6, 169–170, 172
  on mastery of countertransference anxiety, 157–164
New York Center for Psychoanalytic Training, 1
New York Freudian Society, 1
New York University Postdoctoral Training program in Psychotherapy and Psychoanalysis, 1
notes used in supervision, 155, 184, 211
Nova Postdoctoral Institute for Psychoanalysis, 1
Noy, P., 62

Oberman, N. C., 1, 2, 7–8, 179, 180, 207, 211–213
  on achievement of analytic identity, 194–205
objectification of patients, 161, 203–204
object-relations perspective, 157–159, 163–164, 169
  on depressive anxiety, 162–163
  on paranoid anxieties, 160–162
  on schizoid anxiety, 159–160
Ochroch, R., 1, 5, 165
  on psychoanalysis and psychoanalytic psychotherapy, 137–138
oedipal conflicts
  in case histories, 53–54, 80–81
  in competition between students and supervisors, 189–190
  in institutes, 196–197
  "pathogenic beliefs" and, 168
  in supervisory relationship, 13
Ogden, T. H., 190
oral impulses, 53–56